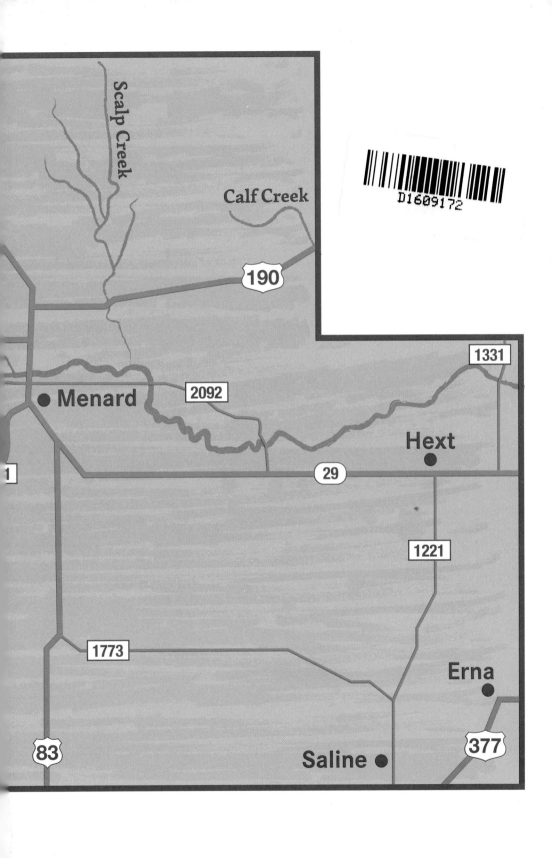

FOREVER MENARD

THE LOST STORIES

FOREVER MENARD

THE LOST STORIES

The Story of Menard County, Texas,
and the City of Menard

Written by students of
Menard High School
Classes 1980-81 & 1982-83

Foxfire project led by English teacher
Patty Miller

Book edited and designed by
Gus Clemens

Mulberry Avenue Books
San Angelo, Texas

Mulberry Avenue Books, San Angelo, TX

Forever Menard : The Lost Stories.
The Story of Menard County, Texas, and the City of Menard
Written by students of Menard High School 1980-81 and 1982-83
Mulberry Avenue Books, San Angelo, Texas, 2017.
pages cm.
Includes index.
ISBN: 978-0-938036-11-1 (cloth binding)
ISBN: 978-0-938036-12-8 (leather binding)
1. Menard County (Tex.)—History. 2. Menard County (Tex.)—Biography.
I. Title.
F392.M45F671 2017
917.64877--dc23

To the students of Menard High School
and their teacher, Patty Miller

Table of Contents

PART ONE: MENARD HISTORY

PART TWO: MENARD PLACES

Part Three: Menard Stories

Part Four: Menard People

City of Menard Maps

SOUTH OF THE SAN SABA RIVER

1–Menard County Courthouse

2–Bevans Hotel

3–Mission Theater

4–Menard News

5–Menard Library

6–Luckenbach Building

7–"Jelly" Bean Drug Store

8–Original Sacred Heart Catholic Church

9–Menard Elementary & Junior High School

10–Bank of Menard Building (First State Bank)

11–Menard National Bank

12–First United Methodist Church

13–Calvary Episcopal Church

14–Grace Lutheran Church

15–First Presbyterian Church

16–Church of Christ

17–First Baptist Church

18–Sacred Heart Catholic Church

19–Menard High School

20–Pioneer Rest Cemetery

21–Country Store

22–Menard Fire Department

23–Old Ed L. Mears Home

24–Wilensky's Store

25–Menard EMS

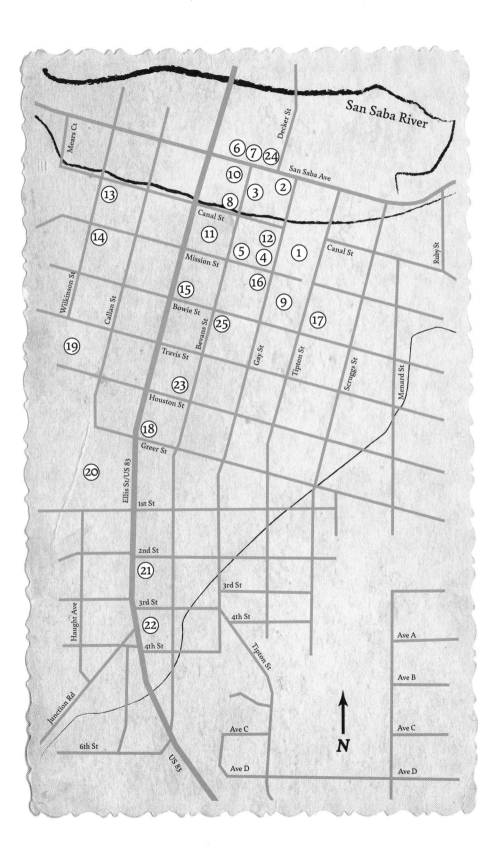

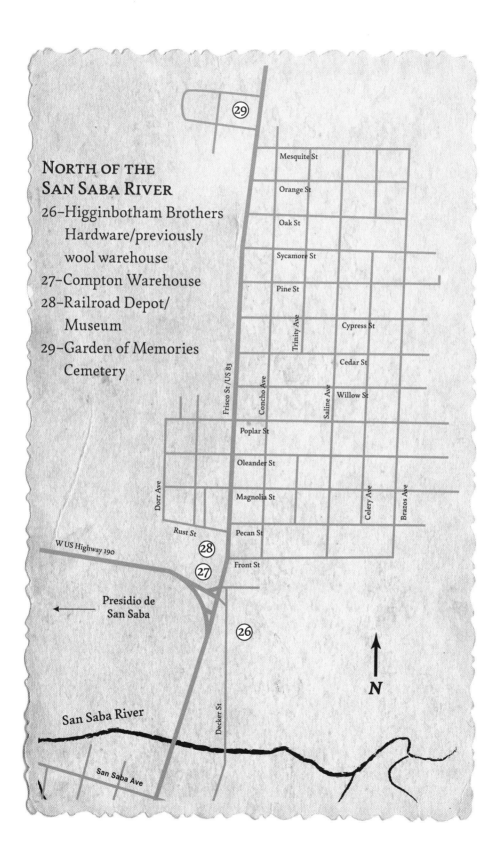

NORTH OF THE SAN SABA RIVER

26–Higginbotham Brothers
    Hardware/previously
    wool warehouse
27–Compton Warehouse
28–Railroad Depot/
    Museum
29–Garden of Memories
    Cemetery

29

Mesquite St

Orange St

Oak St

Sycamore St

Pine St

Trinity Ave

Cypress St

Cedar St

Frisco St /US 83

Concho Ave

Saline Ave

Willow St

Poplar St

Dorr Ave

Oleander St

Magnolia St

Celery Ave

Brazos Ave

Rust St

Pecan St

W US Highway 190

28

27

Front St

Presidio de
San Saba

26

N

Decker St

San Saba River

San Saba Ave

Introduction

By Gus Clemens

"A bombshell just happened in my room!" Jake Landers exclaimed in an email. "Brent Bratton, whose grandfather was Billy Joe Haney [longtime Menard County sheriff], brought me two missing volumes of the Patty Miller English class project for 1980-81 and 1982-83. Brent has no memory of how they got into a box in his barn… I am still in partial shock."

Thus began, *Forever Menard—The Lost Stories*, the second volume of a Menard history created by students at Menard High School.

The first volume, *Forever Menard*, was published in 2016 using 122 student papers held for decades by the Menard Museum. In 2014, Landers, a Menard treasure and historian, examined the papers and began turning the handwritten and typewritten efforts into word processor documents. The *Menard News and Messenger* and its editor, Dan Feather, another Menard treasure, began publishing full versions of the original efforts on a weekly basis.

In a process explained in detail later in this introduction, the 122 papers originally archived then were extensively edited and fact-checked and turned into a 480-page, hardcover book, *Forever Menard*.

Everyone involved in the project thought our work was done when the book was published in November 2016. Then came Jake's email on February 1, 2017. Fifty-two lost stories—stories no one knew existed—had been found.

For those unfamiliar with the first volume, here's the story behind this project.

In the 1970s, Menard High School English teacher Patty Miller learned about the Foxfire project, an education effort in a rural county school in northeast Georgia.

Students at the Rabun Gap-Nacoochee School began a magazine which captured stories about local people, local history, and aspects of local culture and local phenomena—such as foxfire, a naturally occurring bioluminescence caused by fungi in forests in northern Georgia. Begun in 1966, the magazine articles were collected and published in book form in 1972. The first *Foxfire* book became a national best seller; more *Foxfire* books followed.

Patty Miller believed if students in rural Georgia could write quality stories about their area, so could students in Menard, Texas. And, beginning in 1979, they did, eventually creating stories over the next ten years, 122 of which survived in the collection of the Menard Museum brought back to life by Jake Landers.

In 2015, Gretchen Noelke, native of Menard and lover of its history, contacted me about producing a history of Menard similar to my histories of other Texas cities and regions.

Jake Landers cooperated with me from the beginning of the project and began emailing digital files as he transcribed the student papers, suggesting they might be useful in my research.

As I read the Menard Foxfire material as part of my work on the potential book Gretchen requested, I realized the students of Menard already had written Menard's history. Not only did the stories cover main topics, they also reflected the people of Menard. The students' decade of work was an important part of Menard's history in its own right—capturing the language of both the students and the people they interviewed and quoted.

Gretchen agreed with that approach to the book, and noted her youngest child, Kenny Parker, had written one of the stories in the first book. He appears again in this one. Gretchen's other children, Jeffery and Lauren Elaine, graduated before the Foxfire project started. "I have always been proud of Menard," Gretchen said. "And that is why I am happy to help preserve the Menard story."

When Jake and I approached Gretchen about finding fifty-two lost stories, she did not hesitate to authorize a second volume.

Both the first book and the second include edited and revised versions of the original student stories. Some revisions were extensive. For example, part of Patty Miller's technique was for stories to include an introduction describing the Foxfire project. The repetitive introductions were removed.

Another common technique was inclusion of a quotation or poem at the start of the work. Sometimes the opening is an original work by the student. In the majority of cases, the quotations are from published works by others. In those cases, the quotations were researched and, when needed, edited to be accurate to the originals and to give accurate attribution to the original source.

In some cases bracketed comments are used to put a statement in context or adjust its accuracy, particularly in murky areas. Bracketed comments are my comments, often assisted by input from Jake Landers. When historical facts or spellings clearly were wrong, they were corrected without notation. Individual names sometimes are problematic. Whenever possible we verified spelling, but with so many names over so many years, there likely are errors. We went with the student spelling whenever we could not definitively correct.

Many of the student papers were handwritten; in some cases, we did the best we could in deciphering some words. The papers were done in the days before word processors and spell check, and type-written pages include white out (those of this writer's generation remember that tool) and some were typed on erasable onion skin paper. Both could make transcription difficult. Reading the original manuscripts transports you back to the challenges writers faced in the 1980s.

We did standard editing of material to correct spelling, grammar, and to conform to a uniform style. Additional changes were made to produce a more polished read and accommodate the space and typography requirements of a book. My wife, Miki Ross Clemens, did superb, yeoman work. So did my staff at Clemens & Associates, Laurel Vincent and Sarah Williamson (granddaughter-in-law of Rusty Williamson, another Menard legend).

It should be remembered these stories were written as an assignment for high school juniors and seniors in Patty Miller's advanced-placement English classes. There was an assigned form to follow. The main body included three parts: the opening quote, poem, or original work; the story itself; and—at the conclusion—what was called a "senses paragraph" where students described what they experienced or imagined when they wrote their stories or thought about their subject. Senses paragraphs are not history, but the closing is included because it is part of the charm of the student efforts.

The material is divided into four sections. Part One covers Menard history and includes larger historical facts. Part Two covers Menard places and focuses on narrower stories about individual locations. Part Three includes Menard stories and is a catch-all category. Part Four presents stories about Menard people and families.

At Gretchen Noelke's request, Part Four includes a story about Fritz and Anna Luckenbach written by Jake Landers (Roger O Landers Jr.), their grandson. Gretchen believed the Luckenbach-Landers family story needed to be included so the *Forever Menard* books would be a more complete history. Jake Landers graciously wrote the story.

Part of the joy of this effort has been meeting or talking to some of the writers. I grew to know them through their writing as high school juniors and seniors, and now meet them as adults in their forties and fifties. They were understandably proud and pleased their student work somehow unexpectedly appeared in print and became part of the tapestry of Menard's long and important history. No one I have met so far dreamed their student work would, decades later, appear in a serious book that would live on in Texana literature for generations to come.

Note: Proceeds from the sales of both *Forever Menard* books are used to help provide scholarships to Menard graduates as well as grants to Menard charitable causes which seek to help make Menard a great place to call home.

Original Foxfire Introduction

By Patty Miller

As in the book *Foxfire*, the Menard High School English classes caught "the fever," after interviewing the townsfolk for their research papers. "If the *Foxfire* students could compile a magazine and book about their small town, why not we?"

Tape recordings, pictures, and stories of conversations between the generations of the old and young began to trickle into class, and then gradually flood the room at completion time. College writing preparation was advanced, but more than that, communication and a thirst for knowledge had begun.

Communication is what English is all about, yet these students learned much history in the process. Above all else, a flame of pride in the roots of our quaint town was kindled. The classes who follow will research other unwritten memories of Menard, but these ground breakers won't be forgotten by those of us in the wings.

It was my pleasure to be the teacher of the *Forever the Past* authors. This was one of the warmest, most challenging, and rewarding experiences of my life. Congratulations to an unquenchable group of enthusiastic young leaders. Thanks for sharing your spirit with me. I'll be watching you grow.

Menard, you should be proud.

Introduction written by Patty Miller in 1979, the first year of the Menard High School Foxfire effort.

Patty Miller

By Gus Clemens

Kay Patricia "Patty" Day Miller was a special teacher and an important contributor both to the civic life of Menard and the preservation of Menard's rich history.

In 1979, after 13 years as a teacher in the Houston area, Patty and her husband, Bobby Ed Miller, moved to Menard, Bobby's hometown. Patty began teaching classes in English, Speech, Spanish, and English as a Second Language. On weekends and evenings, she coached University Interscholastic League poetry, prose, journalism, and one-act play competitors, helping them achieve regional and state honors.

Beginning her first year in Menard and continuing for a decade, Patty's English class students at Menard High School created essays/reports as part of the Foxfire project, an opportunity for students to interview local personalities to learn and record the history and culture of their area. The project lasted from 1979 through 1988, and the 122 stories the students generated are contained in the first book, *Forever Menard*, and fifty-two additional "lost" stories are included in this book.

Patty's impact on Menard went well beyond her ten years teaching in Menard.

In 1988, Patty wrote and performed in *Song of Silver*, an outdoor musical pageant that was an integral part of Menard's Jim Bowie Days celebration for 17 years.

She helped charter Menard's first EMS service and instructed EMT and EMT Special Skills classes throughout the region. She was an officer in the Menard Volunteer Fire Department Auxiliary, served as historian for the Presidio de San Saba Restoration Association, and was choir director at First United Methodist Church of Menard.

Patty was named Citizen of the Year by the Menard Chamber of Commerce in 2000. While teaching at Wall High School, she was named Secondary Teacher of the Year by the Education Service Center Region XV for 2000-2001. In 2010, Patty joined her husband in the Menard High School Hall of Fame.

A beloved wife, mother, and grandmother, Patty enjoyed a full life, well lived. When she died in 2012 at age 68, family and friends gathered by the San Saba River on the Miller Ranch to sing and celebrate her life.

You will learn more about Patty Miller and read samples of her work in this book. Her spirit lives in every page—a teacher who inspired students to chronicle their county and town and preserve its legacy.

Menard History

The Beginning of Menard
By Sherry Cannon

TWENTY YEARS AGO

I have wandered by the village, Tom—I've sat beneath the tree,
Upon the school-house playing-ground which sheltered you and me,
But none are left to greet me, Tom, and few are left to know,
That played with us upon the green just Twenty Years Ago.

The grass is just as green, dear Tom, bare-footed boys at play
Are sporting just as we were then, with spirits just as gay,
But master sleeps upon the hill, all coated o'er with snow,
That afforded us a sliding place just Twenty Years Ago.

The old school-house is altered some, the benches are replaced
By new ones, very like the same our penknives had defaced;
But the same old bricks are in the wall, the bell swings to and fro,
The music just the same, dear Tom, 'twas Twenty Years Ago.

The boys are playing some old game, beneath that same old tree,
I do forget the name just now—you have played the same with me;
On that same spot 'twas played with knives, by throwing so and so,
The leaders had a task to do there Twenty Years Ago.

The river is running just as still—the willows on its side,
Are larger than they were, dear Tom, the stream appears less wide;
The grape-vine swing is ruined now, where once we played the beau,
And swung our sweethearts, pretty girls, just Twenty Years Ago.

The spring that bubbled 'neath the hill, close by the spreading beech,
Is very high—'twas once so low that we could almost reach;
But in kneeling down to get a drink, dear Tom, I started so,
To see how sadly I am changed since Twenty Years Ago.

Down by the spring, upon an elm, you know I cut your name—
Your sweetheart is just beneath it, Tom—and you did mine the
*   same;*
Some heartless wretch has peeled the bark—'twas dying sure but
*   slow,*
Just as the one whose name you cut did Twenty Years Ago.

My lids have long been dry, dear Tom, but tears come in my eyes;
I thought of her I loved so well those early broken ties;
I visited the old churchyard, and took some flowers to strew
Upon the graves of those we loved some Twenty Years Ago.

Some are in the churchyard laid, some sleep beneath the sea,
But few are left of our class, excepting you and me;
But when our time shall come, dear Tom, and we are called to go,
I hope they'll lay us where we played just Twenty Years ago.

—Dill Armor Smith (also attributed to anonymous)

This paper is going to tell how and when Menard began and how hard it was for it to become a town.

Col. Michel Branamour Menard, after whom Menard was named, was born in Canada of French parentage in 1805. He came to Texas in 1833 after a number of years spent with the Shawnee Indians. He gladly cast his fortunes with the struggling Texas colonists to break the yoke of Mexico.

Fitted by inclination and natural endowment, his great industry and capacity enabled him to render conspicuous service to the Texas patriots in this great cause that had its happy termination in San Jacinto. Shortly thereafter, Menard gained rights to Galveston Island and helped organize the Galveston City Company, which began selling lots in 1838. He is credited as the founder of Galveston. Menard died in 1856.

Menard County, on the Edwards Plateau of southwest Texas, was created from Bexar County in 1858 and named for Michel Branamour Menard.

The area of 914 square miles chiefly is prairie and valley lands broken by hill ranges and traversed west to east by the San Saba River and its tributary creeks: Clear, Rocky, Celery, Las Moras, Dry, and Elm. The average altitude is 2,200 feet, annual rainfall 20.05 inches, and average temperature 64.8 degrees.

The soils are dark and gray, sandy loam and clay, fertile along the streams. Timber includes mesquite, live oak, Spanish oak, and pecan. The principal industry is stock raising with dairying and poultry production also of commercial importance. There was more industry than you would think there would be.

The area that now is Menard County was explored by the Spanish as early as 1541. Francisco Vásquez de Coronado possibly reached the San Saba valley on his Quivira expedition, but there is no direct evidence.

There is certainty Spaniards returned in the 1750s in an effort to protect San Antonio and other locations in northern Mexico by establishing a mission and a presidio on the San Saba River to convert the Apaches, serve as an outpost against French settlement, and afford a base for searching for silver.

Mission Santa Cruz de San Sabá and Presidio San Luis de las Amarillas (later named Presidio de San Sabá) were established in 1757 on opposite banks of the river, the mission on the southern bank and the presidio on the northern bank west of present-day Menard. Diego Ortiz Parrilla commanded the presidio. The Indians called the area "Liltamilpa" (summer land).

The presidio served as a way station between San Antonio and Santa Fe, New Mexico.

In March, 1758, a raid by Comanche, Wichita, and other northern tribes resulted in destruction of the mission. The presidio was abandoned in June, 1768 and briefly re-occupied in 1770.

In the early 1830s, James and Rezin Bowie attempted to find the site of a mine near or at the presidio from which legends claimed Lipan Apaches were securing silver. The only result was the Battle of Calf Creek in November, 1834, in which the Bowie party was defeated.

After the annexation of Texas, the United States in 1853 established Fort McKavett on the headwaters of the San Saba west of Menard, and the country was opened to pioneer cattlemen.

The 1858 act creating the county called for the establishment of a county seat to be called Menardville. A townsite was laid out that year, but lack of settlers and the Civil War meant the early effort to found a town were unsuccessful.

In 1867, Menardville had a store operated by Adam Bradford

in a one-room log house. A blacksmith shop, a saloon, and a grocery opened. All supplies were hauled overland from Burnet. The settlement was a trading post and overnight stop on north and west cattle trails, with the old compound of the Spanish missions used to corral as many as 3,000 head of cattle.

A second attempt to organize the county was successful in 1871, and the first term of the county court convened under a live oak tree. A two-story court house was built in 1872. Australian William Saunders opened the Australian Hotel in 1880; J.S. Evans operated a saddlery in 1885; A.H. Murchison opened a store in 1887.

The Ben Ficklin flood of 1882 devastated the San Saba River valley and did much damage to the small town in 1882, but settlers rebuilt.

Originally called Menardville, the name was shortened to Menard at the request of the Fort Worth and Rio Grande Railroad Company that was building tracks to the town. The railroad wanted the shorter name to facilitate painting of signs, and the town complied.

The seat of Menard County in 1966 had thirteen churches, two banks, and a retirement home operated in conjunction with the hospital.

Menard County primarily is a sheep and cattle raising area, with cash receipts from livestock and products totaling $4,500,000 annually in the early 1970s [$29 million in 2017 dollars]. Major business concerns of the county are sheep shearing, livestock feeding, and furniture manufacturing. In addition, the county has a church-operated hospital.

Tourists are attracted by hunting and fishing. The county built Camp Sol Mayer for the Boy Scouts of America. Fort McKavett State Historic Site attracts tourists to the western edge of the county.

Other information the author found in some court records included:

On September 5, 1911, there was the first regular meeting of the city council of the City of Menard with all members present except W.R. Burrier. The mayor called the meeting to order and the following officers were appointed:

J.G. Callan, city secretary and treasurer

Russell Callan, city attorney

F.M. Hamby, pound master

F.M. Hamby, city assessor and collector

Committees appointed included:

J.T. Westbrook, H.J. Westbrook, D.G Benchoff—streets and alleys

D.G. Benchoff, W.R. Burrier, J.T. Westbrook—finance

E.B. Hallinger, H.J. Decker, W.R. Burrier—claims

H.J. Decker, D.G. Benchoff, J.T. Westbrook—taxes

H.J. Decker, J.T. Westbrook, E.B. Hallinger—police

W.R. Burrier, D.G. Benchoff, E.B. Hallinger—fire & water

D.G. Benchoff, E.B. Hallinger, W.R. Burrier—printing

J.T. Westbrook, H.J. Decker, W.R. Burrier—sanitary regulations

W.R. Burrier, H.J. Decker, D.G. Benchoff—ordinances

D.G. Benchoff, W.R. Burrier, E.B. Hallinger—cemeteries

There was another meeting of the city council on September 19, 1911. Officers present included Mayor N.P. Bevans, E.B. Ballinger, H.J. Decker, W.R. Burrier. An ordinance was passed granting to J.W. Estes and J.J. Rowe their successors and assigns the right to erect, construct, maintain, and operate a telephone system and exchange in the City of Menard, and to erect, place, and maintain such wires, posts, conduits, cables, and other appliances as shall be necessary.

On September 27, 1911, another ordinance passed that granted George J. Clank, his successors and assigns, a franchise to maintain and operate an electric light and power plant and water works system in the City of Menard.

By the permission of the city council on April 18, 1912, Stuart Bros. were granted permission to erect a photographer's tent on the Ed. L. Mears lot on the south side of San Saba Avenue.

On August 6, 1912, a meeting allowed J.R. Walker to erect necessary stalls for his livery stables located on Stucken Street.

On July 22, 1918, it was found unlawful for any person between age eighteen and fifty to be found unemployed and remain unemployed, or found loafing on the streets of Menard, and they must be employed at least thirty-six hours per week.

This paper explains the beginning of Menard: it was a hard beginning.

This author's reaction to creating this paper is that the beginning of Menard and how it grew and kept going was interesting. The author would like to have been there.

One can see how the first building of Menard was constructed and hear the hammering of the boards. The smell of the dust which the wagon wheels stir up brings loads of memories back and forth. It is easy to touch the evidence when they are finished and to taste the coffee when the men go on their breaks. The town grows on.

Floods

By Scott McHorse

THE BROOK

I come from haunts of coot and hern
    I make a sudden sally,
And sparkle out among the fern,
    To bicker down a valley.

By thirty hills I hurry down,
    Or slip between the ridges,
By twenty thorps, a little town,
    And half a hundred bridges.

Till last by Philip's farm I flow
    To join the brimming river,
For men may come and men may go,
    But I go on for ever.

I chatter over stony ways,
    In little sharps and trebles,
I bubble into eddying bays,
    I babble on the pebbles.

With many a curve my banks I fret
    By many a field and fallow,
And many a fairy foreland set
    With willow-weed and mallow.

I chatter, chatter, as I flow
    To join the brimming river,
For men may come and men may go,
    But I go on for ever. — Alfred, Lord Tennyson (excerpt)

Floods have been a regular part of Menard's past. Menard, however, always rebuilds.

The flood of 1899 was the worst of them all, although there also were bad ones in 1936, 1938, and 1980.

Austin Callan was the first owner of a newspaper in Menardville; it was called the *Menard County Enterprise*. Callan owned the paper during the flood of June 6, 1899, that devastated the valley. What follows is an account of that flood.

Noah Rose took the only photograph of the flood. He had a photograph gallery in a tent during the flood and lost everything he owned except a camera and two plates. He rescued those items when the flood was at its height. He took the picture on the west mountain of Menard. This is located near our present water tower. Rose commented:

"It rained heavily on the river above town, and early Monday morning, the river began its first rise. It rained a great deal during that day at Menardville, and the old San Saba came up to within four inches of the highest watermark ever registered near my parent's house, which was built in 1882.

"Then it went down rapidly, and by noon it had cleared my garden. The garden had been under four or five feet of water.

"It began to rise slowly all the day, and by nightfall it found itself as high as it was during the morning and was still rising. As darkness over-shadowed us, moments became real serious for the townspeople. Though the water was still rising slowly at 10:00 p.m., my folks decided to evacuate to Mr. Staton's nearer the hillside.

"When this task was finished, my brother Roland and John Staton, Nat Saunders, and myself went back to his ranch located near Sonora. I made arrangements to go with him to Sonora and then on to Menard. On Sunday, we teamed together and returned to our house to await developments. Then we went to where my tent was located and rescued one camera and two plates I was to use early the next morning. We stayed up all night. I can honestly say, it was the longest night of my life.

"It rained several days starting on June 1, 1899, before the big flood. All Sunday afternoon a big cloud hung over the entire country, which was drained by the draws and creeks of the river. As night came on, the cloud headed downstream. It rained hard along the river's valley. It was thought that the river would rise by dawn, but it took until 8:00 a.m., June 5, 1899, for it to come down. Within four hours it had overflowed its banks. By this time, half the crops in the valley were already destroyed."

Jimmy Crowell also wrote about the flood:

"The only people living on the north side of the river near town were John, Nell and Leo Decker, who had a cotton farm near Celery Creek, eastward about three miles. He said he had a steam engine that irrigated their cotton, which was washed away by the flood. It was located near the Low Water Bridge, which then was called 'Ballinger Crossing.' The water soon began to recede as rapidly as it rose. Many thought the flood was over, although Menardville only had a few people in it. The clouds never left the valley. It rained lightly throughout the valley. Early in the afternoon, the water began to rise again. Some of the cautious began to evacuate.

"By 6:00 p.m., the big rise was coming through the town. Some retired to bed because they thought the worst had already passed. They were soon awakened by the people of Menardville. The men and boys helped the old and the women and children to safety. The water was four to five feet deep in downtown Menardville."

Jimmy Crowell also remembered people telling him: "Some men were wading horses from the stables at the Australian Hotel, which is now owned by Dick MacTaggart and is still standing, across the park, which is the present day Legion Park. The school house was opened and refuge could be found there."

Jimmy Crowell also talked about the house Ida Mae Davis lives in today: "One-half the people of Menardville stayed at this house. It was just built and had beautiful floors on which mud was tracked."

The author learned about heroism from Jimmy Crowell: "There were deeds of heroism that were talked about for generations after the flood. Many people were financially ruined, as was Professor Cook, who ran the Bevans Hotel at this time, although I don't think it was the present-day hospital because that building was built at a later date. The people stayed on the balcony. They saw Dr. McKnight's office, John Callan's drugstore, and then the Frisco saloon wash down Main Street. The drug-store and saloon were stranded opposite the hotel, but the doctor's office went down with the current. Many people sustained a lot of damage to their houses. J.N. Maddux's was wrecked and everything ruined. The Crowell's house washed just a few feet from its foundation."

Jimmy Crowell also told the author: "My family lived in a Puckett House where the West Texas Utilities is now located. Oliver's store was nearly completely destroyed. Lee Russell's new house was destroyed, but a few houses escaped damage. Among other things that were damaged were the bridges along the irrigation ditch—they were all washed out. Every family was moved across this ditch to assure their safety. It was amazing that nobody was hurt seriously. Losses in businesses were estimated to be from $50,000 to $75,000, while the entire valley's loss was $150,000 [$4.2 million in 2017 dollars]. Seventy-five percent of the county's finest crop was destroyed. Other things destroyed were the Noyes's farm houses. Dan Patton's house split in two; half stayed on the foundation, the other half went with the current. A lumber building located near the Legal Tender Saloon washed away."

Jimmy Crowell continued: "The river bottom wasn't cleared out the way it is now. Harris Hollow wasn't either. This caused the water to back up more than it would now. Only eight to ten houses were south of the ditch. Losses to people who lived down toward Five Mile Crossing suffered the most. Everybody on the south side of the river from J.J. Callan's to Five Mile took refuge.

"Nobody lived on the river because there were too many flies and worms on it. There were great losses of crops, while very little livestock was lost because it was too brushy to keep livestock on the river."

Jimmy Crowell call this flood "the hill-to-hill flood."

Another tragic flood happened in 1938. An account of it notes rain measured in amounts of 13.13 inches to 23.38 inches throughout our county, causing the San Saba to reach a height of 23 feet on Saturday, June 22, 1938, causing an estimated $10,000 damage in the city [$173,000 in 2017 dollars] and from $250,000 to half a million dollars damage in the entire county. The ranchers lost a lot of livestock, farmers lost their entire feed crops. Floodwater rose two to three feet in the downtown streets.

During the flood two people lost their lives. Mr. and Mrs. M.E. Hensley drowned while trying to escape from their home. Fred Crawford and Jim Matthews died of heart attacks caused by the excitement of the flood. A lot of water flowed through the county when they drowned. It was said that as much water flowed through Menard as in 1899, but the underbrush was cleared out on the river bottom. Harris Hollow rose to an all-time high and flooded the residential part of Menard. Also, the businesses were flooded, but most escaped from much damage.

Irene Lovelace recalled the 1938 flood: "My mother was telling me to cut the water off in the kitchen. I looked outside and saw two feet of water standing around the house. This was about daylight. Some men, she couldn't remember their names, helped us get to the courthouse. The water was above our knees and really swift. She called these 'scary times.'"

Finally, there was a bad flood in 1980. It was the worst flood since 1938.

The river crested twenty to twenty-one feet. Muddy water got into most of the buildings. It rained 5.27 inches on Saturday afternoon. Electricity was off during the day Monday. About 145 miles of fence was damaged. It was the worst flood this author has ever seen.

This paper has shown how many times Menard has been flooded and rebuilt. Although many floods have come and gone, Menard will always be here. No matter how much the floods destroy our county, we always build back. Menard will always be the author's home. There are many people throughout our little town who have memories that need to be shared with others. The author hopes this paper leaves the reader with greater knowledge of our past, which will live on forever. The author enjoyed and learned a lot from this research paper while living through and writing about it.

The author closes with these thoughts:

The author has walked down by the river lands of the San Saba River many times, enjoying the magnificent scenery that lay before his wondering eyes. Most people who live in this small, yet unique community, never realize just how beautiful and dangerous the river really is. The writer has experienced the sight of deer going to water, just as the sun was rising in the east. This left a special feeling which cannot be put into words. Mother Nature, however, periodically disrupts the wonderful thing she gives us.

Rain comes late in the summer, after the almost drought-like months which lie behind us. There are many tributaries which contribute to the seemingly calm and peaceful river before the rain. Inch by inch the rain comes, ranchers enjoying it, for they have had none since early spring. The rushing wall of water that the rains bring us comes and leaves as though it was a one-night stand. The destruction which the flood leaves behind takes weeks, even years, to rebuild. These may not be memories that anyone would like to remember, but the people of Menard have grown accustomed to this way of life.

[Note: Scott McHorse, Terry Danford, and Kyle Kothmann experienced the 1980 flood only weeks before beginning their papers. All three subsequently wrote about flooding in Menard. No students wrote specific stories about floods in the 122 stories in the first *Forever Menard* book.]

The Flood of 1938
By Terry Danford

> **BY THE BEND OF THE RIVER**
> *The swaying trees sigh contentment to the sky;*
> *Ceaseless flow of murmuring water*
> *soothes the harried feet;*
> *soft music song of the wild peace for my soul...*
> *This I find...*
> *   at the bend of the river.—Arthur J. Weber (excerpt)*

The flood of 1938 was the worst flood since 1899. This paper will describe the night and day the flood of 1938 and its extensive damage.

After a week of heavy rains and several visitations of flood-waters, in 1938 the San Saba River went to the highest flood stage in forty years. It was on Saturday. The river began a rapid rise about four o'clock that afternoon and in a short time was running down the main streets.

Merchants worked desperately to strengthen the barricades built earlier in the week when it became evident the water was going much higher. San Saba Street became flooded, in many places waist deep, and water was about a foot deep in the lobby of the Bevans Hotel.

The water gradually crept farther into town until a peak was reached about 10 p.m. From then on it receded rapidly and, by midnight, the danger was over.

The lights and power remained on during the flood stage, but were expected to go out at any time. The high school was opened as a refuge for people forced to leave their homes. Several houses in the low areas were washed from their foundations, though none were seriously damaged. Several cars were held up in Menard until it was possible to cross the bridge. Harris Hollow was next to overflow.

The first effect of high water was felt early Friday morning when Harris Hollow overflowed and flooded much of the town.

At that time, the San Saba entered the streets, but soon subsided. That Friday was marked by the drowning of Mr. and Mrs. M.E. Hensley as they were fleeing from the water west of town. Their bodies were recovered the following Monday. They were the only human casualties, but monetary losses were high.

The average estimate of the loss in Menard and Menard County was approximately $10,000 in town [$172,000 in 2017 dollars] and a possible $500,000 in the country [$8.6 million in 2017 dollars]. The relief office also was hit hard. Demands were heavy on the office, and the Red Cross assisted in the work. Efforts were made to secure a one hundred percent inoculation of the town against typhoid. Here is the *Menard News* account of the flood:

"Steady downpour of rain over the county last week ranging from measured amounts of 13.13 inches at the Bureau of Entomology to 23.38 inches at the C.W. Wilkinson ranch caused the San Saba River, aided by its tributaries, to reach a peak stage of more than 23 feet Saturday night in the city of Menard and causing an estimated damage of $10,000 in the city when the water rose two-and-a-half feet on Main Street, however, much damage was done.

"The waters that flooded the length of the county as well as adjoining counties, caused a total damage close to $250,000 in the county [$4.3 million in 2017 dollars]. Damages west of town were mostly washed out fences and drowned stock, but most of the farms along the river east of town lost almost their entire feed crops, which were in most cases ready to be harvested.

"Two persons, Mr. and Mrs. M.E. Hensley, were drowned while trying to escape from the home and two men, Fred Crawford and Jim Matthews, died of heart attacks caused by the excitement of the flood.

"Old settlers say that was as much water flowed through the city as it did in the flood of 1899, but because of clearing of underbrush, the water did not come up quite as high, and many homes were damaged.

"Yards around the homes in town were damaged when Harris

Hollow south of town rose to an all-time peak stage and flooded the residential district from the Hills to Main Street. Across the river, homes and one store was flooded when a hollow at the northwest end of the hills drained water into the valley."

Most of the stores in the business district were barricaded with flour and sand, and escaped with little or no damage. As it was impossible to barricade the Mission Theatre and Bevans Hotel, both places received several hundred dollars worth of damage from water, but the flood also did some good.

The five-day rain covered the four corners of the county and, despite the flood damage, was a boon to the county, as shown by the already greening of grass needed so badly to feed livestock. The measurement of rainfall was very high.

Rainfall all over the county was not officially recorded besides the reading at the Bureau of Entomology, but at the C.W. Wilkinson place, John Treadmill reported 21.75 inches; August Broghel recorded 22 inches; Herbert Mears recorded 15 inches.

This paper certainly bears out the thesis the flood of 1938 was the worst since 1899. In reading about all this, the author was filled with great anticipation as he started this paper. He felt he had fulfilled this feeling by the time he was finished. He concludes his paper with the following paragraph:

As the author sat reading about the Flood of 1938 he wondered what it would be like to see the bridge wash away. As he read the story, he could hear the kids yell happily when they got out of school early, and he could smell the dead carcasses floating down the river. He envisioned the people scrambling to get their possessions from their houses until the high water from the flood flooded their property and one was unable to get near without drowning.

This was the biggest flood Menard had experienced since 1899, and the people hope there will not be another like it.

City of Menard Floods
By Kyle Kothmann

THE BRIDGE BUILDER
An old man going a lone highway,
Came, at the evening cold and gray,
To a chasm vast and deep and wide.
Through which was flowing a sullen tide
The old man crossed in the twilight dim,
The sullen stream had no fear for him;
But he turned when safe on the other side
And built a bridge to span the tide.

"Old man," said a fellow pilgrim near,
"You are wasting your strength with building here;
Your journey will end with the ending day,
You never again will pass this way;
You've crossed the chasm, deep and wide,
Why build this bridge at evening tide?"

The builder lifted his old gray head;
"Good friend, in the path I have come," he said,
"There followed after me to-day
A youth whose feet must pass this way.
This chasm that has been as naught to me
To that fair-haired youth may a pitfall be;
He, too, must cross in the twilight dim;
Good friend, I am building this bridge for him!"
  —Will Allen Dromgoole

Floods have plagued the city of Menard from its very beginning. Several times the San Saba River has stretched from one hill to another. In this paper, the author plans to tell of the floods and their destruction.

It is said that some of the first settlers in Menardville were aware of the flood risks in the valley because of the drift and fallen logs left by previous floods. In fact, in the late 1860s the settlers met to decide whether to move the town of Menardville to a hill behind the old Spanish fort, presently part of the Kothmann feed lot. After a heated discussion of many hours, it was decided to leave the town in the present valley. Menardville was undisturbed by floods again until 1899.

On the morning of Tuesday, June 6, 1899, the San Saba began to rise. It quickly subsided. Many people thought the flood was over and the danger no longer existed. Heavy rain clouds hung over the section of the country around the river. The river began to rise again early in the afternoon. Several families started to evacuate the town. Water was still rising higher and faster by evening. A full evacuation became effective.

Acts of heroism in helping people evacuate were numerous. The results of working together was the loss of no lives, except that of a Mexican man who was reported to have floated down on a drift, but this was never confirmed. Losses were heavy, but easy to bear, for only that one person was thought to have been killed [and no proof of that emerged]. Since that day in 1899, there have been two people to drown in San Saba River floods, both in the flood of 1938.

On Friday, July 22, 1938, the San Saba River once again unleashed its wrath on the town of Menard. It reached a peak of about twenty-three feet. Two people drowned—Mr. and Mrs. M.E. Hensley—while trying to flee the water. Fred Crawford and Jim Matthews also died, both from heart attacks caused by the excitement of the flood.

Mr. Jim Matthews, with his wife, his son Norton, and his son's wife Louise (who at that time was expecting their only child, Janet Matthews Rabun) and several other families fled to a neighboring farm house to safety. Mr. Matthews had returned to his pickup for their belongings. There, he suffered a fatal heart attack. His body was laid out on the kitchen table until water subsided. There were other stories about the flood told by Mrs. E.A. Davis in an interview:

"Thirty-eight was when we had all the Boy Scouts camping in our cabins along the San Saba River. There were thirty-two Boy Scouts, two scoutmasters, and a Negro cook."

Mrs. Davis paused as if she were in a different time. Looking toward the sky with a blank expression, just wishing to be back with her family, alive and healthy, she continued:

"Houston Miller and the two Bruce boys had come across there. He said, 'Mrs. Davis, you better get those boys out if you can. It's coming down again. We can help you get them out.' The two scoutmasters agreed, so they had a team take a change of clothes in the backpack. They were dressed in their bathing suits."

Mrs. Davis looked as if she was a rose about to bloom. With a gleam in her eyes, she turned and said:

"I was dressed in my bathing suit and had on an old floppy hat and was carrying a walking stick. I looked like Moses leading the children of Israel out of Egypt."

Mrs. Davis told of how they managed to get those boys to town. One could sense the excitement in her voice as she proceeded:

"The only way we could get across the Las Moras was to get on top of the flume where the ditch goes across at Dr. Westphal's. The water was plum to the top. We spread the bigger boys out across the flume and passed the smaller ones on without ever letting them touch the water. The Las Moras was just sweeping under us. We made it across and started toward town. We had to climb the hill to get there. We'd take one step up and slip back about two steps backwards. It was so muddy! Well, anyway, we made it in. The whole town came out to greet us. They were so worried about the boys."

As Mrs. Davis gazed into the distance, a grin came to her face as she said:

"In thirty-eight, people were driving motor boats down Main Street. People say this last flood we had [1980 flood] was as high as it was in thirty-eight, but it wasn't. I know because we worked so hard to get those boys out, and half of them were in those motor boats.

"I walked on down toward the bridge and asked a man there if he had seen a Jersey cow go by? He said, 'Yeah, I saw one go by and busted its brains out on the bridge.' Oh, I just knew that was my cow, but it wasn't. She swam down to the Rambo place below town."

Mrs. Davis told of devastation, for it too came down with its fist raised in fury.

"The water got three feet in our house. The mud was just about two feet deep. I scooped that mud out of the window. Oh, Lord, you can't imagine, you just can't imagine! Our car was washed bottom side upper.

"Water had gotten three feet in the house, but we found out that it was only nineteen inches where I presently have our house. We moved the house from down there away from the river to right upon this ridge next to the river. The other day, when the river got up so high, it just came to my yard. This proves the flood of 1980 wasn't as high as the flood of 1938."

Monday, September 5, 1980, Menard County had its worst flood since 1938. The San Saba River crested about twenty-one or twenty-two feet about noon, following a rapid morning rise, resulting from heavy rains the night before. Losses from the flood waters were numerous. It's estimated losses of 5,000 Angora goats, 1,000 sheep, and 100 cattle, plus a few horses and pigs. One hundred and forty-five miles of fences were lost at a price of approximately $5,000 a mile [$15,000 in 2017 dollars] in Menard County.

The town of Menard has had its share of floods. Since the first settler arrived in the valley, floods have continuously plagued the existence of people in the Hill Country. This paper bears out the facts of the thesis. The author thoroughly enjoyed the research that was involved in the development of this paper. He got to know his aunt, Mrs. E.A. Davis. He now realizes there is a lot that can be learned from older people. The author wants to leave you with these thoughts:

As the writer walked down to the river the other day, one could see the drift in the tops of the trees. He smelled the pecan leaves and tasted the cool water of the revived springs. The writer could reach down and touch its chilling, refreshing water. He then sensed a feeling of terror, of the awesome power that this calm river could bestow. One could almost hear the roar of the rivers as if it was a monster destroying everything in its path.

Fort McKavett Sutlers

By Michelle Stockton

Horace Greely's newspaper, the *New York Tribune*, wrote of fort sutlers in the 1860s:

"Communication with the North is so easy that sutlers and their goods are allowed to come to the front. One may see any morning at City Point and Bermuda Hundred heaps of mellow apples, peaches, and vegetables, and fresh fish not twenty-four hours from the sea.

"Jellies and wines, pies are all brought from the vicinity of Norfolk and may be had of your enterprising sutler, if one will bear the swindle. Mr. Sutler often deals in literature. He will sell you *Atlantic* or *Harper's* for half a dollar, the latest novel for twice the sale price printed on the cover, or he will sell you a half-dozen rolls of cough candy, or quinine by the case, or a pair of spurs, or a shirt, or perfumed notepaper fit for letters to your sweetheart. He keeps postage stamps. He deals in Bibles. He has several carts of canned fruits, as well as pocket knives and corkscrews, scissors and surgical instruments.

"Great is the sutler. Like Shakespeare, he is a many-sided man. Like Sam Slick's wife, one cannot live without him nor scarcely with him. Like the Miller's daughter, he has grown 'so dead, so dear.' At last, we have a paymaster among us. Several millions of dollars have been paid to this army within a fortnight, and how the sutlers do thrive!"

By U.S. Army regulations of 1861, the federal sutlers were appointed for a three-year period unless sooner removed.

Every military post was allowed one sutler to be appointed by the secretary of war. Only those sutlers who could show officially recognized appointments were permitted on the post.

The paymaster general and other commanders in the field realized many articles which were essential to the soldier could be procured only from the sutler. The government ration consisted almost exclusively of hardtack, beef or pork, and coffee.

With such an unbalanced diet, is it any wonder men had scurvy or intestinal disorders which followed them through the war and to early graves.

On many occasions, the sutler's tent was empty when the men had no cash. Many sutlers displayed very little on their shelves until the men had cash in their pockets. As long as the cash held out, the sutler had plenty to sell, but after the first week of each month, his tent was bare. This was because of the large purchases made by the men and the sutler refusing to replenish his stock until the men were flush again.

According to Frances Nixon in an interview by the author:

"The government furnished soldiers with most essential items of clothing, but these were easily worn out, lost, or stolen, and then the soldier was forced to buy such items from the sutler or go without."

It was very common when the paymaster arrived there also came wagons loaded with all kinds of items for the sutler's tent. According to Frances Nixon:

"Liquor was one of the nonessentials that the sutler handled—Champagne, ale, and whiskey being the most popular. Much more important than liquor was smoking and chewing tobacco. The Confederate government realized this and issued its soldiers a tobacco ration, but the federal government did not. If the soldier bought from a sutler in the North, they paid fantastic prices, often half a month's pay for a common plug of tobacco, which the government could have issued for twenty-five cents. There were teamsters, whose occasional trip to supply depots netted them thousands of dollars because they sold at profits of 500 to 1,000 percent."

Army regulations of 1861 showed that no sutler could sell to an enlisted man on credit or items amounting to more than one-third of his monthly pay in the same month.

On December 16, 1851, Brevet Major General Persifor Smith ordered construction of a military post on the San Saba River. The regiment, commanded by Col. Thomas Staniford, arrived at the headwaters of the San Saba on March 14, 1852, and established a camp known as the "Camp on the San Saba". By the end of May, however, the post was relocated permanently at a more suitable site near a large spring about two miles downstream. Later, it was named Fort McKavett. As the garrison came, so came the sutler.

Sutler was a household word before and after the Civil War. There were two basic questions every soldier became accustomed to answering: where his regiment was camped and where the sutler had set up his hut or tent. Sutlers were subject to official inspections.

On July 20, 1856, Col. Joseph Mansfield arrived at Fort McKavett during an inspection tour for the department. In his report, Mansfield indicated a sutler at the post named Lane supplied other food items, tobacco, and whiskey to the troopers at their expense. Plats and records of Col. Mansfield's inspection showed that construction of several new buildings outside the square had occurred. Two stone and shingled structures built for the use as officers quarters and a sutler's store stood in the southeast corner of the reservation. In lieu of change at the store, individual sutlers issued their own money. Money for the soldiers was metal tokens, usually about the size of a penny, or small cardboard chits. Many of the sutler's metal tokens have been found bearing the name of "J.T. Traynor, Ft. McKavett Sutler". This was in 1858. In 1859, however, the post was abandoned and reverted back to civilian life.

Fort McKavett was reoccupied on April 1, 1868, when Company A, 4th Cavalry, under the command of Brevet Lieutenant Colonel Beaumont arrived on the banks of the San Saba. The nine years, he observed, had taken their toll on the post. It was found to be a mass of ruins, only one house was habitable, and the whole command was compelled to go under canvas. During the first month of reoccupation, the duties of the troops at the garrison centered on reconstruction of the old buildings and involved all the men. The sutler, however, knew what job he was to tackle and how to tackle it.

The sutler was the one who followed the army and sold provisions, tobacco, liquor, and knickknacks to the troops. Unquestionably, the prime reason for men seeking sutlerships was mercenary. The sutler was a civilian and his prices were set by the military authority. The list of items he sold was almost endless. One well-known sutler in Fort McKavett was Samuel Wallick.

From Pennsylvania, Samuel Wallick and family came to this country and bought ranch land, now owned by Joe Hunter Russell. Wallick applied for and attained the sutlership on the Fort McKavett post. Wallick did not have to pitch a sutler's tent nor build a lean-to; he was allowed to use a building on the post.

After receiving his appointment, Wallick purchased a stock of goods from various wholesale merchants, which were brought by freight wagons. Wallick then was settled as the post sutler. Wallick was a well-known and very prosperous man. He began to make a home for himself at Fort McKavett.

When the history of Fort McKavett as an army post ended in 1883 and its life as a pioneer town began, a number of the residents remained. Among them was Samuel Wallick.

On September 9, 1885, Samuel Wallick bought acreage and buildings from Joshua K. and Robert Robinson. One purchase was the sutler's quarters. This was used as the Wallick home for many years.

In summary, the author feels this quote from Francis A. Lord, author of *Civil War Sutlers and Their Wares*, is appropriate to encapsulate the material in her paper:

"History yields few parallels to the absolute obliteration of the sutler. The pension roles bear many hundred thousand names, but this hold there no objurgated blazonry... When we hale campaigners, meet and point to ourselves with pride (who dare gainsay our right?) his place is filled with yawning vacancy. River pilots of the war era, St. Vitus-stricken from dodging guerrilla buckshot, have coveted the Grand Army badge, and sons of sanitary heroes have pleaded for the Loyal Legions perquisites vicarious, but no residual sutler, nor the lineal progeny thereof, signs drafts like these on honor's ample funds. Hence, there is no sutler extant. Q.E.D. Seek ye his obituary in the thin, cold records of the almshouse. Find his flat or sunken resting place in the crowded silence of the potter's field and be therewith content. He lives now only as a fond and fragrant memory."

Although the above quote was not her own, the author's reactions about the Fort McKavett sutlers were very deep and involved. "Sutler" used to be a term not known in her vocabulary, only to be opened and hopefully used as more than just as a term in historical reading.

The author felt that the sutler deserved her thorough research. The sutler's hard work, yearning dreams and desires paid off well, and 1982 was the time for the sutler to come forth to receive his medal. Whether hard times or good times, the sutler always faced them with his head held high and would always leave a memory of pride in the word "sutler".

The cold has left a numb sensation in his toes; however, he must move on to his tent to supply the soldiers with their goods. Business should be good today, thanks to the cold weather. He sticks his tongue out to catch a snowflake upon it, only to taste the chilling wind instead.

The harshness of the wind reaches his ears and sends goosebumps down his spine. He feels an ever-present pain for the men who have to survive this deadly weather. Just the sight of their weak bodies and their dire longing for home takes over the chilling factor of the wind. The memories of the war, pain and discomfort, would also always leave an unpleasant place in this sutler's life.

Jake Wilensky Talks About Menard
By Olga Rodriguez

CHARACTER
The sun set; but set not his hope:
Stars rose; his faith was earlier up:
Fixed on the enormous galaxy,
Deeper and older seemed his eye:
And matched his sufferance sublime
The taciturnity of time.
He spoke, and words more soft than rain
Brought the Age of Gold again:
His action won such reverence sweet,
As hid all measure of the feat.
　　—Ralph Waldo Emerson (excerpt from Essays: Second Series)

While many stories have been forgotten about Menard, Mr. Jake Wilensky has helped relive these moments. The purpose of this paper is to bring back precious moments in story form and never let them die.

This is an interview with Jake Wilensky:

"There was a restaurant by the Bevans Hotel. Before it was a restaurant, it was an old-time bar; Menard was mostly made up of bars. There was a little bar owned by Jack Windle in the Bevans Hotel."

At this time in the interview Anna Bess Wilensky, Jake's wife, disagreed with him.

"Barton Crabb owned a liquor store in the Bevans Hotel," Jake continued. "He sold liquor by the bottle.

"As you go into the Bevans Hotel, the first part was a barber shop. At the first, it was a bar. The bar opened to the corner of the liquor store. Barton Crabb had beer and something else in the center of the hotel. It was there when I came a long time ago.

"There was a drug store named Jellybean's Drug Store. It was where the doctor's office is now.

"There was a dance hall above the Wilensky's Dry Goods

store that is still standing. People were not allowed to drink upstairs in the dance hall. Anyone that had to or wanted to drink had to go downstairs."

As the author listened to Jake talk, she was reminded of Hondo Crouch, the Clown Prince of Luckenbach, telling his tall tales, full of life, and important to the recording of the memories there, as Jake is here.

The writer asked Jake if there was a bar in the dance floor, the one above the boot shop. Jake replied:

"No, it was strictly a dance floor. Beer or liquor was not allowed in the dance hall because of the women. It was the proper thing to do; it showed respect toward the women. If the men wanted to drink, they had to go downstairs and drink in their cars."

Later in the interview, Jake referred to an incident that happened at a restaurant across from the dance hall:

"It was early in the morning, and we heard one shot, and then another. This guy was running around the building. Now, when he shot him or which bullet got him, I don't know. One fell. Then another fell. It was a one-man restaurant. The owner of the restaurant accused one of the men in there that he was messing around with his wife. When that happened, the owner of the restaurant came around and shot, then shot again. I heard two bullets. Where they went, I don't know. I think both of the bullets went in this guy's body. The cause was that the owner of the restaurant accused a customer of trifling. That's the modest way of putting it."

As the interview continued Jake's wife, Anna Bess, put in her few cents worth:

"Sam Mathews had a cleaning press where the Curry Freight building is now. There was a place with a two-story building. You had to climb the stairs, and that's where the Eastern Star met. That's where they had their meetings. That was torn down when John Landen built his building there.

"My two sisters were married in the ballroom in the Bevans Hotel. They were married in 1930. Orchestras were brought in to play. It was a fancy ballroom. Mostly everybody dressed in formals. It was very high class. They had the wedding in Menard because they had flowing liquor. One lady would outshine the other.

"Where Golda Mauldin's office is now," Anna Bess continued, "is where John Landen had a drug store. Next to the Busy Bee store that is still being operated, there was another drug store. Ole' man King ran that drug store.

Jake talked more about Menard then:

"Menard was very prosperous having all the bars. Brady and Brownwood were dry. People came to drink in Menard. Menard was wet in liquor. Soldiers would come in to drink. They were stationed in Brownwood. Menard was known as a 'wet' town. People came from miles around."

The above shows Jake Wilensky was, and still is, a very important part of Menard. The facts in this paper not only reveal some of the things that were in Menard, but that some people still remember little Menard as it was long ago.

The author learned many things about Menard while working on this paper. She felt very privileged she got the opportunity to relive those moments. It doesn't matter how modern Menard grows, the old memories will live forever. The author leaves you with her final feelings:

As the author walked into the old building, she could feel the warmth of the store. Happiness was at her side as she neared the counter. The twinkle in the man's eye was like a star falling from the sky. As she got closer to him, she saw an old, kind man who was willing to tell about Menard's past. He had lived through a golden age that almost everybody had forgotten. He knew these memories must survive. He was ready to relive the memories and share them with us. As the author walked out of the building, she knew that these precious moments would live on because the twinkle in his eye was like a new horizon.

The Menard Volunteer Fire Department
By Jack Cannon

WHAT IS A FIREMAN?
He's the guy next door.

He's the man's man with the sharp memory
of a little boy who never got over the
excitement of engines and sirens and smoke and danger.

He's a guy like you and me with warts
and worries and unfulfilled dreams.

Yet he stands taller then most of us.
He's a fireman.
He puts it all on the line when the bell rings.

A fireman is at once the most fortunate
and the least fortunate of men.

He's a man who savors life because he has seen too much death.
He's a gentle man because he has seen too much of the
awesome power of violent forces out of control.
He's a man responsive to a child's laughter because his arms
have held too many small bodies that will never laugh again.

He's a man who appreciates the simple pleasures of life...
hot coffee held in numbed, unbending fingers... the flush
of fresh air pumping through smoke and fire convulsed lungs...
a warm bed for bone and muscle compelled beyond feeling...
the camaraderie of brave men and women... the divine peace of
selfless service and a job well done in the name of all men.

He doesn't wear buttons or wave flags or shout obscenities
and when he marches, it's to honor a fallen comrade.

He doesn't preach the brotherhood of man...

He lives it.

> —Poem posted at many fire stations, author unknown

In the early days of Menard, before 1920, all fire fighting was done by bucket brigade until some civic-minded city fathers built a cart to carry a hand-operated pump and hose and nozzle. With this, they could pump water from the river or irrigation ditch which ran by almost every house in town. As early at 1920, there were mains laid and a few fire hydrants constructed.

The first fire station was located in an old livery stable which Moser Motors later occupied. One night in January 1924, when the weather was very cold, Emery Childress and Jim Thigpen, two of the fire boys who were staying in that livery stable, decided to put a light bulb in their bed to warm it up and go for a ride in the meantime. The bed caught fire and burned the livery stable.

Otis Moser, who was active in the fire department in the early days, said that they then fixed up an old barn and used it for a fire station. Mr. Moser said they obtained a couple of pool tables, and they wouldn't let anyone use them unless they joined the fire department.

In March of 1924, the city, which had provided financial support in purchasing the equipment for the fire department, agreed to pay Steve Martin $75 for a Ford chassis on which to mount the fire fighting apparatus, and to pay $100 for a fire alarm. Soon the fire department decided to buy a truck for a chemical apparatus. Two months later, both of these articles were purchased. The alarm, which could be heard for miles, was mounted on top of the Bevans Bank.

William Parker, a present trustee of the fire department, was a member for fourteen years and has seen improvements made, but not as many as in the past few years. For instance, the fire department was relocated to its present location in 1959.

Today, the Menard Volunteer Fire Department is a well-run organization with twenty-seven active members and four honorary members. The fire department is ready for almost any emergency and has people taking courses in cardiopulmonary resuscitation (CPR) as well as advanced life saving courses.

The purpose of this paper, to tell how the Menard Volunteer Fire Department was organized, was fulfilled through an interview with Otis Moser and W.W. Parker, as well as the women's fire auxiliary.

It tells of early days of the fire department and the modern nature of today's organization. The author closes with a paragraph written in his English class:

As I watched the burning house and saw the smoke billow up in a black cloud, I felt the incinerating heat upon my face. I smelled the searing wood as it burned. I heard the hum of water come running through the hose I was holding and knew the taste of success was near.

The Ambulance Service
By Kelly Miller

Auto Wreck
Its quick soft silver bell beating, beating
And down the dark one ruby flare
Pulsing out red light like an artery,
The ambulance at top speed floating down
Past beacons and illuminated clocks
Wings in a heavy curve, dips down,
And brakes speed, entering the crowd.
The doors leap open, emptying light;
Stretchers are laid out, the mangled lifted
And stowed into the little hospital.
Then the bell, breaking the hush, tolls once.
And the ambulance with its terrible cargo
Rocking, slightly rocking, moves away,
As the doors, an afterthought, are closed.
   —Karl Shapiro (excerpt)

The call comes over the scanner for an ambulance crew. The ambulance rolls within two minutes of the call. The present day ambulance service has been an asset to Menard for many years. The purpose of this term paper will let the reader learn about the new ambulance service. Time rewinds on a reel-to-reel, only to be played back...

The old ambulance service was not as efficient until the new program began to develop. The old service operated out of the back of a hearse. Precious minutes were wasted as a driver and attendant had to be called. The emergency crew was basically well trained, but often arrived too late to help. As Steve Whitson noted in an interview:

"I called it the old armpit and ankle ambulance crew. They would grab the patients by the armpits and ankles, load, and haul to the hospital."

The faults included more than time factors. Whitson, president of the newly organized ambulance service explained:

"The coordination between the members wasn't up to par. Whoever could be reached went with whomever else could be reached. The training techniques used were basic first aid methods. The level of training probably wouldn't reach the standards of our present-day service."

After much controversy, fund raising, and training, the service began improving. With the purchase of two ambulances, equipment, and hiring personnel, the process of a new mold began. It was a small step in the right direction, as seen through the eyes of the author. It was a beginning, like Squad 51.

Squad 51 [a special-built emergency vehicle used in the television show *Emergency*] rolled with millions of viewers getting the perspective of the camera crew. The author was intrigued with the "clean-cut emergencies" the actors handled without a flaw, but never saw the sometimes bloody and gruesome scenes portrayed on the television program. Johnny Gage and Roy DeSoto [fictional firefighter/paramedics stationed at Fire Station 51] became heroes to many across the nation as they saved lives every week. The squad had deeper roles than just entertainment. It gave the public a message of life and death and inspired the author of this paper.

Menard's telephone company employees, mechanics, school personnel, oil field workers, and ranchers became Johnnys and Roys after long hours of practice. They were never to become television stars except, maybe, in the eyes of a child's mother—the mother of a child who had been saved by them.

The author sat spellbound as he listened intently to tale after tale of EMS stories told by Steve Whitson. After one of the tales, he asked about improvements and how they affected the community. Whitson responded:

"The ambulance service recently organized into the voluntary organization much like the fire department. The results have been uplifting. There has been better coordination between the people in the organization. Financial stability and everyone becoming involved has been the trend since we organized. When everything smooths out, service to the community will be more effective."

The ambulance service was organized August 23, 1982 [this paper was written in October 1982]. After a need was seen for improvement, the current crew met and decided to upgrade the performance. The members selected officers and began forming a constitution. The first officers to be representatives of the new service included: Steve Whitson, president; Terry Zimmerman, vice president; Bob Miller, secretary-treasurer; David Hanna and Bob Brown, captains; and Don Zimmerman, training officer.

Thirteen charter members, in addition to the officers, included: Bobby Danford, Skeet Rodgers, Norman Tanner, Frances Guest, Mary Lee Castleberry, Sylva Speck, Clayborn Powell, Patty Miller, Amy Frazier, Stanley Frazier, Kelly Miller, William Williams, and Dan Feather.

The purpose of the ambulance service organization was to provide competent, effective, and efficient emergency medical care and transport for the county by properly trained, licensed, and certified members. The objectives included:
·   To meet the physical, emotional, and spiritual needs of each patient.
·   To help the patient understand his or her condition.
·   To give support to the patient and his or her family during an emergency and help identify and cope with his or her fears and anxieties.
·   To plan emergency care to meet the patient's immediate and future needs.
·   To comply with the physician's plan for diagnosis and therapy accurately and promptly.
·   To orient new personnel to the organization.
·   To maintain a high standard of emergency care and to provide an atmosphere conducive to learning for the group members.
·   To establish and maintain community awareness of the needs, challenges, and desires of the EMS.

The objectives seem large at times until the author became personally involved with the service. Then he looked into the community's involvement in the ambulance service.

It was three o'clock in the morning as the ambulance and fire truck rolled towards their destination, seventeen miles down the road. Ranchers, store owners, rig drillers, and housewives re-enacted drills to help save three badly injured car wreck victims. The author compared the medical skills of different personalities around town to a company in a large city.

The company initiated an internal first aid/emergency medical program that provided care for incidents that ranged from the simplest of problems, such as headaches and cut fingers, to treatment for serious injuries and sudden illness such as heart attack, stroke, diabetic reactions, to readying the patient for full paramedic care and transport to the hospital. The company had employees trained in the Emergency Care Attendant (ECA) and Emergency Medical Technician (EMT) levels for emergency situations, much like the present ambulance service in Menard.

The author saw the true vision of the EMT ambulance worker also summarized by Harry D. Grant and Robert H. Murray, Jr. in their book, *Emergency Care*:

"Few jobs are as frustrating, physically and emotionally draining, and even at times as terrifying as providing emergency care.

"But, then again, few jobs offer such rewards as seeing color return to the cheeks of a non-breathing child, watching a man walk from a hospital free from the effects of a spinal injury, and participating in the miracle of birth.

"In the sixties, the major thrust was to upgrade ambulance attendants to advanced Red Cross and CPR training. The picture was indeed grim.

"Today, all states, including D.C., Puerto Rico, Virgin Islands, and Guam, have full-time staffs administering EMS programs at the state level."

After the author studied the viewpoint of the EMT, he saw the need for further training and greater need for community involvement. Steve Whitson added to the subject:

"Everyone should become involved, not just to ride the ambulance, but to learn the life-saving skills to maybe someday help or save someone."

The author sat with an open ear as the night progressed and stories spun through Steve's apartment. One particular story of Steve's first experience on the ambulance brought the author to attention:

"I guess this is my most outstanding run, in fact, it is the one I always recall. Two girls rolled a pickup out towards Angelo. The one I was working on had major facial damage and lots of bleeding. The second girl had broken the seventh vertebra in the spinal column. We didn't know this at the time. We took the precaution of applying cervical collars and treated each as if a spinal injury was involved. I made mistakes, but we got her to Angelo. After x-rays were taken, I was glad we had not mishandled her.

"There have been times when I felt like quitting after messing up or not handling a situation correctly. I've made it a point all the way through to give help to the best of my ability, and that's all you can do."

The purpose of this paper was fulfilled by describing the ambulance conception, stories of Steve Whitson's ambulance runs, illustrations, and showing how the service was an asset to Menard for many years.

The author was able to see a flimsy emergency service that grew after a long period of being inadequate. He saw that the dedicated members of the community made it work.

In closing, the author wanted to share with the reader his thoughts:

The radio breaks the silence like a screech owl in the night. "We need an emergency ambulance crew at the hospital," barks the dispatcher. The cold feel of a plastic steering wheel is the only grip of reality at three o'clock in the morning. The red and white lights are flashes of warning as the ambulance flies toward the destination. The smell of fear bounces like a ping-pong ball from the author to the others on board. He tastes the rushing wind as it hurriedly brushes past. The life-saving unit stops deep in the night. Suddenly, the crew is enmeshed.

"Give me a blood pressure reading," asserts one EMT.

"He's not breathing, and there is no pulse," claims another.

The author works to help the victim until spontaneous heart functions and respiration occurs. One tired ambulance attendant rides back in total exhaustion from the night's affair, while the rest of the Hill Country sleeps in silence.

The Law Men
By Joe Hough

> *It is fatal to enter any war without the will to win it.*
> *—Douglas MacArthur*

The attitude expressed by Douglas MacArthur must have been the attitude one had to have had in the early days of Menard-ville to make this town survive. Later, feeding the prisoners, answering the two-way radio, and handling the constant ringing of the telephone was the atmosphere of this writer's early years. He thought that all children had trustees to entertain them. His father was a Texas lawman.

His home was the meeting place of area law officers. The family lived in the jail house of Sonora, Texas. Naturally, in choosing a topic for this paper, this author's interest is in the fascinating profession of the lawman, because the lawman is the symbol of respect and authority. The purpose of this paper is to describe the life of the lawmen of Menard.

One of the early Texas Rangers in Menard was Dan W. Roberts. He was born in Winston County, Mississippi, October 1841, and migrated to Texas with his family two years later. Dan joined the Frontier Battalion of Texas Rangers in 1874 and was soon promoted to lieutenant. He led several successful forays against the Indians in Menard and Mason counties, and on the Staked Plains during 1874 and early 1875. The following was a list the author found giving the names of other lawmen who served as sheriff in Menard County:

Louis Wilson, 1871-72
J.L. Howard, 1872-73
C.P. Nunley, 1873-74
J.W. Cart, 1874-75
W.C. Harter, 1875-76
J.M. Blackeley, 1876-77
J.H. Comstock, 1878
H.W. Merill, 1879-84

J.W. Mears, 1884-86
R.R. Russell, 1886-96
T.G. Robertson, 1896-1900
Jno. N. Tipton, 1900-04
Fred L. Napier, 1904-06
R.H. Spiller, 1906-16
F.M. Slaughter, 1916-26
Cecil Walston, 1926-40, 1943-44
Max Menzies, 1940-42
J.L. Gibbs, 1945

The sheriff at the time of this paper [1982] is Billy Joe Haney, and this writer thought that made him a prime candidate for an interview.

I asked Sheriff Haney why he chose law enforcement as his profession; he answered:

"I needed a job, and people around town asked me to run. I did. That was twenty-two years ago. I didn't figure I would stay with it that long, but I guess that I became addicted. I worked in San Angelo, but I wanted a job closer to home."

I asked Sheriff Haney about serious crimes while he has been sheriff; he responded:

"Well, I guess the most serious were murders. There have been about four of them while I have been here; most of them were by drunks."

I asked if being a lawman had changed over the years, and he responded:

"It has and in every way. The biggest was the code of criminal procedure that dealt with the rights of the accused. For example, we used to be able to get a prisoner and bring him right back. Now, we have to go in before a judge before and after we take him anywhere."

I asked when this law came into effect.

"About ten or twelve years ago. Maybe 1968 or 1970."

I asked Sheriff Haney if he had any amusing stories.

"Well, yes," he laughed, "but you can't turn them into your English teacher."

I asked for one that could be turned in; he thought for a moment and responded:

"There was this drunk downtown, stumbling all over the road. He must have been from out of town, because none of us knew him. I asked him where he lived. He said: 'First Street.' Back then, there weren't but a few streets named, and those were just the main ones. Anyway, I was sure that there was not a street named First. I said, 'If there is a street named First Street, I will take you home. If there isn't, you go to jail.' He said, 'Okay', and got in the patrol car. He pointed us to go toward the railroad tracks. As soon as we finally got there, much to my surprise there was this big sign saying 'First Street', so I took him home."

The author thought of how dangerous this job could be and asked Sheriff Haney if he had any scary stories to share:

"Yes, and this will be amusing, too. This man escaped from Big Spring's crazy house. I received a call on the radio that he was in a house on the outskirts of town. When I finally got there, about five large men were sitting outside saying, 'Don't go in there, he is crazy. Don't go in there.' There was a car sitting outside that he had just driven into the river. When I opened the door, all I could see was a strip of light across the room. It was pitch dark, and I was afraid to turn on my flashlight because I thought he might jump me. I headed straight for that light. When I got there it was a folding door, and I could hear something behind it. Scared out of my pants, I flung open the door as fast as I could. There he stood, a small man shaving. He turned to me and asked, 'What ya gonna do with me?' I replied, 'I'm gonna take you to jail.' 'Okay,' he said. So I took him to jail. The next day, I took him back to Big Spring. Boy was he crazy."

Knowing the sheriff could not do the entire job by himself, the author interviewed his mother, Belinda Fleming, about her work as deputy sheriff in 1972:

"When you [the author] were in first grade, Billy Joe [Sheriff Haney] separated the sheriff's office from the tax collector's office. He needed an office deputy. He came over and asked me if I would come to work for him. I had talked to him and his wife,

Mary Haney, for about five years on the radio. You see, I was the official voice of Sutton County, and they were the link to the outside world from Menard County in those days."

The author asked about frightening experiences:

"Family problems are the type you have to watch out for. One day we got a call to a family disturbance. When they arrived, the people who were having trouble quit fighting each other and turned on us. A heavy-set woman jumped on a deputy's back and tried to take his gun out of his holster. I thought to myself, 'Why did I pick this profession?'

"Another time it rained about five inches. Almost everybody in Menard had traveled to Eldorado to the football game, where it had rained about four inches during the game. All the local officers were on a road block between here and Junction. I think they had an armed robbery. Anyway, the house across the street from Gonzales Restaurant blew up. I had to leave the kids at home and go to the courthouse and get the officers on the radio. This was back in the days before these walkie-talkies and more sophisticated equipment... anyway, I had a heck of a time reaching them, as they couldn't hear me. I think I finally called the game warden in Junction and had him drive toward Menard until he could get them on the radio.

"Everyone's records and stolen items are stored in this computer... so today's officers have an easier time getting information than in the old times."

Belinda Fleming shifted the topic of the conversation to the author:

"You used to come up to the sheriff's office at 2:30 when you got out of school—it was just across the yard—but you got pretty bored. You were glad when five o'clock came and we could go home. You were more interested in playing football than in solving crimes."

After interviewing his mother, the author wished he could interview the law officers of fifty to seventy-five years ago. There would have been a lot more information between Dan W. Roberts fighting the Indians in Menard County and Belinda Fleming working the two radios in the courthouse, but this paper did describe some of the history and lawmen of Menard, as told by Billy Joe Haney and Belinda Fleming. Through long hours of research and organizing, the author leaves the reader with these feelings:

Walking into the old jail, the author feels the stale air against his face. Reading the writing on the wall, he can almost see the people who have stayed there and taste the food that they have eaten. Suddenly, the doors close to the small cell. He can't seem to find his way out of this horrid place. As each day goes by, there is a mark on the wall for it. The only time to look forward to is mealtime. The food isn't half as bad as people say. The time between, however, is long and dreadful. A drunk is brought in arrested, for instance, and put into the cell. The smell is almost too much to bear. He stinks as if he had slept in a trash can. As the author starts to become nauseous, the ringing of the school bell brings him back to reality. He thinks how ironic it is to see the little children playing after thinking such thoughts.

Waddell School House
By Johnnie Nasr

SCHOOL DAYS
School days, school days
Dear old Golden Rule days
'Reading and 'riting and 'rithmetic
Taught to the tune of the hick'ry stick
You were my queen in calico
I was your bashful, barefoot beau
And you wrote on my slate, "I Love You, Joe"
When we were a couple o' kids.
            —song by Will Cobb and Gus Edwards (1907)

Schools were a necessary institution for developing the young county of Menard. In 1908, the Waddell School, therefore, was built. The purpose of this paper is to describe the Waddell School history and preserve its memory.

In 1908, the ranchers met and decided that there were enough children in the neighborhood to build a school. Four ranchers donated land: George Eckhardt, Jim Harper, E. "Babe" Waddell, and Robert Winslow. Each of the men donated one acre on the corner of their property. The others donated labor, tools, or money.

The ranchers built a two-room school with two bathrooms outside. These were called "privies". They named the school "Dry Creek". It stayed in use from 1909 to 1926. The most students ever enrolled at one time were about forty-five. There were many different teachers, but only two taught at a time. The students ranged in age from first grade to tenth grade. Most of the teachers were paid twenty-five to seventy-five dollars a month. The school was used by many people, but the structure was wood, which was very weak.

In 1926, the community decided to rebuild the school into a more permanent structure. The same four ranchers furnished labor and materials. This time, cement was used. They added an auditorium with a platform. It took three months to rebuild. This was when the name of the school changed to Waddell School.

The lumber from the old school was used to build a teacherage. This was where the residing teacher lived. The teacher's salary was paid by funds raised by holding dances on the weekends. The books and supplies were paid for in this way, too. At one time, the funds were running low and there wasn't enough money to pay for a teacher. One woman, who felt that the need of the children getting an education was more important than all else, taught for no money at all. Her name was Fay Callan. The enrollment of students at the time she taught there was always under ten. Many of the ex-students still remember their days at the Waddell School.

"I walked into the school room and looked around, expecting to see a lot of kids," reports Edith Nasr, one of the last students to attend the Waddell School. She continued her story to say:

"I was only in the school for six weeks, but I enjoyed it. There were only eight enrolled in the school, I was the only second grader, so they moved me to third grade, because there was only one third grader. The teacher's name was Hannah Mahoney. She was very nice. When my friend and I wanted to get out of class, we had a plan. I would ask to go to the bathroom, which was outside, and then my friend would ask, too. We would stay outside and play until classes were over. Miss Mahoney never noticed us not coming back. That was probably because of my brother and cousin. They used to make her mad by throwing erasers at the blackboard. Even though it was just a few short weeks. I can still remember going to Waddell School."

Edith Nasr was one of the lucky students to attend the Waddell School. Many of the future students of the Waddell School were forced to ride twenty to thirty miles into town just to get to school. This happened because Menard County gained control of a larger district.

Menard expanded their school district to include the whole county. This made it necessary for the ranchers to take their kids into town for school. The ranchers protested this and tried to think of a way to keep the Waddell School open.

Some of the ranch owners refused to pay school taxes because they felt it was too far for the younger children to go for school. They took it to court and lost after many long trials. This closed the Waddell School and many other schools in the district.

After the school was closed, the land reverted back to the original owners or their descendants. The school building was located on Waddell property, with the teacherage and the windmill. The girls privy was on Harper's, the boys on Winslow's, and the cemetery on Eckhardt's land. The school officially was closed in 1944.

The building was abandoned from 1944 to 1951. The community then got permission from the owners to re-open it as a community center. Dances, barbeques, and other activities were held there to improve the social life of the community. A kitchen and indoor bathrooms were added. Home demonstrations and first aid courses were taught there. People also held many fund-raising events there. This lasted until 1954.

In 1954, Eddie and Ann Mears bought the school. They renovated it into a beautiful home. The interior was re-decorated and the walls and ceilings were painted. The original structure remained the same. This is how the Waddell School House stands today.

The Waddell School, in summary, was a big part of many people's lives. It was built as a school and later has served many other uses. It was used as a community center, dance hall, and meeting place. Even as the doors to the Waddell School were closed for the last time, the memories of the builders, teachers, and workers of the school always remained in Menard, reminding the author of these words:

Time, like an ever rolling stream,
Bears all its sons away;
They fly, forgotten, as a dream
Dies at the opening day.
　　—"Our God, Our Help in Ages Past" hymn by Isaac Watts

The Golden Rules
By Sandra Gail Castillo

School Days
Certain schools
are just big 'fiddles'.
Riddled by rules
and ruled by riddles. —John Roscoe

Menard Elementary School will always be a memorial and a historical building for education in Menard County. This paper will tell more about teaching, however, than the building itself.

Over the years, the school itself has changed very little, but additions have been made. The elementary school was built in 1940 by the WPA (Works Progress Administration). The school is not the only thing that has changed.

What one would like to ask is, "Have you ever thought about how teaching has changed?" The author went to the Menard Elementary School and interviewed one of the first grade teachers, Mrs. Virginia Hendricks. Some of the things the author found out include: kids nowadays like school, but back then kids did not have television and they were eager to learn more. This doesn't mean they were smarter, but students today like to learn at their own speed. Students nowadays are eager to learn, but it is more fun.

It has only been eight weeks of school, and the first grade kids have two books to read: *Pug* and *Sun Tree*. These are the first two books in the first grade. Mrs. Hendrick says: "They get so excited when they pick up a book and can read."

Everything that is taught, like English, math, etc. is taught in a group. Reading is taught by groups, like group one and group two. The students who can read faster do so, while the other group gets more help. This is only right because it is not fair to keep the students behind who learn faster.

Reading is learned by teaching phonics first and, then, after that, the students are shown a word. This word is spelled to them by the teacher. The teacher then tells them what the word is. The students then spell it and say it. An example of this is, if the word was "dog", the teacher would say "D-O-G, dog", and the students have to write the word on paper. They then have to spell it again. After all this is done, the teacher writes on the board "dog" and "hog". The students have to pick out the word they just learned.

The author thinks this is very good. It seems like the students will look at the word more than once, and this new way makes the word appear easier to learn. This is the new system that they are using in the first grade. The author is sure that the other grades might do it differently.

Reading is done the first thing in the morning. Mrs. Hendricks says that in the morning the students are most alert. This way they are fresh and haven't been running around outside. While one group reads, another group does penmanship.

Another thing that has changed in the first grade is students take dictation. They also have to read a story and write a story. "This is so much fun because they make the cutest stories, and they are really funny," according to Mrs. Hendricks.

Their grading system has really changed. They have "E" for excellent, "S" for satisfactory, and "N" for needs improvement. If the child talks or fights, an "X" is put on the back of the report card for the parent to know how the child acts in school. Mrs. Hendricks tries to cope with the problems by herself, but if a solution does not happen, she will call the parents.

Mastery tests also are new in the first grade. There are eight words that have to be read in eight seconds. The pupils really like this because it gives them a challenge and a chance to win a star.

The pupils also have to use the word in a sentence, and they have to do this orally. In the higher grades, they have to write it.

Dressing has changed a lot. It seemed back then, the little boy or girl would wear the pants and short or dress for a whole week, go home, take them off, wash them, and wear them back to school the next week. Kids nowadays do dress better because they have more money and can afford to buy more clothes.

Mrs. Hendricks said students tell her funny stories. "If only some parents knew what their kids tell me, they would never want to come back to school," she laughs. "One student told me her mother took her daddy's clothes and threw them out in the yard."

Punishment has changed the most from older times. One used to be allowed to hit a child if there was a witness to the punishment. Now, if a teacher spanks somebody, that teacher has to let another teacher watch, fill out a form, and have the form signed by the principal. Now, Mrs. Hendricks says a teacher needs all these papers, witnesses, etc. Back then, one just spanked a kid because they felt the child needed it. The author remembers when she was in the first grade and they put a "tattle tail" sign on your seat if you told on somebody. If one rocked back on his or her chair, they got to sit in a chair with the front legs cut off. This way, the student couldn't lean back or rock, but you did slide forward.

The Golden Rules of school might be rough and the work might get tough, but in the long run, isn't it wonderful? The author learned that teaching little children is a lot of fun, and it makes her feel good that one can accomplish such things as does a teacher.

The author finishes with these feelings: As the author walked into the building to get the interview, she could see the children running around after the pep rally. The spirit was so great that the author could feel the chill bumps run up her arm. The smell of the cafeteria was still in the air. One could almost taste the rolls. It is terrific fun to be part of the school, even after you have moved on to high school.

The Old School

By Bruce McCain

> *Nothing now is left*
> *But a majestic memory.* —*Henry Wadsworth Longfellow*

On the morning of October 17, 1948, an event took place that will live in infamy: Menard High School burned down.

From the *Menard News*: "Almost the entire building was ablaze when the fire alarm sounded at 4:00 a.m. Sunday morning.

"The fire started sometime Saturday night, and was of undetermined origin. The entire local fire department and many volunteers fought for several hours to save the building, but were unable to save anything except the football suits and other athletic gear that was stored in the concrete addition at the west end of the building.

"The loss has been estimated at about $150,000 [$1.5 million in 2017 dollars] with about $75,000 insurance carried. The building was built in 1930 at a cost of $30,000, and the principal fixtures installed at that time cost $2,985. Several hundred books had been added along with other equipment that was completely destroyed. One good thing about the time the outbreak began was that there were no people inside who could have been trapped in the burning structure."

Could this fire have been planned? If so, what were the arsonists motives? Why were no clues found? What took so long for the fire alarm to be sounded?

Questions such as these bring to mind some interesting possibilities. The fire may have been a practical joke gone wild. Another town may have been unhappy because of a lost football game. Had there been a grudge against Menard?

The *Menard News* states: "The walls, which were of very flimsy construction, gave way."

Could the electrical work also have been of poor quality? Poor insulation could have been the problem. John Ed Jackson recalls the fire very plainly:

"When I was a kid, I always thought that the best thing that could ever happen would be for the school to burn down. Well, it's not quite like that.

"I remember watching the walls fall in, and tears running down my face. To me, it must be one of the worst tragedies that could happen to a young person, or to anyone for that matter.

"All that was salvaged was the football equipment. I remember that because we had a game Friday night, and the equipment was still on the bus. They thought that the stage could also be saved, but it was no use.

"The fire had probably been smoldering all day, then caught fire and burned most of the night. I think it was about four in the morning when the alarm sounded.

"The following Monday, we met at the high school, or what was left, to look around. Mr. C.R. Brace, the principal, let us go to our lockers. There was nothing left in my locker except ashes. My bottle of ink for my fountain pen was empty except for black soot, which was the ink.

"There were a few class rings left in the safe. They were melted like melted lead. You could not tell one ring from another because they had all run together."

The future of every student could have been threatened.

"All of the records in high school were destroyed," John Ed Jackson continues. "I don't know what the people who went on to college did. They may have gotten into college on the weight of their grades after the fire and on the fact that they just didn't have any grades."

Even with the fire, school had to continue.

"We continued school in several places in town," John Ed Jackson remembers. "We went to a few places in the junior high, the courthouse, and several of the churches. The pastors were a big help here, for they had enough problems anyway. It made the day longer, but we made it. We still managed to have a little fun.

"When we were still in the high school and lunch came around, we all went to the lunchroom to eat. Well, it took us about five or six minutes to walk to the junior high. By then, all the little kids were cleared out. When we were moved to the junior high and lunch came around, 'Bam!' we were there. Well, there we were, having to wait five to ten minutes for lunch. Now, that did not set too well. It was getting close to Christmas and fireworks were plentiful. I lit me a handful of them firecrackers and threw them down the stairs. When I did that, all hell broke loose. Those little kids came running out, and the lunchroom help came running out. We started down the stairs and there were still some kids standing on tables crying, 'I want my mommy!' We did that a couple more times, and they were usually out when we came along. It was a mean thing to do, but it was fun."

Even with the fire, school still had all of the everyday activities it normally would have.

"I am a bona fide graduate of the Mission Theatre," John Ed Jackson continues. "That is where we held graduation. The junior and senior play was held at the theatre also.

"If I had it to do all over again, I don't think I would say, 'I wish the school would burn down,' because it just isn't that much fun."

Wanting the school to burn down is something many students say they want. Faced with the actuality of having no school, the thoughts would probably change drastically, as shown in this paper's account of the aftermath of the Menard High School fire in 1948.

The author's feeling toward this subject are mixed. A student spends nine months out of the year going to school. During this time one comes to love his or her alma mater and would not willingly wish any harm come to it.

There are no words that can describe the feeling one gets when an old school is mentioned. One can still see the students walking to class and hear their conversations. The rough brick walls can still be felt while memories of school linger.

The Word Gets Around—Menard Newspapers
By Brenda Blakeley

> *Carrier of news and knowledge, instrument of trade and commerce, promoter of mutual acquaintance among men and nations and hence peace and goodwill.*
>
> *Carrier of love and sympathy, messenger of friendship, consoler of the lonely, servant of the scattered family, enlarger of public life.*
>
> *—Inscriptions on the east and west pavilions of the Washington, DC Post Office.*

Thin sheets of printed paper crackled as the reader stood, his pride showing through his overcoat, reading his name mentioned in a small town's newspaper column. The purpose of this paper is to relate the history of one such paper in Menard, Texas, the *Menard County Enterprise*, which after much water flowed under the bridge, came to be the present *Menard News and Messenger*.

Printing was nonexistent before 1450. All books were hand-written by monks in monasteries. This was all changed by Johannes Gutenberg. He had invented a printing press prior to 1450, although he thought it was too crude. By 1450, the Gutenberg press was working, and the old method of handwriting was no longer necessary. Also, with this new invention, fifty to sixty pages an hour could be printed. Through the many years, the printing press was modernized to increase speed and productivity. This was also realized in the newspapers of Menard.

According to the *Menard News and Messenger Centennial Edition* in 1971:

"Menard County's first newspaper was known as the *Menardville Monitor*, established in 1887 or 1888 by Columbus Redmon. The printing plant was located in the upper story of the old courthouse building. However, Redmon shortly moved his plant to Ft. McKavett and began the *McKavett Breeze*, a short-lived weekly.

"B.L. Bourland began the *Menardville Record* in 1889 and had his offices in the old Vander Stucken building on Main Street.

Bourland sold the *Record* to J.W. Hunter and he and his family operated the paper for a year before they founded began the *Mason Herald* in 1892.

"The *Menard County Enterprise* was established in 1893 by Dave Maddox who published the paper for several years. He was succeeded by Austin Callan, who published a long account of the flood of 1889.

"A firm of Brady lawyers, J.E. Shropshire and Sam Hughes, purchased the *Enterprise* in 1903 and J.W. Hunter returned to become the editor and manager. Hunter resigned in 1904 to begin the *Kimble County Crony* in London.

"The name of the *Enterprise* was changed to *Menard Messenger* in 1908. The Callans—Claud, Austin, and L.E.—operated the paper for several years during this period.

"R.E. 'Josh' Billings was the publisher of the *Messenger* in 1915. He also published a monthly magazine for a new organization, the Texas Sheep and Goat Raisers Association. This magazine was of considerable help to the sheep and goat industry.

"The first linotype machine was installed by J.W. Munsell in 1923. Mr. Munsell began printing more and better papers with the addition of this machine. Until this time, all type was hand-set, with a full day's work for one typesetter being an average of five columns of type.

"Owners of the *Messenger* following Billings for the next several years included Len Warren, who later sold the plant to N.H. Pierce in 1941. N.H. Pierce established the *Menard News* November 5, 1936, and upon acquiring the *Messenger* in 1941 merged the two papers, thus forming the present-day *Menard News and Messenger*.

"Several honors were awarded to the *Menard News* and to the young *Menard News and Messenger* in this period. Included in these awards were: Best Mechanical Appearance in Division B of South Texas Press Association; First Place News Photography, Division B South Texas Press Association, 1942; Best Weekly Newspaper, West Texas Press Association, 1939; Best Mechanical Appearance, South Texas Press Association, 1938; Best Front

Page, South Texas Press Association, 1939; Best All-Around Newspaper, South Texas Press Association, 1941; and Second Place in National Editorial Association for Excellence, 1940."

The many owners of the award-winning paper following N.H. Pierce included: Hugh B. Thompson, Lyle Young, Robert S. Weddle, and a trio of David Young, Jerry Lyon, and Ted Polk. Jerry Lyon and Ted Polk sold their interest in the paper, and David Young took on ownership with Don Wilkinson as a partner for a short time. Dan Feather acquired the paper in 1972, and he was the sole owner of the *Menard News and Messenger* and the accompanying office and party supplies business.

When the author interviewed Dorothy Kerns, reporter for the *Menard News*, she learned many useful facts, such as Dorothy Kerns said that a typesetter was two things. One was a machine that puts the article in columns; the other was the person who operates the machine. The author then asked about linotype machines.

The reply was the *Menard News* office does not use a linotype machine, which creates a line of type or a row of type. At one time, however, it was a very up-to-date machine that helped in the printing of the newspaper.

Dorothy Kerns continued: "Dan and I start the paper Monday morning and it is printed Wednesday at 7:00." She also said the newspaper is taken to Fredericksburg to be offset printed. The author inquired about offset printing:

"Offset printing is done by a computer that photographs the typed article and sets it into columns," was her reply. [Offset printing is a type of printing; the computer setting type likely was doing so to allow the building of the page, which then would be used through a photographic process to create the negative or plate for offset printing.]

The author next asked what was Ms. Kerns favorite aspect of the paper. She said she enjoys pasting pictures, but she least liked selling ads.

The writer then asked if one needed formal training to be a photographer or columnist. The answer was no, although Ms. Kerns did have formal training in those fields.

The essayist's final question was: "What has been your most humorous event working on the newspaper?"

Dorothy Kerns said it was the April Fool issue. "Everything was printed upside down and backwards. I loved the expressions on people's faces when they read the front page."

Even though there were humorous events, the author knew the newspaper business was not an easy one, and one must be able to take sides on a controversial issue.

In this paper, changes in the newspapers of Menard were shown to be basically in the many changes in ownership of the paper. Certain changes lay also in the span of newspaper names from *Menardville Monitor* to the *Menard News and Messenger*, and the variety of equipment necessary to prepare it for the people. And, as one of the people who reads the paper, the author feels a sense of the newspaper business.

The author, at the end of her research, knew much more about the printing of a newspaper.

A sign of age shows as I grasp the big, brass door handle; the handle is big and heavy, not like the new hand-fitted knobs. As I pull open the door, the hands of history grab my arms and lead me into the past. I touch the old typesetter, while hearing sounds coming from the new, updated model. I smell the aroma of freshly printed papers, and see them stacked, ready for the morning's delivery. The taste of years gone by leaves my mouth as I exit, knowing that someday, after returning to Menard, both presses will sit, side-by-side, and wait silently for the arrival of another.

The Kothmann Commission Story

By Lisa Kothmann

YOUNG LAMBS

The spring is coming by a many signs;
The trays are up, the hedges broken down,
That fenced the haystack, and the remnant shines
Like some old antique fragment weathered brown.
And where suns peep, in every sheltered place,
The little early buttercups unfold
A glittering star or two—till many trace
The edges of the blackthorn clumps in gold.
And then a little lamb bolts up behind
The hill and wags his tail to meet the yoe,
And then another, sheltered from the wind,
Lies all his length as dead—and lets me go
Close bye and never stirs but baking lies,
With legs stretched out as though he could not rise. —John Clare

The Kothmann Commission Company was founded twenty-seven years ago [at this writing in 1980] by two young brothers, Jamie and Carlton Kothmann. The Kothmann brothers of Menard, Texas, have shown that management and teamwork pays. The purpose of this paper is to explain that thesis.

Jamie and Carleton, only two and one-half years apart in age, have always done things together. When money was scarce and the decision had to be made as to who could stay in college, Jamie quit Texas A&M in 1947 to run a sheep operation. After leaving college, Jamie married June Cates the same year. Jamie ran a small sheep operation on eight leased sections south of Fort McKavett to provide money for Carlton to get this degree in animal husbandry.

"James would run the ranch, and I'd get the education," Carlton noted.

Jamie and Carlton were born in London, Kimble County, and moved to Menard when Jamie was about nine-and-a-half years old. They both went to Menard schools, three years apart, and have always been quite independent partners. Carlton says: "We were typical brothers; we fought, and Jamie usually came out on top."

Carlton helped Jamie during the summer while he was still attending school.

"At odd times he did all the work," Carlton said.

"It was quite a load, but I got a living and so forth out of it," Jamie replied.

The brothers both decided the big load was worth it when Carlton returned from college, but the drought soon came.

The drought hit in 1952; Carlton was fresh out of college. He had received his bachelor of science degree in husbandry, but there were no animals to work with.

"The land dried up and the owners went up on the lease, and we were forced out," Jamie said.

Carlton then joined the United States Air Force, and Jamie went to work in a feed store in Menard. The drought made the future look dismal at the time, but it was the best thing that could have happened. It forced Jamie into the beginning steps of what would become their future business.

In 1953, Jamie and Carlton's father, well-known Menard livestock buyer W.L. Kothmann, died and Jamie went into the livestock buying business. A year later, he expanded into the feed business, working as a salesman for a feed company.

"Order-buying business was real good in the spring and summer, but not so good during the winter," Jamie said.

Carlton returned from the Air Force in 1953, newly married to Barbara Rue Cannon. He went into partnership with Jamie in the livestock order-buying business, and Kothmann's was formed. Jamie also took on a sales territory for the feed company in Schleicher County.

In 1956, the brothers leased warehouse space for their own feed store and added a mill the next year. Both Jamie and Carlton stated: "The business just sorta gradually grew."

They moved into a modern feed store, their present location, in 1961. Their capacity was 25,000 head of sheep and cattle.

The Kothmann feed pens are located in the sheep raising region called the Edwards Plateau. They feed sheep of all breeds, but a popular breed is a Suffolk-Rambouillet cross with a trace of Delaine.

There are two main phases of the Kothmann Commission Company operation. The first is the feeding and fattening of lambs. The second is the feed mill and service to the ranching industry in the surrounding area.

Lambs are bought from area ranchers, as well as out-of-town ranchers, to be placed on feed. The weight and price of these lambs vary throughout the year. When the lambs arrive, they are placed in a starting pen. While there, they are drenched, vaccinated for over-eating, given vitamin A, and implanted. The drench is to kill stomach worms. The implant is a tiny pellet shot into the ear tissue to aid in a faster, more efficient gain. The vitamin A is to correct any deficiency which the area usually has.

The lambs are sheared when they have adjusted to the feed and overcome the stressful period. Lambs generally will gain weight faster out of the wool. The Commission Company contracts with a local shearing company because there are sheep to be sheared almost every day.

"Age determines the wool crop. A lamb six to eight months of age will shear four to five pounds. Sheep, one year or older, will carry five and one-half to seven pounds of wool," Jamie stated.

The lambs are taken from the starting pen and placed in regular feeding pens. These pens are designed to hold 500 to 1,000 animals. This begins the feeding process. There are five feed numbers that the lambs are fed. Number one is made up mainly of cotton seed hulls with Aureomycin and a small amount of milo. The Aureomycin is an antibiotic used to control the over-eating disease. The number two through number five increases in milo. Number five is considered a full or hot feed, and the lambs are maintained on this until they reach the desired weight to be shipped.

The weight of the fat lambs ready for market varies from 105 to 110 pounds. The price varies according to the current supply and demand at supermarkets and restaurants.

The marketing of lambs usually goes to Swift Meat Company in Brownwood and Monfort in San Angelo. A few loads are trucked out of state. The lambs are sold on a guarantee of sixty-one percent dressed yield weight. If the lamb yield is more or less than six-one percent, the price is added or subtracted according to butchered hanging weight.

The weather environment cannot be controlled during the feeding process. When it rains, the pens get very muddy along with the lambs in them. The company has a sheep washing machine. The machine is a shed that hold 450 head of lambs. The lambs are wet with Tide soap and watered for a period of time. One of the employees then hooks up a fire hose to an electric pump and washes the lambs until they are ninety percent clean. The water is recycled several times through use of a slatted floor. The slatted floor aids in the draining of the excess water. The lamb washing machine is one of a few in the United States. The market price of the lamb would be docked if the lamb pelts were dirty.

Lambs do not gain at the same rate. They are run through a cutting chute. Lambs weighing 105 to 110 pounds are cut off to be shipped to market. The others are returned to the pen to eat more feed and gain more weight.

Kothmann Commission Company has expanded their pens over the years. The pens average from 15,000 to 30,000 head of lambs. The pens are designed with alleyways between each pen. This allows the bulk feed tractor to drive along slowly, filling the open feeders along the edge of each pen. This type of arrangement cuts down the expenses of labor.

The feed program from beginning to market usually takes an average of 60 to 120 days, depending on the size and condition of the lambs coming to the company. Most people buying lambs at their local market don't realize the many hours of hard work that go into getting the meat ready for their tables.

The feed mill operation is a major part of the feeding program of the company for area ranchers. The feed is hauled in by company-owned trucks and stored in bins.

The feed must be mixed with the right balance of ingredients for a complete feed ration. The milo is heated by a steam boiler and crushed flat between two large rollers. This process enables the animal to get more digestion juices around the ingested milo and results in faster weight gains. These steps are very important to the success of the feed program.

The next function of the mill and warehouse is the complete service to the livestock producers. This service includes all feeds for pasture, range, and a full line of healthcare products for all livestock. The Kothmann Commission Company even carries feed for deer and domestic animals. There are also many other products available to the customers.

Jamie and Carlton Kothmann began a small partnership business twenty-seven years ago. Hard work and determination helped Kothmann Commission Company become one of the largest businesses in Menard County. The lamb feedlot is one of the largest in the United States. The Kothmann brothers' methods helped to improve their operations and that of area ranchers. Carlton and Jamie have shown management and teamwork pays off.

The author took in a great amount of information about the sheep occupation and dealing with the difficulties of running a business. The author learned hard work and lots of time are involved in running a business, especially one starting before the drought, having one's business forced out, and then coming back in the end to have one of the largest feedlots in the United States. Reflecting upon all these things, the author leaves with her thoughts as she entered the Kothmann Sheep Commission:

As the author walked into the feed store, she could smell the newly mixed feed. She could almost taste the molasses that was being blended in with the feed. She saw all the workers scurrying around, getting their jobs done. She heard the trucks as they were backing up against the chute to unload the fat little lambs. One could just imagine touching the young lambs' wool, yet wondered what would become of them in the end...

Banking Institutions of Menard

By Laura Rabun

Take care of the pence, and the pounds will take care of themselves.
   —Lord Chesterfield

A pioneer cattleman twisted the hat in his hand nervously, hoping the banker seated across the desk would grant his loan. He was an example of the importance of banks in Menard's early growth. Without the birth of banks, the continuing growth of Menard might never have occurred. The purpose of this paper is to relate the important history of banks in Menard with first a look at the early banks of Menard.

According to N.H. Pierce in *The Free State of Menard*, Menard has never had a bank failure. From sources about Menard's history, the author learned that even though one bank was liquidated, it was true Menard never had a bank fail. This was fortunate because when the railroad came to the little town, there was indeed a need for a place to record currency exchanges and borrow money. According to *The Free State of Menard*:

"The need for banks rose as more money was traded in Menard. The nearest banks before 1903 were in Mason and Brady. Much of the trading took place in San Antonio. The money bags were frequently robbed on the way back from the city. The first bank in Menard began the business in 1903."

In an interview with the author of this paper, William A. Carter (a former president of the Menard National Bank) said the Bank of Menard had more history available than the other banks in the community. It was organized in 1903 by R.R. Russell and William Bevans. "William Bevans was president, C.B. Mason was cashier, and W.P. Bevans worked as the bookkeeper," according to Carter.

The bank had been located on the corner of Canal Street and San Saba Avenue throughout its history, although its name changed.

In 1919, the Bank of Menard became a national bank, and

was then known as Bevans National Bank. The officers at that time included: William Bevans, president; W.P. Bevans, vice president; George C. Stengel, cashier; W.A. "Willie" Cannon, assistant cashier. The bank then changed from a national bank to a state bank.

According to Carter: "On January 1, 1928, the City Central Cooperative of San Antonio bought control of the bank from Mr. Bevans and the name was changed to the Bevans State Bank, as it is today." [The Bevans State Bank of Menard changed its name to First State Bank in January 2004.]

At the time of the change in 1928, William Bevans was president, W.P. Bevans was vice-president, George C. Stengal was vice-president and cashier, and Joe Glasscock and William Carter were assistant cashiers.

The presidents from 1903 to date were William Bevans, W.P. Bevans, A.J. Lewis, and A.B. Williams. These men were assets to the bank, but two men in particular worked at the bank for many years.

William Bevans was president for twenty-eight years. As one of the founders, he was indeed the backbone of the bank. Another man who was with the bank for many years was George Stengal. He was employed at the establishment for sixty-two years.

At the time this paper was written [1982], the board of directors consisted of Carl G. Kothmann, A.J. Lewis Jr., J.L. Smith, A.B. Williams, and Alton Williamson. These men and the Bevans State Bank helped the economic development of our town.

The coming of the railroad also brought the opening of the Menard National Bank on November 29, 1919, as stated in *The Free State of Menard*. The bank was organized in 1919 by R.M. Heyman, J.A. Heyman, J.R. Smart, Carl A. Martin, and G.W. Bradford. Smart was elected president and Martin vice-president.

According to Carter, "In 1963 control of the bank was sold to Carter and Gene Whitehead by Heyman and associates. Whitehead became chairman of the board and Carter president."

At the time of this paper, Whitehead was chairman, Drake

McKinney was president, Martin was inactive vice-president, while Jack Walston served as vice-president. The cashier was Shirley Lewis. Murph Compton, W. Roy Jacoby, J.R. Kothmann, Drake McKinney, Martin, and Whitehead formed the board of directors. These people were responsible for the construction of a new bank building.

The new 7,000-square-foot facility was constructed of native stone. It was built on the corner of Bevans and Canal streets and Highway 83. Completion date was August, 1981. The new building was constructed with a three-lane drive-through, a community room with adjoining lounge and kitchen area, a five-station teller area, and a night depository. The bank had been located in the old location on San Saba Avenue since its organization in 1919.

Although there has never been a bank failure in Menard, Menard had another bank at one time. In 1914, the First National Bank of Menard was organized by William Bevans and Dick Russell. Much of the stock was owned by Bevans and Russell. The president was D.G. Benchoff. L.G. Callan was cashier. Without loss to depositors or stockholders, the bank liquidated after operating for only a few years.

With a peek inside the Bevans Bank door, the author summarizes her paper.

As bank notes, coins, checks, and currency passed through the old teller's bars at the Bevans Bank, the author realized that her paper's purpose had been fulfilled. The history of the banks, the founders, and the functions of their business had been researched through the eyes of William Carter, N.H. Pierce's *The Free State of Menard*, and the author's own banking experiences. The paper showed that without the births of the banks, the birth of Menard could not have occurred.

The author felt she had researched the banks of her community as thoroughly as possible. There was a feeling of satisfaction knowing her paper was complete. That satisfaction was shown in the closing paragraph, written for safe-keeping in another age.

The year is 1903. The writer walks into the newly constructed bank building. The look of workers busying themselves is thrilling to the author's eyes. As the bank employees try to please the many new customers the bank has acquired, the author can smell the new wood aroma surrounding her. The iron bars, which enclose the teller, are shining. The tellers seem as anxious as anyone in the bank to please customers. As the reporter stares through the remodeled windows, she is drawn back to the present and finds herself scrubbing off the white shoe polish with which she, as a cheerleader, had written spirit slogans to spread excitement for her school.

Electrical Companies
By Keith Bundick

A RHYME ABOUT AN ELECTRICAL ADVERTISING LIGHT
I look on the specious electrical light
Blatant, mechanical, crawling and white,
Wickedly red or malignantly green
Like the beads of a young Senegambian queen.
   —*Nicholas V. Lindsay (excerpt)*

A power station electrifies a town. A town's survival may depend upon the electricity from the power station. Electricity heats and cools homes. It allows businesses to operate efficiently. The purpose of this term paper is to describe the present and past of electrical power in Menard and Menard County.

Ruby Wagner explained early electrical power in an interview:

"In the early 1900s, Menard was supplied with electricity by a generator. The generator was driven by two 125-horsepower oil engines. The generator was owned by Pete Anderegg. This was the only means of electricity during this period. The generator was turned on in the evening for townspeople with electrical lights.

"In 1913 and 1914, Pete Anderegg, owner of the Menard Power and Ice Company, started to supply electricity to the City of Menard. He installed six street lights at a cost of $235 per year."

The City of Menard has grown since the early 1900s. At the time of this paper [1982], Menard has approximately ten times as many street lights to service than in the early 1900s.

The situation changed in 1925. According to the City of Menard council minutes:

"On July 13, 1925, the City of Menard granted a franchise to West Texas Utilities to supply electricity to the city and surrounding area."

The ordinance was approved by the city council of Menard. The ordinance passed on July 13 and approved on July 21 by the city council and the mayor, J.W. Munsell. A building then began to be erected by West Texas Utilities in October, 1925.

The building, in which West Texas Utilities was still located in 1982, was located on West San Saba Street. West Texas Utilities also purchased the Menard Power and Ice Company. According to an interview with Marvin Bryant and Ruby Wagner:

"At this time, Menard Power and Ice Company had 216 customers to serve and twelve street lights. The population was around 1,500 people."

West Texas Utilities had many customers at the time of this research. The growing pains occurred with difficult transportation means. According to Bryant:

"As Menard was being prepared for a sub station, men started building power lines to Menard. From Eden to Menard and from Mason to Menard poles and line were carried to construction areas by team and wagon and Model T pickups."

West Texas Utilities, from then to the date of this writing, had five managers. The first manager was Joe Whaley, and his bookkeeper was Mrs. Bluitt. Crawford Lehmberg became the bookkeeper after Mrs. Bluitt. Crawford Lehmberg later became the second manager, and Doris Lankford became the bookkeeper. Lankford was still the bookkeeper when this paper was written in 1982.

John Agnew was the third manager. The fourth was Robert Conner. The fifth, and current manager in 1982, was Marvin Bryant.

The author had some hard times working on this research paper. Working for the present-day electric company, studying, and playing football presented some obstacles. Though it was hard, it helped me get an understanding of the history of Menard's electrical sources and inspired these closing remarks.

As I touch the light switch, I see the brilliance of the light fill the room. I remember the past of electricity. I feel heated and cooled air being circulated by electric power. I smell the aroma of cooking coming from the electric stove. I listen to the stereo that helps me finish this paper.

The Steam Engine of Menard

By Mark Menzies

In the crisp light of a November morning, the author stands in the midst of the tools of a blacksmith. They are brought with the years—the steam engine, lathe, and forge. Is that burning wood which the author smells as he thinks how the steam engine served its purpose to the blacksmith? He hears the story of grapes grown for wine, and in his mind's eye he can see the first windmill in Menard. A taste of wine, tinged with the flavor of the past, and now it is time to go back to town. —Mark Menzies

The steam engine made a great impact on the lives of Americans in industry and in agriculture.

This paper explores one such steam engine in Menard County, showing how the effects of steam power affected a community even of Menard's small size. The author found a perfect example of this on the Beyer farm, which is approximately seven miles west of Menard.

The author interviewed Charles Beyer at his ranch, who told of his grandfather, Gus Beyer, who came to this country in the late 1870s on a steamboat. It seems there was some trouble with the steamboat's engine while en route to the United States. The captain asked if there was anyone aboard capable of repairing the steam engine. Gus Beyer said he could—and he did. Because of Gus's steam engine knowledge, some interested parties wanted Gus to stay in New York where he landed, but Gus decided to go further west.

Gus moved to Fredericksburg for a while, then moved to Menard in 1879. He brought the first windmills to Menard and was laughed at because he thought he could use the wind to pump water. Gus's trade was blacksmithing, as it was for many members of Beyer family before him.

Gus set up his shop at the place it now stands on the Beyer farm. In this shop he set up his steam engine with pulleys and belts to run his equipment. His equipment was very complete in that he had both a wood lathe and a steel lathe which were brought from Germany. He also had a corn grinder and a forge, the latter being a necessity for a blacksmith. He used the steam engine to run the lathes, the blower in his forge, and the corn grinder. The forge also was equipped with a hand crank for small jobs.

At one time, Gus had seven employees working in his blacksmith shop. He would go to the ranches and help the ranchers with their blacksmithing needs. As well as being a blacksmith, Gus Beyer was a jack-of-all-trades.

Apparently, Gus also was very proficient in the skill of producing crops and farming. On the Beyer farm he planted seven acres of grapes which he used to make wine. In his time, Gus Beyer was noted for his ability to make good wine, a tradition which is now carried on by his grandson.

The wine was made in fifty-five gallon barrels, where it was fermented and stored. While Gus was producing his wine and knowledgeable about such things, he would go to Fort McKavett to help Col. William L. Black run the cannery at the fort.

Charles Beyer gave the author a sample of the wine. It tasted very good, but had something different from other wines. What made it different? Perhaps it was the addition of the most-frequently missing ingredient: the flavor of the past.

The author feels that there is a certain fulfillment in the gaining back of a little of the past. He can't think of a better way than simply getting in touch with those around him. The past is only an arm's length away if one will just reach for it.

Fort McKavett Masonic Lodge
By Maela Kothmann

There were a lot of good men who were Masons. —Merlin Rogers

As smoke fills the air, wet eyes sting and nostrils tingle from the rank smell. The old general store and previous lodge hall burned to the ground in a matter of minutes. Masons gather from near and far to help their fellow man, and Fort McKavett, Texas, is no exception.

The purpose of the following essay is to show the development of Freemasons and the Masonic history of Fort McKavett. Freemasonry refers to the principles, institutions, and practices of the Fraternal Order of the Free and Accepted Masons.

The largest worldwide society, Freemasonry is an organization of men based on the fatherhood of God and the brotherhood of man, using builder's tools as symbols to teach basic moral truths generally accepted by persons of good will. It is religious in that a belief in God is a prime requirement for membership, but no religious test is used. The purpose of Freemasonry, thus, is to enable men to meet in harmony, to promote friendship, and to be charitable. Its basic ideas are that all persons are related to each other, and that the best way to worship God is to be of service to other people.

Service to people is a very important part of Freemasonry. The Masons join in unity to help the benevolent, widows, orphaned children, and people in need. Some examples of the Lodge's charity were listed in *The New Age Magazine*, a publication of the Supreme Council, Ancient & Accepted Scottish Rite, in September 1982:

"December 9, 1916—Motion was made and seconded that Lodge donate ten dollars to the children of the Masonic home to be used in assisting 'Santa Claus' in paying them a visit.

"May 25, 1918—A motion was made, seconded, and carried that we buy $100 Liberty Bond providing the Lodge is able financially.

"May 27, 1927—The meeting was called for the purpose of taking up donations for relief of the Mississippi Flood. All members present contributed one dollar for the relief."

Charity is an important part of our society. As Masons, symbols represent them and remind people of their community service.

The most visible symbol of Masonry is the Masonic square and compass. In Masonic symbolism, the square and compass refer to one's duty to the craft and to Masons, thereby becoming an emblem of brotherhood. The symbol consists of three parts: the square, upon which rests the compass, with points extended, and the letter "G" lodged within the center.

The symbol is patented and displayed publicly as a symbol of Freemasonry because of the first Masons having been builders. From this, carpenter's tools are also used as symbols.

The "G" represents the Deity. Masonry is based on religion; hence, one sees the Creator represented in the symbol. Masons honor their symbolism and are pride-filled whenever it is seen. The symbol is seen on the buildings of Masons throughout history.

The previous and present lodge halls carry many memories for Masons in Fort McKavett. This history is reviewed and re-lived in the author's interview with her grandfather, Merlin Rogers, who said:

"When it was first built, first Masons were in Fort McKavett. Well, they held their meetings at that old, two-story building, the officer's quarters, upstairs. Then a man by the name of G. Baker had a grocery store that had an upstairs to it. Later, they moved their meetings up there."

Thus, on March 20, 1897, an order was made and approved that twelve dollars rent be paid to G. Baker for rent of a lodge meeting quarters. The 1897 annual report showed the furniture at a value of fifteen dollars. The Masons did not own the building.

The building, however, became the property of the Fort McKavett Lodge on May 28, 1910. A deed from Brother Baker was presented and signed by him. The Fort McKavett Lodge now owned the building formerly known as Baker's General Store.

Some conflict, of which the author is unsure, arose questioning the ownership of the building in June 1924. The committee appointed to see if Miss Baker's report was favorable. The committee was retained and instructed to draw up a deed and have a notary attend to the deed. The building then was officially owned by the Fort McKavett Lodge.

The Fort McKavett Lodge continued meeting there until the early 1940s. The old general store, however, burned to the ground in a matter of minutes. The wood structure no longer existed. All the possessions were also burned, though a small safe was salvaged. Its contents included minutes of lodge meetings, which allowed the author to learn some of the Fort McKavett Lodge history. The Fort McKavett Lodge faced the problem of finding a new meeting hall. Rogers reported:

"Well, when that building burnt, we were already organized and everything like that, and we had to have a meeting place, and we held our meetings in that little rock sentry building out there until we could get a lodge built. They only have to meet once a month, but they can only miss two meetings or they lose their charter. We met in that sentry building and when we had a candidate, we brought 'em to Menard to put the work on 'em."

Meetings were held in the small structure for approximately fifteen years. Even though Masons were packed like sardines into the sentry building, they always held together as brothers.

In March of 1942 discussion was put into action and plans were made for a new lodge hall. After plenty of discussion, it was decided that the Fort McKavett Lodge secure plans and cost of a rock building, two stories high, the size of twenty-four by twenty-eight feet inside. The following committee was appointed: Bros. J.D. Cowsert, J.F. Webster, Merlin Rogers, and J.M. Treadwell. The secretary was instructed to see about repairing the old safe. After many meetings in the small building, preparations for a new lodge hall were beginning.

The process was a long, time-consuming and a tedious job for the Masons, but they were determined to see a United States flag fly over their lodge hall. The minutes from September 18, 1943, reported a building committee composed of Merlin Rogers, Asa Tomlinson, and Henry Murr was appointed to see a contractor. Plans for a new building were examined, discussed, and a few changes were made on July 16, 1946. The following turn of events then occurred in this order of dates to bring the reader up to date on the present lodge building at Fort McKavett. According to the Fort McKavett Lodge minutes:

"July 15, 1947: A discussion was had about the school building being used for meetings until the other accommodations were made being leased on a 99 year basis, so the Master appointed the Master (Jr.) and Wardens (Chester Murr, J. Dennis Lehne, Charles J. Murr) to see about the building and lease contract.

"May 22, 1948: Contract between the Menard Independent School Board read and resolution motion was made, seconded and carried that we accept the foregoing contract and authorize the Worshipful Master and Secretary to sign the same and enter into said contract for the purpose therein contained in said contract.

"June 8, 1948: The building contract was read and approved and the agreement from the Menard Independent School District was read and unanimously agreed to.

"January 15, 1949: Worshipful Master appointed a new building committee composed of J.F. Webster, Joe H. Russel and J.M. Treadwell to investigate the prospects of a one-story air conditioned building to meet the approval of the Grand Masters.

"December 10, 1949: Letters and bids from three contractors on the erection of a new building: three bids are of $4,575, one of $6,874, and one of $8,716, each was not complete, but are close estimates.

"March 4, 1950: The building committee gave a report and two bids were read and the bid of Floyd Napier was accepted. The bid was $5,367, the other bid was $8,795. The committee set Sunday, 2 p.m., March 5 to meet with Mr. Napier and have a further understanding of plans and so on.

"April 8, 1950: Building committee gave a report that they are waiting on the permits from the Grand Masters which had been applied.

"December 12, 1950: Building committee dismissed."

That dismissal recognized that the building was, or would soon be completed. An exact date was not recorded. For financial support of the new structure, new dues and meeting dates were established.

In 1893, the Masons met the first Saturday of every month, charging fees of twelve dollars for every degree conferred per year.

In November of 1896, however, meeting dates were changed to Saturday night on, or after, the full moon of each month.

The present date of meetings had been the second Tuesday of each month at seven thirty. Dues are $15 annually and increase with each degree. These were established the first day of July in 1950. With an established meeting date and dues, the Masons of Fort McKavett Lodge continued their services. That benevolence is the helpful side of Freemasonry; worldwide respect for the dead is the other.

When asked the meaning of a traditional Masonic funeral, Merlin Rogers explained:

"Well, the only thing I would know, it be a showin' that all Masons are brothers, and a showin' of brotherly love for their fellow members."

Information about Masonic funerals was the most impressive knowledge gained by the author.

The traditional funerals were held to show the utmost respect for the Masons. The church held their services for the deceased and the body was then turned over to the brothers. In procession, the casket was taken to the cemetery for special services. The following is a story of the first Masonic funeral at Fort McKavett, taken from the Fort McKavett Lodge minutes that survived the fire in the small safe:

"To the Worshipful Master. Wardens and Members of Ft. McKavett Lodge #750 A.F. & A.M.

"The lodge is called to mourn the death of a worthy brother and upright man, Brother William Mullenhauer was ruthlessly shot down by the hand of an assassin at his ranch in Schleicher

County on the sixth day of June, 1896, while of pursuing his daily calling and although friendly and faithful hands done all that they could to relieve his sufferings, he died before reaching medical care.

"In token of the esteem in which Brother Mullenhauer was held by the members of this Lodge, we be to submit the following resolutions and ask their adoption.

"Resolved that in the death of our Brother this Lodge has lost a faithful member who lived up to the full measure of his duty as a just and upright man and Mason.

"Our community mourns the loss of a good citizen, his friends as a genial companion and a faithful friend.

"Resolved further, that in respect for the departed, the Lodge be dropped and the numbers wear the usual emblems of mourning for 30 days; that these resolved resolutions be recorded in the minutes of the Lodge and a copy be sent by the Secretary under seal of the Lodge to the relations of the deceased and a copy be published in the county paper."

Respects and love were thus displayed for the final time at a Masonic funeral in Fort McKavett.

The knowledge gained from the above research brought the author closer to her father, who she loves very much. The strongest realization was that she someday wanted to become a part of her family's organization of Masonry through Eastern Star. This history has been a joy to uncover and the author learned that one must always start uncovering with an open mind.

In summary, the author brought together all the attainable information about Freemasonry in Fort McKavett for the reader. In Merlin Rogers' interview, history was retraced through eighty-nine years of Masonry. From soldiers to modern-day citizens, the paper reveals Freemasonry has flourished. The author hopes the term paper is a trip down memory lane for all those who read it. In closing, the author leaves the reader with these words written during her research:

The meeting will come to order! The familiar words ring in the author's ears as she dreamily sees herself walking into Baker's General Store of 1893. The staircase's arms open wide and beckon her to attend the first Masonic meeting in the old general store. The ascending of the staircase is a long task, for dust fills her nose and stings her eyes. The old timbers creak their protest in despondent tones from the author's weight upon them. On the second floor, men gather in the unity of God. The meeting is held to help one another. When the meeting adjourns, the author conquers descending the old stairs. She is filled with love when realization of what Masonry means to her father, grandfather, and great grandfather, and now to her.

Fort McKavett Lodge

Original thirteen members: L.D. Collins, W.W. Crockett, C. Champie, Tom Elliot, Rufe Holland, H.J. Kneid, W.W. Lewis, Wm. Prescott, W.S. Robinson, J.W. Ruley, T.I. Terry, and Sam Wallick.

GRAND MASTERS

1894–Sam Wallick	1914–C.H. Holland
1895–Sam Wallick	1915–L.L. Ball
1897–Rufe Holland	1916–J.M. Treadwell
1898–J.L. Parchman	1917–Ed Lehne
1899–G.B. Baker	1918–Clay Holland
1900–Sam Wallick	1919–Charles S. Black
1901–Sam Wallick	1920–J. Warren
1902–Rufe Holland	1921–J. Warren
1903–E.L. Martin	1922–Ray Wyatt
1904–Rufe Holland	1923–Lawrence E. Callen
1905–E.L. Martin	1924–C.H. Holland
1906–Sam Wallick	1925–J.D. Cawsert
1907–G.B. Baker	1926–Joe N. Wyatt
1908–E.L. Martin	1927–Henry T. Murr
1909–W.S. Wilkinson	1928–Johnny Webster
1910–C.D. Wyatt	1929–Floyd Baker
1911–C.D. Wyatt	1930–Ray Holland
1912–E.L. Martin	1931–Rufus Baker
1913–C.H. Holland	1932–Jack Sykes

1933–Tillman Landers
1934–Tillman Landers
1935–J.D. Cawsert
1936–Merlin Rogers
1937–Merlin Rogers
1938–Robert Flutsch
1939–John Winslow
1940–J. Dennis Lehne
1941–Charles Murr
1942–Charles Murr
1943–Joe Russell
1944–Chester Murr
1945–Chester Murr
1946–J. Dennis Lehne
1947–Chester Murr
1948–Chester Murr
1949–Charles J. Murr
1950–Charles J. Murr
1951–W.A. (Bill) Stockton
1952–Joe Russell
1953–Elmer E. Hubbel
1954–Elmer E. Hubbel
1955–Curtis Stockton

1956–John Troy Vaughn
1957–G.E.O. Burleson
1958–G.E.O. Burleson
1959–J.D. Murr
1960–James Pullen
1961–J.L. Robbins
1962–John Henry Murr
1963–Charles Kothmann
1964–Thomas W. Murr
1965–W.E. Edison
1966–W.A. Edmiston
1967–Jack Bloch
1968–Audie Murr
1969–Audie Murr
1970–G.E.O. Burleson
1971–Paul Garrett Murr
1972–Paul Garrett Murr
1973–Jim Lehne
1974–Alton Murr
1975–Fred Ellis III
1976–Walter Russel
1977–Darral Ray Lewis

The Menard Gun Club

By Barcy Jackson

...the right of the people to bear arms shall not be infringed.
—Amendment II, U.S. Constitution

Any dream can come true if one works hard enough to achieve it. In the case of the Menard Gun Club, the dreamer was John Ed Jackson. His dream was to have a range where everyone could go to practice his or her shooting or participate in organized matches. The purpose of this paper is to show how that dream came true.

The first attempt to establish a rifle range was in 1948. The group was known as "The Menard Sportsman's Club". They had to disband when they failed to find land upon which to build a range.

In the years following, John Ed Jackson continued the search for land. He intensified the search in 1965, and in 1975 he finally located land that was both available and suitable.

The land was owned by Vernon Crawford. He leased it to Jackson with the stipulation that a club be formed. The range would be locked and only members and their families could use the facilities. The lease between Vernon Crawford and the Menard Gun Club was for the price of fifty dollars a year. Later, at the first meeting of the club, Crawford was made an honorary member.

The first meeting was held at the Cafe 83. Officers were elected. They were John Ed Jackson, president; Franklin Gainer, vice president; and Betty Jackson, secretary-treasurer. About twenty interested people attended.

It was decided membership dues would be ten dollars a year. It was also decided twenty people would pay an additional ten dollars and become charter members.

Work parties were organized to clear the land and build the range. A trap shoot was held on August 24, 1975. The grand opening was at a turkey shoot on October 26, 1975. The turkey shoot had been advertised in surrounding towns and attendance was excellent. The Menard Gun Club had made its debut.

For the protection of individual members, the club became incorporated in July 1976. This was soon followed by other projects designed to benefit members of the club.

Since the invention of firearms, man has longed to shoot competitively. As a result of this longing, the club joined the Transcontinental League in 1977. The Transcontinental League was an organization designed to promote competitive shooting. Another organization to which they belonged was the National Bench Rest Shooters of America.

In 1977, the NBRSA formed the hunter class. The Menard Gun Club held the first registered hunter match in the state of Texas. George Belcher won the match with a perfect 250 score. It was the first recorded perfect score in the hunter class. The following quote from Warren Page, author of *The Accurate Rifle*, describes the feelings most shooters had toward competitive shooting:

"It was hotter than hell in August that Texas summer of '64, but the special undercurrent of excitement which earmarks any national-level competition was much in evidence. Exotic-looking rifles, super-tuned to near perfection, adorned benches along the firing line. In the shade of the covered reloading area, competitors clustered in random groups to discuss the mysteries of wind and mirage, to debate the merits of bullets and case design, perhaps even to speculate the outcome."

The club had become more involved in competitive shooting. In 1979 they hosted the state championship match. They continue to shoot in competitive matches through the Transcontinental League and the NBRSA.

In 1982, the club won their division and finished fourth in the national championship. Despite the excellent record, the club had few active members. Interest had dwindled among Menard residents, while staying high among members from other counties. It was hoped, however, that interest in the club was on the rise.

Future plans to encourage such interest included doing

needed maintenance work and hosting the state championship in 1983 or 1984.

The author, at this point, reviewed the main points of the rise of the Menard Gun Club. The first idea for a gun club was in 1948. The search for land was rewarded in 1975. The club was incorporated in 1976. In 1977, they hosted the first hunter class match in the state and the first perfect score of 250 was fired. In 1979, they hosted the state championship match. In 1982, they placed fourth in the national championship. The author now states her feelings about his project:

The author enjoyed writing this paper. She liked researching a project that was important, not only to her father, but to her entire family and community.

To close this paper, the author leaves a reminder that any dream can come true if—and only if—the dreamer is willing to fight for it.

I am sitting at the firing line observing the match in progress. I can see the concentration in the eyes of the shooters. I can hear the click as they close the bolts on their guns. I can feel the reverberations of the shots and smell the acrid scent of gunpowder. When the match is over and the trophies given out, one can taste victory.

MENARD
PLACES

The Mission and Presidio

By Steven Edwards

> *Generations are born, they live and pass on.*
> —*N.H. Pierce*, The Free State of Menard

One good reason for studying history is to know how we arrived where we are and to understand the influences which shaped our past and our present so we may better cope with the future.

The purpose of this paper is to describe how and why the Mission Santa Cruz de San Sabá and the Presidio San Luis de las Amarillas (later renamed Presidio de San Sabá) were built.

In 1725 an aged Franciscan priest, a veteran of the East Texas missions, looked with pain upon the ravages of the bellicose Apache on mission settlements along the San Antonio River. Father Francisco Hidalgo was equally aggrieved by the behavior of his own people toward the Apaches. It was the practice of the Spaniards to answer Apache raids with retaliation, taking captives and selling them as slaves.

This policy had failed utterly to deter the Eastern (Lipan) Apaches from their attacks. Father Hidalgo believed the answer was to establish missions for the Apaches. Effective Christianity, he knew, could change their ways, and he felt making Christians of the Indians was entirely within the realm of possibility. Father Hidalgo died a short time later, but he had sparked an idea that was to grow until the Mission Santa Cruz de San Sabá finally came into being. The vision of mortal man is infinite; this new mission led not to peace, but to more bloodshed and strife.

Orders came from Mexico City to San Antonio in April 1752 for exploration of Apache country.

With only a few men from the San Antonio de Béxar Presidio, Lieutenant Juan Galvan and Father Miguel de Aranda explored the Pedernales River country and the Llano River region without finding a desirable location. Then, on the San Saba, Galvan found what he was looking for: an abundance of water and an alluvial plain with good arable land.

In the autumn of 1755, some thirty years after the aged Father Francisco Hidalgo had offered to risk his life to go alone into Apache country to seek conversion of the Indian tribes, action was taken in Mexico City toward establishing an Apache mission in Texas. By October, the project had the support of Juan Galvan and Pedro de Rábago y Teran. The viceroy, Juan Francisco de Güemes, 1st Count of Revillagigedo, then referred the matter to the auditor, who raised questions about how the proposed garrison of 100 men was to be provided for on the San Saba and suggested the plan be taken up by the Royal and Supreme Council of the Indies.

At this point, Texas governor Jacinto de Barrios y Jáuregui uttered his final protest. He did not believe the Apaches when they promised to come and live in the proposed new mission, and he was supported in this disbelief by the Apaches' own bloody history.

The governor was not opposed to converting the Indians, but he insisted the practicality of such a project must be considered.

A Spanish mission like that planned for the Apaches on the San Saba River was more than just a church in the wilderness. It usually included a group of small houses where the Indians lived arranged on a square; carpenter, blacksmith, and tailor shops; looms, granary, and kilns; houses for soldiers assigned to protect the mission: a cemetery, garden, and orchard. The buildings generally were enclosed by a stockade wall with fortified gates. Outside the village, or mission, were irrigated fields cultivated by the Indians, and beyond were pastures for the mission livestock. Christians needed food to survive.

The mission's main purpose was to Christianize the Indians. Another important purpose was to teach Indians civilized customs and habits in order to transform them from savages into useful citizens.

From timber available nearby, they would build quarters for the missionaries and a temporary church. A typical mission took shape inside a strong stockade of logs. Along the river, they cleared fields, planted crops, and started an irrigation ditch.

No Apaches were seen for the first several months. In mid-June, the Franciscans found a glimmer of hope when some 3,000 Apaches arrived and camped near the mission. They were not coming to join the missions, however; they were seeking revenge on their old enemies, the northern tribe [the Comanches]. The Apaches returned later to warn the mission of their enemies—the northern tribe was planning an attack on this mission.

As the mantle of night closed over Mission Santa Cruz de San Sabá, an aura of peace seemed to envelope the little log mission on the south bank of the river. The padres said evening prayers and retired to their cells for quiet meditation. While servants finished the day's chores, the eight soldiers from the presidio set the guard for the night.

Outside, among the shadows, a more sinister movement was taking place. From all directions the shadowy figures came, advancing stealthily under the cover of night, toward the point of rendezvous. While the little mission slept, the Indians held their council of war.

At dawn, Indians [primarily Comanches] swarmed from every side. The chief claimed it was a peaceful visit. The Spaniards soon found the Indians were lying. The Indians stole everything they could get their hands on. The padres were murdered in cold blood.

Somewhere along the south bank of the San Saba River the bones of the two martyred priests and the soldiers who died in defense of the mission still lie in their secret graves. The mission cemetery has never been found. Any markers erected by presidio commander Diego Ortiz Parrilla and his men have long since disappeared, covered by silt or swept away by the river's floods.

A Texas Historical Commission marker near where the mission was located pays tribute to the two priests and the sacrifice they made in attempting to advance Christianity and the frontier of New Spain. It reads:

Site of Mission Santa Cruz de San Sabá.

Founded among the Lipan Apache Indians by Franciscan Missionaries in 1757 through the financial aid of the Count of Regla. Sacked and left in ruins by the Comanches in 1758. Here perished padres Alonso Giraldo Terreros, José Satiesteban, Martyrs to the Christian cause.

The Spanish did not give up easily. Several years later, a campaign against the northern tribes [Comanches and their allies] was made, but it proved to be a failure.

For many years Mission Santa Cruz de San Sabá lay as a heap of ashes. Presidio San Sabá, on the other side of the river, was an empty shell abandoned to field mice and lizards. The Spanish, who had advanced to this remote point on the frontier, had turned in retreat after a dozen blood-spattered years.

No matter how dismal the Spaniards' failure on the San Saba River, they left a legacy for the permanent settlers who came later.

The old presidio served one last purpose. Its stones were used to build a town. The inside walls which formed the soldiers' quarters came down first to be used in courthouse, jail, and school construction. The outside walls were left to pen cattle. Then as the longhorns vanished and trail driving and the unfenced range went away, the outside walls came down, too. A saloon, fences, and homes were built from the ready-made supply of stones. Some of the stones quarried by the Spaniards still may be seen in the walls of business buildings along Menard's main street. If those stones could talk...

In an interview with Dimple Noguess, the author learned the mission was used as a picnic place by the high school students in her class. The class used the stones as picnic tables.

Jim Menzies has several stones he intends to use in the fireplace of his new home. These stones serve as an exciting reminder of the past. Such enthusiasm inspired this author to write the following:

As I walked up to the old stone fort, I felt an eerie excitement all around. It was as if guns were firing. I could smell the gun powder as it tinged my nose. It was as if arrows were flying. I could hear them whizzing past my ears. I touched the walls and felt their strength. I looked at the large cactus inside the walls. They were as great knives stabbing our future. Now, as we all well know, our cacti have been cut out so we may live on.

Fort McKavett School

By Yvette Calderón

In School-Days

Still sits the school-house by the road,
　　A ragged beggar sleeping;
Around it still the sumachs grow,
　　And blackberry-vines are creeping.

Within, the master's desk is seen,
　　Deep scarred by raps official;
The warping floor, the battered seats,
　　The jack-knife's carved initial;

The charcoal frescos on its wall;
　　Its door's worn sill, betraying
The feet that, creeping slow to school,
　　Went storming out to playing!

Long years ago a winter sun
　　Shone over it at setting;
Lit up its western window-panes,
　　And low eaves' icy fretting.

It touched the tangled golden curls,
　　And brown eyes full of grieving,
Of one who still her steps delayed
　　When all the school were leaving.

For near her stood the little boy
　　Her childish favor singled:
His cap pulled low upon a face
　　Where pride and shame were mingled.

Pushing with restless feet the snow
　　To right and left, he lingered;—
As restlessly her tiny hands
　　The blue-checked apron fingered.

He saw her lift her eyes; he felt
　　The soft hand's light caressing,

And heard the tremble of her voice,
  As if a fault confessing.

"I'm sorry that I spelt the word:
  I hate to go above you,
Because,"—the brown eyes lower fell,—
  "Because, you see, I love you!"

Still memory to a gray-haired man
  That sweet child-face is showing.
Dear girl! the grasses on her grave
  Have forty years been growing!

He lives to learn, in life's hard school,
  How few who pass above him
Lament their triumph and his loss,
  Like her,—because they love him. —John Greenleaf Whittier

People who lived in Fort McKavett long ago did not have to go out of town to get to school. They had their own school.

The author will write about the school building, the teachers, and even a student who attended the school.

The author walks into the old rock building feeling very excited. As she opens the door, she sees herself being pulled back into the past. The author's interview is very special because Mrs. Godfrey's world at one time was the school and its children.

"My teaching career began in 1949," Mrs. Godfrey said. "The reason I chose to teach there was because I did not have a bachelor's degree and they needed a teacher. I taught for three years, and those three years were some of the best years of my life.

"During the months of September and October, I had only three children. From November through May, I had eight children. I had to teach eight grades in one big room.

"Math was our first subject, followed by geography. Since I had only three eighth graders, they would help me with the children in the lower grades. In geography, I would ask the smaller children where they lived. If they said Fort McKavett, I would give them an A. That would be their lesson for the day."

Mrs. Godfrey told the writer about a funny incident.

"Come December, the children decided to burn some old tires in the old wood stove for heat. There was so much smoke everywhere that people thought the school was on fire. Before we knew it, several parents were inside the school trying to rescue their children. School was let out early because of all the confusion.

"During recess, the students would gather scraps of iron. One day a man came to buy our iron. We sold it for forty-five dollars. With the money we bought apples, oranges, and lots of candy. Every day the students could eat until they were sick. We collected more iron after that and sold it for thirty-five dollars.

"With the money we bought lots of wienies. After we got all our work done, we would all go down to the river and have wiener roasts.

"When it was cold on Fridays, we would have talent shows. I'd bring evening gowns and makeup from home. The boys would model the gowns for all the class. The best one would get a prize.

"When we had a few students, all of us would go outside and build a fire. During recess, we would get the coals and put them on our stove inside. I would take potatoes and the students would carve their names in them. When we got back from lunch, we'd eat them. The children really enjoyed doing that. Some days, we'd even make soup."

Mrs. Godfrey has been known to discipline students when needed. When the author asked about this, she got a feeling that no one misbehaved in her class.

"I had a leather strap," she said. "If the children would talk ugly, I would make them carry rocks. When they misbehaved, they would have to clean out the restroom."

Mrs. Godfrey told about two students who always misbehaved.

"They would talk to me in Spanish when they knew they would get in trouble for it," Mrs. Godfrey said. "When the boys talked in Spanish at school, I would put a dress on them. They could only talk in Spanish until they got to the dirt road in front of the school. One boy kept the dress on most of the time.

"Many parents began to protest against the things I would

do. The school board had already decided that it would be best if the school was closed down. They thought the children would get a better education in Menard. The school board gave me the old bell. It is one of my most prized possessions."

As the author's interview was coming to an end, she summed it all up: "Lord, I loved it." The author felt like crying. The author knew she would always remember the information Mrs. Godfrey shared with her.

The author's research continued with Elissa Calderón, who was a student at the Fort McKavett school.

"All the students in the school were Mexicans," Mrs. Calderón said. "We didn't know any English when we first started school. The teacher told us the first day of school if we needed to talk to her we needed to raise our hands until she called our names. If we had to go to the restroom we thought we had to say 'May I go to the excused.' That would mean we needed to go to the restroom. Years later, we learned that was not the way to ask if we could go to the restroom. The restrooms outside were cold, as was the big classroom.

"During the winter months, there were two big, wooden stoves to heat the building. The kids would all cooperate by going into the pasture and bringing in wood. When we didn't need to gather wood, during recess we would sit around the teacher and watch her grade papers."

The author felt good during this interview. She thought to herself how special the little school was, being that all the children helped in doing everything. Mrs. Calderón told me about something funny that happened during recess one day.

"Everyone was outside during recess. There was a little girl rolling a bat up and down the side of the school. The bat slipped and hit Mrs. Godfrey, the teacher, on the back of her neck and knocked her out. We were all so dumb we thought she had fallen asleep. Later, when she came to, she let school out because she had a headache.

"Her headache was over when they finally closed the school, and that's when the heartache began.

"The year I graduated from school, they closed it down. There were just three of us. Mrs. Godfrey arranged it so we had our commencement exercises at the high school in Menard. We wore black and gold gowns and black caps with gold tassels."

To end the interview, Mrs. Calderón said: "If I had to do it all over again, I wouldn't change a thing."

The author's feelings about this paper are very special. She will always have a place for the old school house in her heart even though she did not attend school there. Here are the author's final thoughts:

As the author walks up the concrete steps leading to the old school house, she feels herself being pulled back in time. Stepping inside the building, she sees a little boy being spanked with a yardstick. She smelled a stale odor in the air. It's the ink wells on the desks of the students, and she sees the antique quill pens lying by their books. As the author looks around the room in amazement, she sees a shiny red apple on the teacher's desk, and she can taste its sweet nectar in her mouth. Then she touches the restored walls of the school and suddenly senses herself focusing back on the present. She walks away feeling a tingle inside her body.

Fort McKavett Hospital

By Debra Valdez

> *What is that old building*
> *As a young lady turns to see*
> *Way behind a big oak tree,*
> *Just what could it be?*
> *What is that old old building*
> *That stands so big and tall?*
> *May she go near and touch it,*
> *Or will it all fall? —Debra Valdez (original poem)*

The hospital at Fort McKavett has played a vital role in the history of the Texas Hill Country. The author intends to describe the hospital and show how important it was and is to that region.

The following is an interview with Gully Cowsert, superintendent at Fort McKavett State Historical Site:

"The Fort McKavett hospital was built in 1852, and it was open until along about the period of the Civil War. It was closed for a few years, and later reopened until 1883. Most of the building was done in 1868, after the Civil War. It was rebuilt by troops and Negro soldiers who were called Buffalo Soldiers because of their curly hair."

At this point, the author wanted to know more about the hospital and fort. She asked about officers who ran the hospital. Cowsert replied:

"They had several commanding officers through the years, however the most famous one was Colonel Ranald S. Mackenzie, who did most of the rebuilding at Fort McKavett.

The author asked about the hospital building, and Cowsert replied:

"This building was the hospital. It was the last hospital built; there were two others built before this particular one. It was used a few years, and the largest room was used as a ward room where they kept the sick people.

"In the other rooms they had the doctor's office, the examining room, and so forth. The back wing was the kitchen and dining room."

Cowsert commented on the work of restoring the building:

"We did quite a bit of repair, but nothing major. The roof and porch were in bad repair when we took it in. That was the first thing done, and when they redid the largest room, they had to repaint and take off some fancy woodwork done by people who lived there after the army left."

The author noted an old, small building near the back of the hospital. Cowsert explained:

"That building out there was plain spoken as the 'dead house'. Today, we would call it the morgue. At that period of time, I don't know how long they kept them in there, but they would put the dead person in a pine box while someone else dug the hole."

This research supports the thesis that the Fort McKavett hospital did, and still does, play a vital role in Hill Country health.

The author shares her feelings:

The feelings about this research will endure. She feels now that even though a building is old and no longer in use does not mean it doesn't have any special historical interest. It does have historical value.

When the author drove into town, she wasn't driving a car. She was riding a covered wagon. Her hands were no longer on the steering wheel; they were on leather reins. She heard the music from the old saloon, the men yelling at each other over a silly old poker game, and she could smell freshly baked bread. There also was some apple pie which someone had put on the window sill to cool. All of a sudden, a gust of strong wind came and, like an eraser waved across a blackboard, everything was gone. She could, however, feel something holding onto her and saying: "Listen to the winds, and let them tell you more about the town in which you live, words which will make you proud."

Scabtown

By Rosemary Ramon

AFTER READING THE SAD STORY OF THE FALL OF BABYLON

O Lady, my city, and new flower of the prairie
What have we to do with this long time ago?
O lady love,
Bud of tomorrow,
With eyes that hold the hundred years
Yet to ebb and flow,
And breasts that burn
With great-great-grandsons
All their valor, all their tears,
A century hence shall know,
What have we to do
With this long time ago? —Vachel Lindsay

Before the author wrote this paper, she never realized there was once a "scabtown" at Fort McKavett. After she had done research on this town, she was made aware that there was an interesting and unknown place around her—Scabtown.

If every great fortune is founded on a crime, a lot of good American towns, especially in the West, were built on whiskey and houses of prostitution.

One such place, close to home, was a settlement which emerged across the river from Fort McKavett when construction began in the 1850s. Originally named Lehnesburg to honor a German merchant, it was called Scabtown instead. It was wide open to the world and was a pretty wild place. As long as the fort was occupied, Scabtown remained profitable to its inhabitants. It was made up of a motley crew of camp followers, outlaws, and prostitutes.

This area proved havens for lawbreakers on the run. Many of the ne're-do-wells pursued their livelihoods in the drinking and gambling houses and various other establishments of pleasure in Scabtown.

Soldiers also took part in this establishment of pleasure.

It drew soldiers into the midst of its lawless breed. Even when the pay reached the soldier's hand, there was no guarantee that he could hang on to it. Good whiskey and bad women were the downfall of more than one. Lonely soldiers in forts far away from home went to drink beer and found women who cured their loneliness. In an interview, Frances Fish explained that in her archeology work at the Scabtown site:

"Even though it was off limits to the soldiers, we found an awful lot of uniform buttons, belt buckles, and other stuff."

Soldiers who went to Scabtown gave the military a hard time, but there was no comparison to the trouble caused by the outlaws who roamed around Scabtown. Frances Fish noted:

"It being a wild place, there were some pretty notorious outlaws. They claim the 'Hole in the Wall Gang' was there at one time. Black Jack Ketchum and different outlaws of the day were also there." [Possible, but Ketcham was born in San Saba County 1863 so he only would have been a teenager during Scabtown's height. Fort McKavett was abandoned in 1883. Ketcham's major crimes were in New Mexico in the 1890s; he was executed for "felonious assault upon a railway train" in New Mexico in 1901.]

The first recorded incident in Scabtown was when the local constabulary became involved in a fracas with several unruly soldiers, one of whom was shot through the mouth and knocked into the river. The trooper jumped up and fired once more at the constable before wading across to report for medical aid.

Another incident occurred on February 28, 1877. Shooting and mayhem broke loose in Scabtown as a group of Kimble County men arrived to try to free two friends who were being held for horse stealing by Menard County Deputy Sheriff Richard Godfrey. The group opened fire on two men who had crossed the river to spend the night with the post sutler. No one was hurt in the skirmish.

Even though Scabtown was rough country, it had homes for people who weren't there for carousing, but tried instead to peacefully make a living. According to Frances Fish:

"There were two merchants. One was Mr. Lewey Lehne, a

farmer and saloon keeper. Soon after the post was built in 1852, he came up there. There was another man, Ferdinand Mayer. He came up there and opened up a mercantile store. You could dern-near call it a supermarket. He carried groceries, hardware, dry goods, liquor, and a few clothes, mostly shoes and hats. He is the father to Sol Mayer, who donated the land for Camp Sol Mayer to the Boy Scouts.

"There was a feller, I can't remember his name, opened up a big saloon. I can remember where that saloon stood. There was some cedar posts on the ground, and I don't know whether when burning up some brush they burned those posts.

"The people what came there and settled were hunters or cut wood for the army. They had their chores and were civilian employees, most of them. One old man, by the name of Mengis, killed deer and antelope. He'd sell from house to house in Scabtown. He hunted for not only the government, but for the merchants in Scabtown. Between the San Angelo Crossin' and the Spring Branch there was a sub-irrigated area there. It's always been called 'Government Garden'. It's grown up in mesquite pretty bad now. That was where they put up a little dam on the Spring Branch so they could water their garden if it got too dry. They never wanted for the soldiers to go down and work on the gardens because the girls and women from Scabtown would come across the river and help them work. It being where it was, I 'magine Scabtown people took what they wanted.

"One building was right where the road is, and the saloon was across the road over in what's Mr. Hurd's pasture now. There was a few permanent houses, but very few. The western-most one, I know of, was up there at Lewey Lehne's land. The flood of 1938 destroyed it. They later used some of the lumber to build the little house that stands there now. The family by the name of Chantleys lived there then. At the eastern end of town, a family by the name of Miles lived over on Milago Holler.

"I believe the man that owned that property before Mr. Hurd bought it was named Shoemaker. I can, of course, remember both those houses. Us kids used to think it was great fun to get out and scout around. There was piles of rocks where the chimneys had been out in the flat between the river and the timber back north of us. There were foundations of houses and cedar posts in the ground, or elm posts, or whatever wood was available. Some people had rock chimneys.

"The rocks had fallen down, but there had been chimneys because they didn't have any electricity or any gas. They had to find wood to stay warm. I guess people lived up in Scabtown alright. They put up this big beer garden down there at the One-Mile Crossing. It's called San Antonio Gardens. The officers would take their wives or lady friends down there. I guess they served meals, I don't know, but it was a pretty nice place.

"There was, of course, a building there, but I've never remembered any sign of that building. It was just purely a beer garden. In its heyday, there was about 2,000 people who lived in Scabtown. Just before they left there with the soldiers going up to Palo Duro, there were about 3,200 soldiers stationed at McKavett. I 'magine Scabtown was a kinda booming burg with that many people around.

"I think most of the soldiers were Northerners, so they were either taken home or transferred close enough to the Mason Dixon line so they could get across that line into the North. While they were gone during the Civil War, either Union patrols or Confederate patrols would come through there. They stayed in the buildings, but as quick as the fort was abandoned in 1883, the people from Scabtown moved up into the rock buildings because their houses down in Scabtown would correspond to a kind of tar paper shack today."

[Fort McKavett was an active military post 1852–1859 and 1868–1883. Scabtown was the name people gave the civilian settlement across the river during the first period of fort occupation. When soldiers returned in 1868, the town changed its name from Lehnesburg/Scabtown to Fort McKavett, Texas.]

In summary, Scabtown was not occupied for a long time, but the time it was occupied, it made quite a reputation for itself. Scabtown was a rough place at one time, but at the time of this paper there was no trace of where Scabtown used to be. Scabtown faded away when the soldiers left Fort McKavett. Scabtown, however, would never really be gone. It would always remain in the minds of one who had the opportunity to envision it.

The author's feelings, too, about her term paper were very special to her. Finding out the history of the town made the author glad she did research on the area. She never once stopped to think there could be a hidden and forgotten place unknown to her—Scabtown. She concludes this paper with these thoughts:

The author sits under a tree. The smell of mesquite creeps into her nose. She notices the stream which is in front of her. Suddenly, she hears wagons, horses, and guns firing behind her. She walks down the dusty road. To her right she sees a tall building. She hears music and laughter coming from inside. She walks to the door and sees cowboys drinking beer and playing cards. Suddenly, two men stand up with hatred in their eyes. One of them yells at the other, telling him to draw. Shots ring out. The author falls to the ground in pain. Everything is a blur. The author tastes something cool touching her lips. She stirs and wakes up, realizing it was only a dream.

Menard Saloons
By Len Clark

PUB
The glasses are raised, the voices drift into laughter,
The clock hands have stopped,
the beer in the hands of the soldiers is blond,
the faces are calm and the fingers can feel
The wet touch of glasses, the glasses print rings on the table,
The smoke rings curl and go up and dissolve near the ceiling,
    This moment exists and is real.

What is reality? Do not ask that. At this moment
Look at the butterfly eyes of the girls, watch the barmaid's
Precision in pouring a Scotch, and remember this day,
This day at this moment you were no longer an island,
People were friendly, the clock in the hands of the soldiers
    For this moment had nothing to say.

And nothing to say and the glasses are raised, we are happy
Drinking through time, and a world that is gentle and helpless
Survives in the pub and goes up in the smoke of our breath,
The regulars doze in the corner, the talkers are fluent;
Look now in the faces of those you love and remember
    That you are not thinking of death.

But thinking of death as the lights go out and the glasses
Are lowered, the people go out and the evening
Goes out, ah, goes out like a light and leaves you alone,
As the heart goes out, the door opens out into darkness,
The foot takes a step, and the moment, the moment of falling
    Is here, you go down like a stone,

Are you able to meet the disaster, able to meet the
Cold air of the street and the touch of corruption, the rotting
Fingers that murder your own in the grip of love?
Can you bear to find hateful the faces you once thought were lovely,

Can you bear to find comfort alone in the evil and stunted,
    Can you bear to abandon the dove?

The houses are shut and the people go home, we are left in
Our island of pain, the clocks start to move and the powerful
To act, there is nothing now, nothing at all
To be done: for the trouble is real: and the verdict is final
Against us. The clocks go round faster and faster.
And fast as confetti
    The days are beginning to fall. —Julian Symons

Menardville saloons are a part of this town's history. The purpose of this paper is to tell of the saloons' entertainment and businesses in Menardville starting in the 1870s.

The Rock Saloon was one of the first saloons built in Menardville. This is a description of how it was started. Johan G. Bremer bought some land from the State of Texas in the early 1800s. About 1870, Gustave Schleicher bought, then donated some land where town lots later were laid out for a courthouse and school in consideration that Menardville be chosen as the county seat. Later, J.J. Callan became owner of the land mentioned.

It is not known how J.J. Callan, land commissioner, transferred the lots where the Rock Saloon later was to be located to Adam Bradford. Bradford sold the lots to John F. Dexter in 1876. Dexter sold it in 1877 to Samuel Wallick. Samuel Wallick and James H. Handy were post traders in Menardville and had a general mercantile store in Fort McKavett. They are believed to be the people who built the building that housed the saloon. Wallick deeded the lots and building to his wife, Katie, who sold it the same year to a Mr. Campbell. In 1882, Campbell sold the lots and building to William Johnson. It is said Johnson was the owner who added the saloon. He gave it to Ludy Johnston in 1891.

It changed hands again when Ludy Johnston transferred the land to William Bevans in 1918, and the saloon closed because of World War I. But, this wasn't the last time it changed owners.

William Bevans transferred the property to Magnolia Petroleum Company in 1924, and they transferred it to Frank Hart-graves in 1925.

Frank Hartgraves was a lawyer and practiced law for years in the same building that housed the Old Rock Saloon. His son, Perry Hartgraves, had a law office and an abstract office there. After his death, his widow sold the lot and building to Estelle Smith, another attorney.

Jimmy Crowell is one of the oldest and most interesting men in Menard. At his age, he still has a remarkable memory, and the author would like to share some of his stories with readers. One of his stories was about a fight between the Sapp twins and Jessie Wright.

"It was on a Saturday afternoon, and they were having a few drinks at the Legal Tender Saloon," Crowell remembers. "When all of the sudden one of the Sapps called Jessie Wright a 'son-a-bitch', then all hell broke out. The sheriff was out of town, so nobody stopped them. After catching their breaths, Jessie told Sapp that he was going to kick his ass 'cause you called me a son-a-bitch.'"

Another story Jimmy told the author was about a killing in the Legal Tender Saloon. It all started in a poker game behind the saloon when a Mr. King accused a Mr. Haby of cheating. After a few rounds, Haby ran out. They couldn't play with three people, so they went to the saloon to have some drinks at the bar. Haby appeared at the door and shot King in the back.

The bullet passed through him and lodged in the mirror behind the bar. There was no trial held, and he was set free.

The bar and mirror are on display at the Menard Museum for all to see. The bar in the Legal Tender was filled with whiskey, beer, and ice. The price for whiskey was twenty-five cents for one-half pint and five cents for a glass of draft beer. Ice cost three cents a glass and had to be hauled in a wagon from Mason. The whiskey and beer came from Brownwood. The barrels that were empty were sold for water barrels. Jimmy mentioned a hanging when he concluded his conversation about saloon supplies.

The only hanging in Menard County was a Negro named

Green Johnson, who murdered his wife in a family dispute. They hung him to a mesquite tree down behind the courthouse and Cottonwood Saloon, according to Jimmy Crowell.

When the author asked Jimmy about entertainment in the saloons, Jimmy noted: "There was a little guitar once in a while, but most people just came to drink, gamble, and talk."

Jimmy also told the author that he took one drink legally. It was just before all the closing of the saloons in 1918.

The thesis of this paper, that saloons were a part of Menard's early history is validated by the discussions, research, and interviews described in this paper.

In doing this paper, the author got to know Jimmy Crowell not just as a person, but also as a friend and the author learned how the older generation worked to give us what we have now.

In closing, the author leaves the reader with this paragraph:

Walking down Main Street, the taste of the bitter grain alcohol reached the author's lip. Upon opening the doors to the saloon, it was smoky, but the author could see the old men sitting or standing around the card tables. Putting his hands on the bar, feeling the rough texture of the wood, and ordering a glass of beer, the writer hoped the bartender would not recognize his young age. Hearing the chips fall onto the table made his head turn to see what was happening. It brought him face-to-face with the sheriff, who was smoking a hand-rolled cigarette. He blew the acrid-smelling smoke towards the author's face, making him feel like coughing. After drinking his beer somewhat hastily and leaving on his horse, he was brought back to the reality of pen and ink.

Saloon of Long Ago—The Legal Tender
By Ruby Gonzales

Not too long ago, far out
In the west,
Lay the little town of
Menard, so alive with zest
Down the street nearby was
Located a saloon
which didn't swing open
till high noon.
Now back then during
those olden times
The cost of a beer was
only a dime.
So everyone rushed down
and had his fill.
Now, what do you
Younguns think about such?
Some folks here still
Haven't lost the touch. —Ruby Gonzales (original poem)

The Legal Tender Saloon reveals many memories that have long been forgotten. The purpose of this paper is to swing open the doors of that old saloon and let its past memories flow. The swinging doors of the old saloon are now being opened with the help of Roy Benson, who I interviewed.

According to Roy Benson: "When I used to come to town, I would stay in the Cottonwood Saloon. This saloon was located on the north side, now the present-day Luckenbach store. The Legal Tender was across the street from the Cottonwood Saloon. It was located in the old building beside the Bevans Bank."

As I listen to Roy, I think about the future and sitting in his place. Then I see in his face that he is bursting with great excitement to tell me and my friend more.

"Now, in this town of Menard," Mr. Benson says, "there

were about five saloons. There probably were more saloons than churches."

That made him giggle, and this author was happy to see him smile. As he spoke it wasn't easy to forget those good old days. He made us realize there won't be any more days like those. Yvette, this author's friend, and the author leaned forward as Mr. Benson's story became exciting. His voice seemed to echo. As he kept talking, we listened more earnestly. Mr. Benson began telling us about an incident that happened in the Legal Tender Saloon: "In the Legal Tender Saloon there was a man that shot at another man."

Here, there seemed to be some confusion. Everyone the author talked with about the saloon told her the bar with the bullet crack is at the Menard Museum.

Mr. Benson continued the story: "They all bought this whiskey together. They got me to haul it out of the cellar and hide it at a ranch. I was about fifteen. I would keep this whiskey because they thought there wouldn't be any more good whiskey [because of Prohibition]. I kept the whiskey until they drank it all. It took them a little over a year to drink all that good whiskey, and plus two wagon loads I hauled from the saloon. By then, all the ranches were making whiskey.

"There were many things always happening, like playing poker. There were many fights, but I was too young to stay in the saloon, so I just sat through it, but I would have to go to the back. In the back, there was a big old room. In that big old room was a heater, which you had to put wood in. That's were I would stay and listen to the people in the saloon. They would cuss and fight, always raising a dickens.

"Everyone would come with their argument to the saloon and get into fights. In the 1930s [1933], whiskey became legal again. They let people make beer; everyone made beer."

The author asked if Mr. Benson ever made beer?

"Yes," he said. "Everyone made beer."

The author asked how he made beer.

"You take Blue Ribbon Malt and then you put in so many

cans of malt and so many cans of sugar. Then you let it stay in a barrel until it quits, and then you bottle it. Everyone would have a cap or bottle capper," he said.

The author did not think beer was that easy to make, and she bet if she tried to go in the kitchen, she would not finish with the whole process of brewing beer. Just like the author wouldn't finish making beer, law officers in those days never finished their jobs. Mr. Benson noted: "Back then, in the courts, they didn't ever really punish somebody for killing someone else. Mostly, the person killed was a Mexican. I don't know of a man who was ever sent to the pen for killing a Mexican."

As the author listened, she wondered about what it would be like to live back then when there was so much prejudice and hatred. Mr. Benson, however, changed the subject to Mr. King.

"Mr. King was a real good man. Mr. Hawby, the deputy, was afraid of Mr. King. Hawby was afraid King was going to kill him, so Hawby kills King first. After the incident happened, people didn't like Hawby."

Mr. Benson had another Hawby story: "Hawby told this Mexican to go home because he was drunk. As the Mexican was going home he was about at the present day dentist's office. Hawby shoots him in the back. He just shot him, I guess, to play tough. That's why Menard was called the Free State of Menard, because they never did anything to people who killed other people. People were always getting by and they were never sent to the pen."

The author asked if he saw Hawby kill the man. Mr. Benson answered with a deep, hurt voice: "Yes, I was about ten steps from them. That made me so... so... I don't know what. In a way, if I had a gun I would have shot Hawby. I thought what he did was the most awful thing anybody could do—kill a poor man when he was doing nothing."

Hearing the small shake in his voice made the author perceive what Mr. Benson was feeling inside.

The author has shared with the reader facts about the saloons of Menard. The author also hopes she has revealed and helped open those swinging doors to the many memories of those old saloons.

The author learned many things in the process of putting together this term paper. She found out that many old people are nice and anxious to tell her about the past. Her first apprehension was that all the older people would reject her efforts, but she discovered older people are the nicest people to know. She closes with a paragraph about all this:

As the author walks into the front doors of an old building in Menard, once the old saloon, she hears the shuffling of cards, and her thoughts begin to escape into the past. The smell of liquor seems to be getting stronger and stronger as her thoughts reach the depths of history. The sight of fights and killings from the past then enter her fantasy. Momentarily, all of her thoughts fade away, leaving behind only the memories of yesterday.

Saline Community
By Reg Royal

THE BUILDERS
All are architects of Fate,
*   Working in these walls of Time;*
Some with massive deeds and great,
*   Some with ornaments of rhyme.*

In the elder days of Art,
*   Builders wrought with greatest care*
Each minute and unseen part;
*   For the Gods see everywhere.*

Build to-day, then, strong and sure,
*   With a firm and ample base;*
And ascending and secure
*   Shall to-morrow find its place.*

Thus alone can we attain
*   To those turrets, where the eye*
Sees the world as one vast plain,
*   And one boundless reach of sky.*
*   —Henry Wadsworth Longfellow (abridged version)*

The Saline Community has been in existence for 120 years [in 1980]. It survived Indian raids in the 1800s to become a well-known community that won numerous awards in state community improvement competitions.

Even though the old schoolhouse is no longer used as a place to teach, it still has many uses. The author intends to show the reader the facts of Saline and how it has progressed over the years.

The story begins with the creek. The Little Saline Creek was a flowing stream in the early 1860s. As it was flowing, it attracted many settlers and Indians because there was plenty of water and the stream had an abundance of fish.

Mr. and Mrs. Henry Parks and their twelve-year-old grandson were among the first white settlers to live in what is now known as Saline. The Parks, who were born in Georgia, had been living in Llano County before coming to Saline. When the grazing for Mr. Parks's cattle grew short in 1862, they moved to Saline, where there was a plentiful amount of grass and a creek with crystal-clear water. The Parks built a log cabin and a picket corral. Things were going well for the Parks until April 2, 1862.

A surprise attack took place during the night at the Parks's home. The Comanche Indians killed all three members of the family. They each were scalped and stripped of their clothes. All three were buried in the same grave. In an interview conducted by the author, Louise McWilliams said:

"Before the Indians set fire to the cabin, they took a feathered mattress from the bed and split it open, scattering feathers all around the scene."

During the years from 1862 to 1870, many Indian raids made for shifting populations. Now and then a new family moved in, and almost always a discouraged family moved out. The following is a saga of one of those families.

In 1867, Gus Shumann arranged to establish a ranch and build a log cabin on the Little Saline. One morning, Shumann and his twelve-year-old son, Billy, went to their new homesite to cut some trees prior to building a cabin and corrals. They went on horseback. They worked until late in the afternoon. At sunset, they stopped working in preparation to returning home.

Gus and Billy rode out on their horses to find a yoke of oxen that were grazing nearby. A band of Comanche Indians rushed in and released a volley of arrows into the Shumanns. The following day, Mr. Casey and some other men who had been trailing the Comanches went with Mr. Reichenau to the site where the Shumanns had been working because they had not returned home. They rode to the scene of the tragedy and found both were dead. Each had been shot with twelve arrows and then scalped. The boy's body was shot with wooden arrows, all in the back. Likewise, the father was shot in the back with twelve arrows, but the arrows used on him were steel-headed.

The bodies were buried under a live oak tree near where they

were found. The Schumanns weren't the only unfortunate settlers.

Frank Johnson was another victim of an Indian killing in the
spring of 1866. He was found with a body full of arrows and one
unused arrow placed across his chest. He was an old man with
long hair and a white beard. He was scalped all the way to the
front side of his head. They had taken his long white beard, too.
His story is as sad as Fred Connaway's.

It is said that Fred Connaway had a cow ranch on Little Saline. In 1867, he was attacked by Indians in the Red Creek valley
and was wounded. He took refuge in a cave and was able to fight
off the Indians. After the Indians left, he tried to make it back to
the Saline settlement on foot. Being weak and suffering pain, he
made his way to Scott Springs, which was more than a mile from
the cave that he had left. After drinking some water, he hid his
pistol, which was later found. He walked up Red Creek near the
mouth, left the creek and then came back. As he knelt down to
drink, he died. One hand was in the water, and a walking stick
lay nearby. Three days later, he was found. He was hurriedly buried under a live oak tree, very near the spot where he was found.
This wasn't the end of the Indian trouble.

The last reported Indian trouble was in 1875. On January 9,
1875, nine Indians and a squaw met five of Captain Dan Roberts's
Rangers on the Saline. There was a short fight of Winchester rifles against wooden arrows, and the five Rangers dismounted to
claim the spoils of war. The dead savages were left to the mouths
of the coyotes, except the squaw. The Rangers gave her a shallow
grave on which they heaped a pile of honeycombed rocks, which
remains the only monument to the fight.

In November 1877, Captain Roberts, passing the spot where
the fight took place, saw a skull stuck on a mesquite limb, grin-
ning one perpetual, ghastly smile at passersby. Afterwards, a
lawyer on his way to Junction took down the skull, as he stated,
for the purpose of making a drinking cup out of it. Also Jim
Gillet of Lampasas Springs, who took one of the scalps from
the fight, covered his revolver holster with it, but afterwards, in

bending over a frying pan at breakfast, he trailed the long hair in the hush puppy gravy, whereupon Lt. N.O. Reynolds applied a torch to the greasy locks, and in an instant nothing was left of the bald skin.

"Bah!" said a Ranger walking by. "You have spoilt my appetite."

Rangers played a part in Saline, and outlaws did, too.

In 1876, Saline had two outlaws living in the settlement. They were Bill and Bob McKeaver, on the dodge and wanted for murder. They were soon arrested and taken away. Things quieted down after that.

After the Indian and outlaw problems settled down, a school was built. The first school was located in Pleasant Valley. Later, the school was moved near the cemetery on the banks of the creek. One time the water got up to the ceiling of the school, probably during the flood of 1899.

The school moved to its present location on August 29, 1901. Mr. A.A. Boyce deeded four acres of land to Menard County for a school, known as District #4. Mr. E.L. Allison was the teacher. In the 1923-1924 school year, there were thirty-six students. There were fifty students in the 1930-1931 school year. The 1946-1947 school year was the last time the building was used as a school. It consolidated with the London school. The school building was three rooms, and it is still used as a voting house for people living in a certain area around it. It also is a community center.

On March 29, 1950, the Saline Community Council organized for the purpose of keeping the school building in repair so it could be used as the community center.

In 1965, the Saline Community Council entered the Texas Community Improvement program and won first place. Each year since 1965, the Saline Community has entered the Community Improvement Contest and won each year.

In an interview with the author, Maggie Phillips said:

"There are twenty-five people involved in the Community Improvement, and our goal is to keep the cemetery looking good and keep the school going as a community center. The Saline

Community hasn't died, because the Saline Community meets once a month and plans many activities."

To enter in the Texas Community Improvement contest a community must be under 1,000 people. Saline has received $1,200 in prize money in community improvement.

Saline also had a quilting club that was started sixty years ago. Two quilts were made each month. There usually were twenty members and dues were twenty-five cents a year. There was a Christmas party every year. The club closed two years ago.

The Saline Community has been a very important part of Menard County's history, from the Indian raids, where many were brutally killed to the participation in state competition for community improvement.

The author enjoyed doing research on Saline. He found out many interesting things about Saline he never knew. The cemetery has some unique tombstones. The school is still in good shape and many activities are still held there. The author was able to become acquainted with Mrs. McWilliams when he interviewed her. The author sums up his feelings toward Saline this way:

As the author walked by the cemetery he could see the tombstones. He read "died in an Indian raid", and he could feel his heart beat faster as he smelled the ashes of a burnt brush pile. He could taste the venison steak as he saw a buck run past him. The author could see the progress the community had made when he touched the fresh-cut cedar from the cedar mill. The same writer could hear Saline Creek and remembered all the stories he'd heard concerning Indians and settlers who were attracted to it. All of a sudden, he heard the whine of a Pontiac Trans Am as it cruised by, and his thoughts returned to the present.

Hext—A Tiny Town of Prosperity
By Tracy Hodges

TRUE LIVIN

I've had the opportunity
To contrast and compare
A lot of towns and cities
And the folks a-living there.
Some people have the notion
That a city is the place
Of a bountiful existence
For the entire human race.
But as one who's dwelt among 'em
I can state, with due restraint,
That there's no place like a city
Where the joys of livin' ain't.
Why you hardly know your neighbors,
And your friends you love so true.
Might as well live in Alaska
For what good they're doing you.
Yes, a big town was invented
Just to make friends grow apart—
Cause ulcerated stomachs
And to chill the human heart.
Sure it's fine to have ambition
And to strive to get ahead,
But most likely you will end up
With hard arteries instead.
Good folks are found in every clime,
But out where my folks live
We'd never trade a cow hand
For a big executive.
And experience has taught us
That true livin' is an art
That escapes most city people
And they really ain't so smart.

So I've weighed the facts and figures
For the quality and worth
And decided that the county
Is the finest place on Earth. —Carlos Ashley

As the author interviewed the people of Hext, she found that a lot of them referred to it as a "tiny town of prosperity." The author will attempt to show the reader why they called it this by showing how it grew, what buildings were established, and where. The author will provide you with some of the statements she received from interviews, starting with Mrs. Myrtle Pope:

"My family moved here in 1900. I wasn't born until nineteen and one. I had three older brothers: Henry, Everett, and R.T. Wagoner, and one older sister. Her name is Mrs. Lee Alexander."

Mrs. Pope recalls that her family was here before Hext got its name. She also remembers the different names the town had and why those names were used:

"There were only four families here at first. My Uncle John had the place where the Baptist Tabernacle is now. My Uncle Glen had the school house lot. My dad, George Wagoner, had the strip next to the London road. This whole area was called Wagonerville.

"My uncles' kids got tired of this name, so they said, 'Let's just name it The Pocket,' and they called it The Pocket.

"About ten or fifteen men met at the school house and suggest a name for the town, but it never took, so my uncle said 'Let's name it after ol' Bob here.' His name was Bob Hext [Joseph Robert Hext]. They all raised their hands, and that's how Hext received its name."

Mrs. Pope proceeded to discuss where the first settlers lived and where they got their food:

"At first, everybody lived in dugouts or tents. Nobody had any water. My dad built the first water well. There wasn't any stores then, so everybody had to raise chickens and handgrub farms for their food. I can remember the river was full of those wild chickens a-squawking at night. They were wilder than a turkey."

Mrs. Pope noted that her father was a conservative man:

"Papa built a log cabin with a dirt floor, and he undoubtedly dropped me in the dirt when I was a baby. The cabin had no windows, only an east door. I lived in the cabin 'til I was six years old.

"Papa was a really conservative man. He wouldn't build a house until he had the land paid for. The house he built had two rooms with windows in it, and it was just like I think heaven will be to look out those windows. Mama warned us over and over not to touch them, but my brother liked to put his fingers on them."

The author asked Mrs. Pope about some of the buildings in Hext, and she reported:

"There was a little post office and store where Gene Low's house is now. They called it Meringo, Texas [this was the name for the area around Hext in the 1870s]. They also had a church and school house up there. The school house was one room. There were eleven grades in one building, and three people sat in one seat."

Mrs. Pope showed the author some school pictures and commented about them:

"Every child who could walk took a school picture whether they were in school or not."

Mrs. Pope commented about rules of the school yard:

"The teacher drew a line down the school yard with chalk, and the boys played on one side and the girls on the other. It was a very serious fine to cross that line."

Mrs. Pope said the school moved to two other places before its location was settled:

"An old man married this beautiful woman named Miss Clark. George Livingston had a camp where the Andersons live now. Well, one morning they came a runnin' to get Papa. George Livingston had been burned up. His tent and all. They buried him right there where he died because, back then, there was no cemetery. Everybody was buried in their yards.

"The old man was suspected of shooting Livingston because of jealousy over his beautiful wife. The old man disappeared, so they moved the post office and school to Lower Hext.

"A man named N.C. Lethal appeared on the scene about that time and suggested they build another school. This was about fifty-seven years ago, which would make it about 1923.

"After Menard and Hext consolidated, Hext took part of the school's departments and Menard took part. Hext leased the school house for fifty-seven years."

According to Mrs. Pope, the post office moved to different locations from time to time:

"After they moved it from Meringo, they moved it down here by the London road in Lower Hext, but they hadn't named the town yet.

"A widow woman was really the first postmaster, but she had to quit because she had to send her two boys to school."

The author had a hard time keeping up with all the different places the post office moved to and who ran the post office. According to Mrs. Pope:

"The A.J. (Andy) Northcutt Merchandise Store had the post office in it at one time. It was then moved to another building, and Barney Westbrook ran it.

"Barney Westbrook was the Baptist preacher who wed everyone in town. He had the prettiest black, curly hair, even when he got old.

"Well, anyway, Mr. Westbrook raised his children in the back of the post office.

"Carol and Ella Williamson took it over for a while, but the government was going to take it away from Hext, so after they decided they wouldn't, Vicky Anderson took it over."

The author asked about two different churches in Hext; Mrs. Pope reported:

"Back then, everyone went to church, and we had a picnic every Sunday at Meringo. The thing I remember that caught my eye the most during those Sunday picnics was the thing they packed their lunches in. Since we didn't have cardboard boxes or paper sacks, we had to pack them in a wash tub.

"Everyone either rode horses to church or came in buggies. Some used wagons and the rest walked.

"When I was fifteen years old, twelve Baptists met at the Lower Hext school house and organized the Baptist Church, but they needed a place to have their meetings because it was really hot in the school house during the summer, and the babies cried when they got too hot, so the men decided they would build a place and cover it with cedar. This became the Baptist Church."

At this point, Mrs. Pope showed the author a ledger with the names of the first members, and it included the following: W.S. Williamson, Eli Wilkerson, B.M. Westbrook, A.J. Westbrook, C.S. Seiners, M.M. Seiners, G.W. Copper, Rebecca Northcutt, J.R. Hext, J.A. Baldwin, and Fannie Baldwin. Mrs. Pope then talked about the land the churches were built on:

"My Uncle John donated some land to the Baptists, but he had the deed fixed so that if they ever quit having church, the land would go back to his heirs. The Church of Christ church has their deed set up the same way.

"A couple of years ago I decided I would write my cousin and see if he would let me buy the land from him.

"Hollis Hodges said that he wanted to help me, but he also suggested we call a church meeting first.

"Hazel Hodges is the church treasurer, and she told us that the treasury had enough money in it to buy the land, so now the land belongs to the Baptist Church."

The author asked Mrs. Pope to discuss the Church of Christ:

"Some land was donated by Wallace Phieffer and a man named Mr. Bingham helped set the church up and organize it. The church was called the Campbellite Church then, and Mr. Bingham, who also was a school teacher, preached there."

The author knew there were other buildings besides the church and asked Mrs. Pope about them.

"At one time we had three grocery stores, a garage, a barbershop, two filling stations, a café, a rodeo, and a tent show."

Mrs. Pope had some deep feelings about the tent show, so she decided to share some of them:

"The tent show was something else. It came every week. A man called Jim ran it. Jim had something wrong with him, and every time he saw a certain color he grabbed for it. Well, one day I was wearing a red dress and he grabbed hold of it. Then after he let go, he walked off without saying a word. Ol' Jim really had some wonderful shows."

Mrs. Pope said a gin was another Hext business:

"Papa had the first steam-powered gin, and N.C. Lethal had the first modern gin."

As Mrs. Pope discussed the next building, the author envisioned its location:

"A man who was a school trustee had a little store right there in Hext. It was across from the old post office." [Tracy Hodges notes the man's name is garbled in her recording of this interview.]

As the interview drew to a close, Mrs. Pope noted:

"Uncle John was a great politician. I remember the fights he used to have with his nephew over elections. Uncle John had fingernails like a bear. Well, they had one fight, and Uncle John caught his nephew on the neck with his nails. The nephew still had the scar on his neck when they buried him years later."

The author asked about other types of recreation besides the rodeo and tent show.

"I remember going to one silent picture show," Mrs. Pope recalled. "It seemed like those horses' heads were right there."

The author found out the name of the man who had the tent show from Hollis Hodges. Hodges said a Mr. Camps showed his movies at a place next to the blacksmith shop. Hollis Hodges also discussed some of the author's relatives:

"Hext got its name from your great-great grandfather Robert 'Bob' Hext because he was an outstanding citizen and he had a short name."

The author also was told that Alf Reeves's name was considered by his son, Nat Reeves, in the naming of this tiny town and learned about other links in the history of Hext and her family during an interview with Hollis and Hazel Hodges:

"John Gabriel Hodges had a freight yard that ran from San Antonio to Fredericksburg to Mason, then to Hext, Menard, Fort McKavett, and then on to Fort Concho. It was one of the largest freight yards around.

"Another uncle named John Hodges was a county commissioner who was appointed by Judge Matthews. John served two terms, and he died during this third term."

Hollis Hodges presently serves as a Menard County commissioner. At the end of this term he will have served as commissioner for ten years.

The author asked Hollis to discuss the Hext volunteer fire department and its trucks:

"We have two trucks. A 1937 Chevy that was donated by the Menard Volunteer Fire Department. The other one is a one-ton Jeep donated by the Texas Forestry Service."

The author asked the date Hollis Hodges owned the café in Hext.

"Hazel and I had it in 1947. We ran it for three years and then sold it to Mr. Chambers, who ran it for two years."

The author asked Hazel Hodges about Jim's traveling tent show:

"I don't know much about the tent show," Hazel Hodges said, "but I do know Hollis and Daine Davis used to fight in wrestling matches because they received free passes to the show when they won."

The author next interviewed Flossy Westbrook, who has lived in Hext for many years, about the names of teachers who had taught in Hext. Mrs. Westbrook was a valuable source of information:

"Mr. E.L. Allison was the first teacher and principal. Mrs. Celia Turner Williamson, Harvey Sutton, Mr. Irie Pearson, and Mrs. Leverett were teachers here at one time. I also remember two sisters name Ned and Mabel Cummings. Coke Stevenson [governor of Texas 1941-1947] and Lamar Faxton also taught school in Hext."

The place where these people taught school is still in use because the school house is now used as the community center, and Hext has its homecoming there every year. The author found some other funny stories during an interview with Mr. Nat Reeves:

"When we decided we were going to get married, my girlfriend and I got in my buggy, drove over to the church, and the preacher married us right there in the buggy."

Mr. Reeves also noted the frontier life in the early days:

"I remember using my horse when I came to the post office to get the mail every morning. They would put the mail in my saddle bag, then I would go home. One morning I came home from the post office to find out that my Mama had thrown boiling water all over some savage Indians that were after the children. They tore out of there in a hurry."

The many different stories told the author differed in some ways, but they were alike in some ways, too. One of the cases of conflict was over how many children were enrolled in the school, and also what the highest population of Hext was. Apparently the population ranged from 1,500 to 2,000 and the school enrollment was from 135 to 150.

The author had conducted her last interview, so she wrote her conclusion by referring to the thesis of this paper, which was the fact people did call this town a tiny town of prosperity. This paper bears out the thesis by showing the once-strong growth of Hext. The author's reactions are as follows in the concluding senses paragraph for the English class:

As the author sat down in the chair, she recalled how people she interviewed swelled with pride as they told their part in Hext's history. She remembered one man telling her how his mother threw boiling water on a group of hostile Indians. She imagined hearing the Indians screaming as the water hit them. These thoughts also made her remember another interview, one in which she was told about the traditional picnics every Sunday. She could almost taste the chicken, which had a delicious aroma.

These stories and others she heard touched the author's heart, and she hopes the readers will be touched, too. She leaves you with a reminder of one of Mrs. Pope's statements:

"It was like I think heaven will be to look out those windows."

The author believes Mrs. Pope's feelings are very true, and she imagines the little windows as the gates into heaven.

The Davis Ranch
By Carmen Davis

It began in South Carolina some years after the end of the Civil War. —Alda Powell Davis

The first record of the Bar Half Circle Ranch is from a patent dated June 26, 1856. Since then, the ranch has changed hands many times.

"Character of instrument: Pat. #117, vol 32, dated June 26, 1856," begins the earliest recorded deed of what is now the Bar Half Circle Ranch. With this instrument, the State of Texas grants to Galveston, Harrisburg & San Antonio Railways Co. or assigns forever six hundred and forty acres of land situated and further described in this paper.

The purpose of this paper is to describe the layout of the ranch and the various owners who purchased it. The abstract of title describes the land:

"In Menard County known as Survey No. 3 in Block A on the waters of the San Saba River about nine and a half miles S.47.W from Old San Saba Fort by virtue of land script No. 1248 issued by the Commissioner of the General Land Office September 1, 1875.

"Beginning at the S.W. corner of Survey No. 233 and N.W. corner of No. 2. Thence S. 1900 vrs to stk. and md. for S.W. cor of No. 2. Thence W. 1900 vrs of Survey No. 235 for B. Heimann. Thence E. 1900 vrs to the beginning.

"This indenture made this first day of February in the year 1876, by and between the Galveston & Harrisburg & San Antonio Ry. Co., a body corporate under the laws of the State of Texas of the U.S.A. party of the first part and Charles B. Goodrich and Jonathon Barrett of Boston in the county of Suffolk and Commonwealth of Massachusetts one of the U.S. counselors at law parties of the second part as supplemental indenture to a certain indenture bearing the date of February 1, 1871. Executed by and between the same parties which other indenture was sign in behalf of said party, Thomas W. Pierce, the president, and Charles Babbidge, the treasurer, of said railway company."

Upon the death of I.W. Pierce in 1886, the following appraisement was made of his real estate in Texas:

"Menard County: 5,120 acres @ $1.00 per acre."

The present price for property is $500 an acre and up. The abstract continues:

"A deed of trust dated November 14, 1885, by the Las Moras Ranch Co. (William F. North, president, and Walter Tips, secretary, both of Travis County, Texas) conveys 640 acres of Survey 3 in Menard County to August Giesen."

An instrument dated December 18, 1906, executed by I.E. Gates of New York, Frank H. Davis of New Jersey and George M. Thornton of New Jersey, transfers the following described lands to W.K. Murchison of Menard County:

"670.4 acres by virtue of certificate No. 1248 situated in the County of Menard in the State of Texas on the waters of the San Saba River about 9 1/2 miles S. 47 W. from Old San Saba Fort."

A warranty deed dated July 19, 1915 conveys by W.K. Murchison and Birdie Murchison to I.W. Ellis Jr. Survey No. 3.

A deed of trust dated November 29, 1920, executed by Irve Ellis and I.W. Ellis Jr. to William J. Callan, secretary and treasurer of the Bevans Cattle Loan Co. to secure an indebtedness of $42,708.05 was approved by the following directors: Wm. Bevans, Julius Rasmussen, Tom P. Russell, James Flack, James Callan, Lee Murchison, Fritz Wilhelm, D.F. Volkmann, Wm. J. Callan, James T. Westbrook, W.F. Jenkins, R.H. Flutsch, F. Luckenbach, Frank C. Wilhelm, Frank Hartgraves, W.P. Bevans, R.R. Russell, Irve Ellis Jr., Wm. W. Lewis, George C. Stengel, Louis L. Ball, J.D. Smith, John P. Kitchens, Charles W. Graham, Ike Wilensky, Joseph T. Callan, R.H. Spiller, Fred Speck, Sam Melinger, A.E. Nauwald, Emil Toepperwein, W.L. Oliver, Walter W. Russell, J.D. Scruggs, W.K. Murchison, J.J. Russell, Houston Callan, Fred A. Ellis, R. Wilensky, Russell Callan, H.H. Wilhelm, Lee L. Russell, Johanna C. Wilhelm.

A deed dated March 29, 1923, executed by I.W. Ellis Jr. and Irene Ellis transfered to E.H. Perry and D.C. Reed, Survey No. 3.

A warranty deed dated January 25, 1925, executed by E.H. Perry and D.C. Reed of Travis County, Texas states: "For and in consideration of the sum of $8,235.45 to us paid by Johnnie Powell of Menard County, Texas, survey No. 6 original grantee, G. H. & S.A. Ry Co. said land sold and awarded to G.M. Jenkins by the commissioners of the General Land Office of the State of Texas as an actual settler, April 23, 1906, @ $3.08 per acre."

A patent dated July 26, 1934, executed by Miriam A. Ferguson, governor of the State of Texas, grants to Joe Powell 661.2 acres known as Section 4, G.H. & S.A. Ry. Co. about 10 miles southwest from Menard, bought and fully paid for on the application of Joe Powell in the General Land Office October 19, 1902 under the laws regulating the sale of public free school land.

A communication dated September 26, 1929, by S.S. Sayers, chief clerk and acting commissioner of General Land Office of the State of Texas certifies that the records of said office shows that the state school sections 4 and 6 G.H. & S.A. Ry. Co. were sold to Sidney Bremner @ $1.00 per acre said application filed in the Land Office June 5, 1882.

According to the abstract of title, the sales covering same were forfeited May 2, 1896 by decrees issued out of the District Court of Menard County, in Causes Nos. 460 and 461, State of Texas vs. Louis H. Runge, et al, certified copies of which decrees were filed in the Land Office April 28, 1896.

A petition deed dated May 31, 1949, name of parties Cora E. Powell and Alda B. Davis conveys to the said Alda B. Davis the following lands. The east one-third of Survey 4 and the west one-third of Survey 3 and the north part of Survey 7.

According to the abstract: "That said Section 4 was awarded to Joe Powell June 29, 1903 on application filed with the county clerk of Menard County, October 11, 1902 to purchase same @ $1.00 per acre as additional to home on Section 243."

Joe Powell made required proof of three years occupancy and improvements on said home tract and additional Section 4.

A warranty deed dated June 11, 1945 executed by Ves Powell conveyed to C.W. Davis and Alda Davis the east two-thirds of Survey 3 original grantee G.H. & S.A. Ry. Co. being 438.9 acres for a consideration $11,342.

A petition deed dated December 16, 1977 executed by 198th District Court of Menard County, Texas in Cause No. 3582 conveyed to Alda B. Powell Davis 353.447 out of the south part of Survey No. 6 G.H. & S.A. Ry. Co.

From here, the author did further research to find the unwritten meaning that lay in these papers. Mrs. Alda Powell Davis explained:

"Why are we here on this, you ask. It began in South Carolina some years after the end of the Civil War. One reason was that those who fought for the Confederacy still had to endure the enmity of a government in power which resolved that 'the South shall not rise again.'

"Couple that hardship with the natural hardships of those times and it is little wonder that Grandpa Joe Powell was looking for some way to better provide for wife Mary—he always pronounced it with a long 'a' and not as if it was part of the Christmas greeting—and his 'chillun. This pronunciation was used by the Negro slaves but originated elsewhere.

"So, he wrote to brother-in-law John Alexander, who was already in Texas, to inquire about conditions here. 'For I knew John would tell me the straight of it.' By this expression, he meant that he knew that his brother-in-law would tell him the truth about the situation here.

"The reply was favorable, so in 1893, Grandpa rented half a boxcar for their household possessions and came by train with his wife and three sons, the youngest of which was my father," Mrs. Davis continued.

"Grandpa worked at first as a laborer for various people, and later for Wm. F. North of the Las Moras Ranch Company.

"He bought a place on the San Saba River, which was not part of this ranch, but laid the foundation for acquiring it. He planted a truck garden and hauled vegetables to Menardville in a hack, peddling them door-to-door to the housewives. With the money thus acquired, he was able to make the down payment on a part of this ranch.

"Life was harsh in those days, and the family endured by eating game, their garden produce, along with the pecans and wild fruits they could gather. A trip to and from San Angelo to acquire barrels of flour and sugar and their yearly supply of coffee was made by wagon and a team and required one week to complete. Wolves prowling around at night kept their dogs confined to the yard.

"It was in these surroundings that my father, Johnnie Powell, grew up. He worked as a cowboy and became foreman of the Bois d'Arc Ranch. There were no trucks in those days to haul feed for the cattle, so they endured the winter on the range. Daddy has told how the weak cows would become mired in the mud of the waterholes and had to be roped and pulled out by horses. When freed from the mud, they would turn on their benefactors and fight horse and man as he tried to remove his rope.

"Sheep had made their way into the country by then, and Daddy supervised the Mexican sheepherders who lived on the range in their covered wagons. They and their dogs herded the sheep as they grazed during the day. For the night, they cut brush for a pen with their machetes, forming it into a horseshoe-shaped enclosure with the sheep inside and the men, dogs, wagon, and campfires in the open entrance. This was for protection against wolves. At this time, Daddy acquired some hounds and began to gradually drive the wolves from the country, making it safe for the sheep, goats, and calves.

"In 1923, Daddy bought some land that eventually became a part of this ranch. Your grandfather and I bought some land in 1945. The remainder was inherited by me from my father, who inherited it from his father," Mrs. Davis said.

The land, as described above, proved the hypothesis that it changed hands many times, and that the people survived many hardships throughout their lives. These hardships, however, made each stronger for the next hardship.

Thus, as the author sits here watching the white-tail deer eating outside the yard, smelling the wood burning in the fireplace, hearing the birds singing and the breeze rustling through the trees, she recalls some of the information she acquired to complete this paper. She can almost taste the intensity of some of the trials and tribulations her ancestors went through. She also feels a little awed to discover there were so many problems and changes in life back then.

The Pegleg Ranch
By Lisabeth Rabun

A pile of rocks, scattered square nails and broken glass and pottery of a bygone day mark the location of what once was Pegleg Stage Station, on the ranch now operated by Clyde (Ray) Rabun, 12 miles east of Menard.
—Menard News and Messenger, *November 19, 1964*

As the author stands on the bridge overlooking the beautiful rush of the water above the dam, she remembers the vast amount of history that lies in the land known as the Pegleg Ranch. Being a part of this history is an enchanting memory in the heart of the author, whose family has had possession of the ranch for almost seventy-five years.

The purpose of this paper is to learn and share the information concerning the evolution of the ranch in the development of the town of Menard as we know it today.

The *Menard News and Messenger* wrote:

"Pegleg, which belongs to Mrs. Rabun's family, extends along both sides of the river, where a concrete dam provides a good fishing hole, and a beautiful waterfall when the river is running.

"Aside from that, the ranch probably has more history associated with it than any one site in this entire region except Fort McKavett and Presidio San Saba. And Pegleg's colorful history extends over a much longer period than either of those two places."

The continuing history of the Pegleg is vast and colorful. It is located in the southeast part of Menard County, about twelve miles from the town. The San Saba River is set in beautiful pecan tree-covered banks that divide the ranch. The rushing water's path pushes over a dam, down some twists, turns, and rapids, then under a bridge. The water talks like one generation to another, trying to tell of the history and stories that occurred there long ago. Information about this place comes from an interview with the author's father, Ray Rabun:

"The land was first patented in 1860 when Menard County

was part of Bexar County and San Antonio was the county seat. I think Sam Houston was governor when the first properties were deeded. Its main operation in the early years was the running of a stage station. The station required a corral for horses and a place the passengers could get a bite to eat and something to drink. Probably that earlier life was more interesting in that it has the mystery and mystique and the Western 'twang' to it.

"Many stories and adventures have been attributed to the Pegleg such as lost treasure and things like this, of which there's little or no proof during the early sixties. A large caliber musket ball was found north of the present crossing and west of the present home."

In 1964, an interview and replay of knowledge about the ranch was prompted by the finding of this musket ball and a cocked pistol. Research of this event was published in the local newspaper at that time. The following is an excerpt of an article written in the *Menard News* at the time these discoveries took place:

"Many events of recent months have led to the unfolding of Pegleg's history, piece by piece.

"Several months ago, Mrs. Lonnie Pollard found, in the Pollard pasture nine miles west of Menard, an old Colt dragoon pistol with the name J.T. Bates stamped on the butt.

"That was the name of the first Concho County sheriff, who skipped out before his term was up and was rumored to have taken part in stage robberies at Pegleg. No rap has been pinned on J.T. Bates, but the discovery of his gun and resultant speculations, served as a spur to the quest of Pegleg's history.

"But for some unexplained reason, Bates left his cocked Colt Dragoon pistol in a live oak thicket in the Pollard pasture. As Lonnie Pollard says, 'There must have been some action around there, or the gun wouldn't have been cocked. A man just wouldn't carry his pistol around like that—not unless he was crazy, or else trying to lose a leg.'"

As the author's father has mentioned, these findings caused an urge to learn more. The *Menard News* continues:

"About the time the pistol was found, J.M. Skaggs, a graduate history student at Texas Technological College, was working on a thesis on the Great Western Cattle Trails, the main stem of which crossed the San Saba River at Pegleg near the mouth of McDougal Creek. Skaggs corresponded with several Menard residents, then came to Menard to look over the site.

"During Skaggs' visit to Pegleg Ranch, Rabun arranged for him to talk with J.D. Noguess, who has a vast store of knowledge of the history of this area, both from personal observation and from information handed down to him by his parents."

The following is a recalling of an interview Mr. Rabun had with Mr. Noguess:

"On top of a hill south of the area where the stage station is located, a little community cemetery was founded. Most of the information I have on it came from an interview and an on-site discussion with J.D. Noguess. At that time, Mr. Noguess discussed his mother coming from San Antonio to the stage station and getting off the stage and staying with the people there for some period of time.

"During that time, one of the sons of the owner accidentally shot himself with a buffalo gun and she helped take care of him for the three weeks he lingered before he died. He is buried on top of the hill out there, along with the sheep farmer McDougal who was scalped by some white men dressed to look like Indians. These two people are the only ones that I know of that are actually buried there, while the size of the cemetery and various other things suggest that there were a number of other people buried there.

"Today, evidence of the stage station and activities surrounding such adventure are still visible along with the old stage coach road that comes off the higher area into the river bottom."

Other parts of the interview were published in the *Menard News*:

"Going over the ranch with Rabun, Skaggs, and the publisher of the *Menard News*, Noguess made positive identification of the Pegleg Station site. Then looking over the pasture, he established a part of the old stage and wagon road.

"On the side of the hill descending to the river, he pointed to markings left on the rocks by an iron-tired wheel as a now unknown stage driver applied the brakes to his vehicle."

Although the evidence of the stage concludes that it ran smoothly, they did have problems. History indicates that the robbers of the time had much to do with how smoothly. The memory of the legendary stage coach robbers still lives in the history of Pegleg. According to my father:

"Immediately west of Pegleg is a hill that was sometimes called Robbers Roost, while the real Robbers Roost is located on Cynthia Martin's ranch some six or eight miles south of the Pegleg. The closer hill was used by the bandits to watch the stage and ensure the fact that there weren't any Rangers or marshals riding shotgun hidden on top of the stage. Once they determined this was not the case, they promptly robbed the stage and were ultimately chased back to the area south of the ranch."

This isn't the only criminal action that has taken place on the ranch. My father continues:

"During the time that the Rangers were active in fighting crime on the frontier, supposedly the Indians were stealing horses in Mason County. They had taken the time to construct a rock wall, in the gate of which they pitched their tepees.

"One side of the corral was a steep hill that they could stack brush on to keep the horses in. Subsequently, they went to Mason County, stole the horses, and brought them up to put them in this corral. This activity was supposed to have been conducted by Chief Quanah Parker. As the story goes, the Indians escaped and later were the same group responsible for the abduction of Cynthia Ann Parker. Whether or not she was with them at that time, I don't know." [Parts of this story are suspect. Cynthia Ann was captured in 1836 and rescued in 1860, although she did not happily return to life with her birth family. Quanah Parker was her son and, at best, a teenager when Cynthia Ann was returned to civilization; Cynthia Ann died in 1870; Quanah did not emerge as a Comanche chief until after his mother's death.]

Evidence of the stage station, cattle drives, and the other various activities mentioned is shown by the wear and tear one can see on the land. According to my father:

"During the period of time when the stage was in operation, a bridge was built over McDougal Creek, that has washed out long since, but evidence of the bridge is still visible. This bridge was allegedly to have been built by the cavalry, and various artifacts have been found to suggest that the cavalry did, from time to time, camp around Pegleg. Old buttons, belts, and harness pieces used by the army have also been found there. Later on, the cattle drives did cross in the area of Pegleg. It has a natural crossing, plus the fact they could replenish some supplies from the stage station such as flour, lard, and perhaps whiskey, cigarettes, or tobacco."

After civilization settles, the ownership becomes permanent. From a wild, rip-roaring cowboys and Indians time, the land on which the Pegleg lies is deeded to the author's ancestors. According to my father:

"In later years, after the turn of century, the north side of the Pegleg was turned into an irrigated stock farm by Joe and Jim Matthews about 1909 or 1910. They cleared some 250 acres and built concrete and cypress pipes for irrigation ditches, some of which are still in place.

"From pictures, apparently a great deal of truck farming was done by Joe and Jim, and large crops of maize and other products were grown."

The ranch's resources were used widely in this area by struggling settlers. My father continues:

"One mark left by the Pegleg has to do with the availability of sand and gravel on the ranch. A number of the buildings, homes, barns, and sheds are built out of concrete. The old ranch home, which was built by Jim Matthews, is still standing. The army obtained sand from the Pegleg to build Fort McKavett and Fort Concho, this being the closest source of sand available to them at this time. Menard County also obtained their sand from the Pegleg when the new courthouse was built. This is the structure we see today."

"In their construction of the old ranch home, Joe and Jim Matthews used all of their cast-off body frames, cable, trash pieces of wire, pipe, and various pieces of farm equipment, chains, and anything else made of steel that could be put in there to add reinforcement. The discovery was made during various bits of remodeling on the ranch house."

The historic ranch is also represented in the political records of the county. From records stated in the book *The Free State of Menard*, the author finds that between 1923 and 1932, Joe Matthews was Menard County judge. He also served as the Precinct 4 county commissioner from 1916 to 1920.

My father says the Matthews made many improvements in the area:

"One of the first dipping vats was located at Pegleg, along with—after the dam was built—a water wheel that was used to power shearing machines. Apparently, in yesteryear, the area ranchers brought their livestock to the Pegleg to have them dipped and sheared when necessary."

The ranch also contains several surprises, one of which remains a mystery. According to my father:

"At one time on the west side of the ranch, there was evidence of an old structure of some sort. It's very small, about ten feet by fourteen feet. While prowling through the foundation of this structure, Norton Matthews dug around and found what he thought was a box. It was late in the evening, so he decided to go back the next chance he had to dig it up. He went back later only to find someone had already been there and dug it up. It was a rectangular-shaped box. It may have been a week or ten days before he went back, but when he did, it was missing. What was in the box? I have no idea, nor did Norton."

The treasure lies, however, not in a stolen chest, but in the natural resources of the land. According to my father:

"Today, the Pegleg still is a farm. It is a farming and ranching operation, with probably more emphasis on recreation as many ranches in the county are. There is hunting in season, and the river is the provider of several forms of recreation."

The author's father, in his interview, says that many large fish have been caught in the ranch's part of the river. "The biggest fish I have caught there weigh forty-one pounds," he said. "But I was told about a seventy-one pounder that was caught in the drought."

With this recreation, rules to protect the animals are provided by the state. The breaking of these rules prompts the formation of committees, such as the following, about which the *Texas Parks and Wildlife Magazine* reports: "Texas' new Operation Game Thief Committee has awarded $2,200 to persons whose tip led to apprehension and conviction of violators of the state's game and fish laws."

This committee stresses that the hunting and fishing laws be obeyed by all. The author remembers the many fishing and hunting experiences enjoyed by her friends and family at the lovely campsite along the river. According to the author's father:

"It has been a popular camping spot from the time of the Indians and Spaniards, all the way up to the present date. People enjoyed the big pecan trees and the pretty river. It has been used as a shady camping ground by people for three or four hundred years. An example of the use of the area back in the earlier days is that, recently, while a backhoe was digging a septic tank, ashes from campfires were buried under a foot of dirt."

As the river runs from the product of rainbows, each beautiful sight in one's mind is shadowed by the destruction of the floods and accidents that have caused death. According to the author's mother, Janet Rabun:

"There has been a number of deaths through the years on the Pegleg. All the deaths I know have been violent deaths. There was one duck hunter who shot himself in the boat when Norton Matthews was a little boy. During the flood of 1938, Jim Matthews died of a heart attack while trying to get his family out of the flooded area."

Because she was almost there, the author's mother recalled the vivid description told to her by her mother while growing up:

"My mother was eight months pregnant with me during the

flood of 1938. My grandfather had gone to start the pickup. As he was turning the key, he died of a heart attack. The family went to a small frame house above Taylor Creek to join several more families to wait for the flood waters to subside."

In keeping with the thought of death, the author wants to include a song written by her teacher, Patty Miller. The death of her father-in-law, while she and his son celebrated their anniversary at his river ranch, was the inspiration for the song:

RIVERSONG

> There's a place by the river
> I know it well
> It comes from my childhood
> And it always rings a bell
>   ...in my mem'ry...

> There's a campfire at evenin'
> The fam'ly's around
> And the music they're making
> Can't be heard in any town
>   ...hear her singin'...

Chorus:
> There'll be sunshine enough for everyone here
> There'll be laughter to ring in your heart
>   and your ear
> There'll be sunshine enough to last us
>   forever
> If you're near me, by the river
>   ...we'll make our own mem'ry, by the river...

> There's a shade tree o'er the bonfire
> Moonlight and all
> There's coals in the mornin'
> With a whippoorwill's call
>   ...hear him callin'...

> And before you know it
> It's time to say good-bye.

Breakin' camp is a thing
That makes you want to cry
 ...but we'll remember...

Chorus

The author remembers many outings taken by her family and friends, and she knows how it feels to say good-bye. In his interview, her father summarizes the intention and information in his final statement:

"While probably a lot of things that you've heard about the Pegleg are fantasy, fiction, and trying to make a good story, I feel like the Pegleg, by the same token, did contribute a great deal to the founding of Menard County. Perhaps more so in yesteryear than today, but it was kind of the gateway or entrance into the county. I feel like most people, early on, that came to Menard County, probably came through and visited the Pegleg."

The author, too, had her reaction to the abundance of information about Pegleg Ranch.

Through the paper, the author felt mixed amounts of drudgery, excitement, and wonderment. The assignment was difficult for a busy teenager to complete, but the satisfaction and enjoyment of the finished report was overwhelming, especially because her relatives before her are involved. The author, a visitor to the beautiful acreage, closes with observations on the stimuli of the surroundings.

As I drive down the dirt road leading to the river, I smell the dry dust in the air. I stand on the bank of the river and hear the hard rush of the powerful water as it falls from the dam. I touch the brown bark of the reigning pecan trees, and I look up in time to see the result of the strong fall winds as they force the leaves to dance. I taste the meat of a cracked pecan and realize that I am standing on a piece of land which is involved with many events from the past, and now has become part of me.

The Black Family Cemetery
By Randy Runge

THE GARDEN OF PROSERPINE
From too much love of living,
    From hope and fear set free,
We thank with brief thanksgiving
    Whatever gods may be
That no life lives for ever;
That dead men rise up never;
That even the weariest river
    Winds somewhere safe to sea.
    —Algernon Charles Swinburne (excerpt)

The Black Cemetery was built in the 1890s by Col. William L. Black. He architecturally planned it to his own specifications. The purpose of this paper is to explain how Col. William L. Black planned and built the cemetery, and to visit the tragic stories of the loved ones buried in it.

There were four persons buried in the Black Cemetery: a mother, father, and two of their ten children. While walking through the cemetery, the author saw that the first to be buried was Delano Black (October 25, 1889–February 24, 1890). Delano, who died when he was only five months old, nearly broke his mother's spirits and heart. Delano died of membranous croup in a very sad and tragic death. Upon the top of Delano's gravestone, there was carved within a little lamb, indicating he was just a newborn, not old enough to enjoy the sweet taste of the fruits of life.

The second person to be placed to rest in the Black Cemetery was Willie Black (November 9, 1876–September 5, 1890). Willie was his mother's pride and joy. At the age of fifteen he was turning into quite a young man and very helpful around the ranch. On September 5, 1890, a tragic accident happened when he disobeyed his father's instructions, saddled up a bronc horse, and rode off into the pasture. When Willie failed to show up for lunch and was again missing at supper, a frantic search began.

The search continued until late in the night. A cowboy named Mayer found Willie. Willie had been drug to death by the wild horse. The family never saw Willie's body because it was so badly disfigured. This was too much for his mother. With the death of Delano in February and Willie in September, their mother never recovered from a nervous breakdown.

Inscribed in the tombstone at Willie's grave is this epitaph:

Dearest loved one we have laid
thee the peaceful graves embrace.
But the memories will be cherished,
Till we see thy heavenly face.

Engraved on the top of the grave is a Peace Rose, symbolizing that he shall lie in the peace of heaven forever.

The third person to be buried in the Black Cemetery was Camilla Bogert Black (1848–1916). Col. and Mrs. Black were married in June, 1869. Mrs. Black died a long, drawn-out death and was once quoted to have said: "After I lost my two sons in one year, my world was empty and I had nothing to live for." Mrs. Black died in Brownwood and was transferred to Fort McKavett to be buried on the ranch.

After the tragic death of the infant Delano and the terrible death of his young son, Willie, Col. Black designed and built the beautiful Black Cemetery.

The Black Cemetery was built in a unique way. It was built in a square. In every corner a desert oleander was planted and a century plant. In the very center was a huge live oak tree. The tree was more than 100 years old at the time of this paper. Col. Black referred to it as "The Big Oak." Col. Black wanted to and did bury his deceased family members in the shade of the Big Oak, and Col. Black himself is buried there, too. The plots and the Big Oak were surrounded by a wrought iron fence embedded in a cement rock wall. The cemetery, overgrown with weeds and underbrush, was a mere shadow of the beautiful place it used to be. A rock walk encloses the cemetery, which a grandson built in later years.

Col. William L. Black (1843–1931) was the last person to be buried in the Black Cemetery. The designer, builder, and founder of the cemetery, he lived a long and industrious life. During his last years he stood nearly six feet tall with snow-white hair and a scholarly beard. At the age of eighty-eight, Col. Black was an old man in those days. He was buried under the shade of the Big Oak, as he requested. Col. Black's death was listed under the death column in *Time Magazine*.

Other people buried in the Black Cemetery include: Robert Winslow (1900-1900) who died of whooping cough at the age of six months. The baby had other complications with whooping cough, which were too much for the baby to withstand, and in two weeks from the time he contracted the disease, he was returned to the Lord. Robert was moved to Menard in 1936 to be laid to rest with the rest of his family.

To accept death was to accept all its aspects. The sadness, fear, anger, mystery and even some humor. Although the fate of several members of the Black family contained no humor, folks look at death nowadays in a more mechanical way. Death was no worse than what tomorrow might bring. Below are examples of humorous epitaphs—words carved on tombstones—by generations who left them laughing.

This inscription decorates the tombstone of an unmarried women in Scranton, Pennsylvania: "No hits, no runs, no heirs"

A Pennsylvania man's tale: "Here lies the body of Jonathan Blake. Stepped on the gas instead of the Brake."

The author found the humor and sadness of the Black cemetery ran deeper than just death. The deaths were somewhat unfair, but as the saying goes, "that's the way the ball bounces."

As the author leaves the cemetery, he feels the cold chill of death. The smell of oldness and deterioration fills one's nostrils. Seeing gravestones leaning awkwardly and overgrown with weeds, one can only imagine hearing all the laughter once emitted from those now deceased. The feeling of death overwhelms the author to the point he must leave the cemetery out of fear of becoming ill.

Mr. Clark's House

By Dorcas Petty

THE HOUSE WITH NOBODY IN IT

Whenever I walk to Suffern along the Erie track
I go by a poor old farmhouse with its shingles broken and black.
I suppose I've passed it a hundred times, but I always stop for a
*   minute*
And look at the house, the tragic house, the house with nobody in it.

I never have seen a haunted house, but I hear there are such things;
That they hold the talk of spirits, their mirth and sorrowings.
I know this house isn't haunted, and I wish it were, I do;
For it wouldn't be so lonely if it had a ghost or two.

This house on the road to Suffern needs a dozen panes of glass,
And somebody ought to weed the walk and take a scythe to the grass.
It needs new paint and shingles, and the vines should be trimmed
*   and tied;*
But what it needs the most of all is some people living inside.

If I had a lot of money and all my debts were paid
I'd put a gang of men to work with brush and saw and spade.
I'd buy that place and fix it up the way it used to be
And I'd find some people who wanted a home and give it to them free.

Now, a new house standing empty, with staring window and door,
Looks idle, perhaps, and foolish, like a hat on its block in the store.
But there's nothing mournful about it; it cannot be sad and lone
For the lack of something within it that it has never known.

But a house that has done what a house should do,
a house that has sheltered life,
That has put its loving wooden arms around a man and his wife,
A house that has echoed a baby's laugh and held up his stumbling feet,
Is the saddest sight, when it's left alone, that ever your eyes could
*   meet.*

So whenever I go to Suffern along the Erie track
I never go by the empty house without stopping and looking back,

> *Yet it hurts me to look at the crumbling roof and the shutters fallen apart,*
> *For I can't help thinking the poor old house is a house with a broken heart.* —Joyce Kilmer

The house which Buddy Joe Clark remembers as a child in Menard contains much interesting history. The author of this paper intends to reveal some of those facts which span more than a century.

The following is an interview with Mr. Clark concerning the same house in which the author now lives. The author asked Mr. Clark if his grandfather ever sat with him and told him stories.

"My grandfather would relate to me hours upon hours as I sat and listened to him in the room, which is now in the back south portion, about his cattle drives and various stories of driving them over the country. He would tell me stories about the Indian fights. Several interesting stories were told over the years as he was driving these cattle."

The author asked about the roof of the house.

"For several years past, it probably had the cedar shingles. Older buildings on the ranch are covered with the type of shingles people use today."

The author asked Mr. Clark which was his favorite room.

"It would depend upon the time of the year. Around Christmas time it would be where the Christmas tree was set. The Christmas tree generally was put in the living room in the northwest portion, and during this time of the year, I would say this room was my favorite. The rest of the time, the room just south of that is a room that was being used as a bedroom. That was my favorite room."

The author felt sentimental because she sat back and thought about all the many happenings she had been told about that had gone on in the house. These facts affirm the old home place of Buddy Joe Clark holds much history of Menard. The author leaves with these reflections:

The author now understands how Buddy Joe Clark feels about

the house and why he does not want to sell it. She can now walk into the house and see in the back of her mind why the wallpaper and curtains have such sentimental attachments for Mr. Clark. They hold so many memories and so much love. She can now walk into the house with a loving feeling, just as Buddy Clark has. Finally, the author can call the house and the memories a part of her because of what has been shared with her. She closes with these thoughts:

The first time the author stepped into the Clark's house, she felt a sensation like she had already been there a year. She walked into the bedroom. While going through it, she knew then the house was old because of the way the wood smelled; the roller closet and other furniture were made out of cedar. As she saw all the curtains hanging in the house, a cold chill ran through her. She could almost taste the past in the Clark's house, the days that had been lived in this house during his childhood. In her mind, she heard the kids running around while the women and men sat around the fireplace talking, like Buddy Joe talking to her just now.

Home—The Low Farmhouse
By Wes Menzies

Mid pleasures and palaces though we may roam.
Be it ever so humble, there's no place like home.
  —John Howard Payne

The Low farmhouse was built in 1909, but the history of the land goes somewhat further back. In this paper, the author will try to trace the house, the land, and the occupants of each as far back as possible and discover the almost-forgotten past of a noble land.

The first recorded owner was W.R. Walston. J.J. Terrell, commissioner of the General Land Office, sold the land, formerly school property, to Mr. Walston in April, 1906, for five dollars per acre. Mr. Walston attained other land and sold it to Sam Low.

Sam and his brother, John Low, moved to Menard from Erath County sometime before 1909. They camped on the Perry and Reed Ranch and worked on the ranch until they could afford the land and lumber to build a house.

The land cost Sam Low $500 for 640 acres. Soon after he got it, he bought lumber in Brady. They made the two-day trip from Brady with the lumber by wagon. They built a barn and lived in the barn until the house was finished.

The original house had four sixteen-foot by sixteen-foot rooms, two on top and two on the bottom with a back shed. It was built by Charles Schuchard, Sam, and John. They planted two oak trees, one to the north and one to the south of the house. The one to the south died, but the tree to the north is alive today. Mrs. Low used it to hang the children's diapers on the saplings. The tree's trunk now is about twenty-six inches in diameter. There were plenty of diapers to hang onto it.

The Sam Lows had ten children, six girls and four boys. To support all of this family, Sam had a team of large horses that he used to work on the road to Junction. He also had a farm and might have had a horse race track. It is rumored that there was a track to the north of the house, and Scotty Menzies found a buffalo nickel on the alleged site.

Sam sold the north 240 acres to John on September 2, 1910, by a quit claim deed.

Scotty Menzies bought the 240 acres on November 15, 1965, and the other 400 acres on February 22, 1967. From then until now, the author can remember many things about the place.

The first thing the author remembers about the ranch is the old, dilapidated two-story house. He remembers walking up the old steps into what had once been a screened-in porch. The screen was almost gone, rusting away. Even in this run down condition, the old house still seemed to hold its head high.

The back shed was torn off, as well as half of the stairs, making it difficult to go to the top rooms. But once he got there, the author found an old television set, probably one of the first ones made. Surprisingly, when it was turned on, it worked! The reception was bad, however, and later it was sold.

The author remembers his father, Scotty Menzies, bringing a trailer house there from San Angelo. The old two-story was used as a bedroom, while the family lived in the trailer house.

The author remembers how he first learned to drive on this land. He would sit on his parent's lap and steer down the long, dusty road from the highway to the house after school.

The author recalls walking around the place with his grandmother hunting for arrowheads, old bottles, or just hunting and enjoying the beauty of nature. These walks always were interesting. There were stories of the past, and one could envision the Indians behind the trees when one found an arrowhead, or imagine hearing the rumble of old wagons when observing an old wagon road with its ruts still deep in the rock after all that time. He also imagines the time before wagons, when there were only wild animals roaming the country, unmolested by man.

The author feels the bumps and bruises he got learning to ride a bicycle there. The author remembers his feelings when, one day, he didn't fall but rode instead into the pasture and down a narrow road cannot be described with mere words on paper. Looking back, the author wishes life would still be as carefree. All good things, however, must come to an end, and these did. With a crash, the author's life changed quickly.

The author remembers his mother as she began to act differently and strange. He watched helplessly as his father tried everything to help her, from doctors, to health foods, to building the present house by moving the old two-story and another house together and building between them.

The author remembers her dying at the age of forty of presenile dementia, or premature aging of the brain—senility. [Presenile dementia is the most common form of Alzheimer disease that develops before age 65.] This scar will stay on the author's heart forever. This is the one time the old house let its head down.

Like all other occupants of the house, the author will one day be part of its past. Only the house will live on.

This paper has covered the land and its occupants. The old house has seen its share of good days and bad. The author believes that it will be holding its head high and defying the elements long after this generation is gone.

The author was inspired to write this about the old house:

As I walk into what is now a bedroom and touch the now-paneled walls, I suddenly seem to go back in time, back to when the bedroom was part of an elegant ranch house. The paneling disintegrates and the rough-hewn walls smell of cured live oak. An old wood stove appears in the corner, and the linoleum disappears to show a wooden floor. As I look out through the translucent window, the trees, huge live oaks, begin to shrink to mere saplings. A wagon rolls into the yard with a squeak of old wheels. Then, like a movie in reverse, all of the memories slowly return to their places in time. Past once again becomes present, and I go to turn off the microwave oven.

If Walls Could Talk: The Old Ed L. Mears Home
By Ginger Nasworthy

The house stood tall above the small child. It seemed to be mocking her, laughing at her, trying to scare her. She slowly crept through the door. The dusty staircase creaked loudly as she started to climb the stairs. She walked out, onto the balcony. There was a strong ache in her chest. She longed to be in the country in her nice, warm house. This huge creature had swallowed her now, and she knew she was here to stay. She hated this place, and she knew she would never accept it as her home... but as children grow older, their thoughts and opinions change greatly, as the author later discovers.
—Ginger Nasworthy

The Ed L. Mears home has sheltered many people since it was built in 1916. The author will share with you some thoughts and opinions of this home from people who have lived here, including herself.

If one has ever been in the old Ed L. Mears home, you probably found it to be a solid, massive structure. Though the author lived there for nine years, there were many things about this house she did not know.

She found the State of Texas granted Survey 191, from which the town of Menardville was established, to Johan G. Bremer. Bremer then sold to Gustave Schleicher and E.D.L. Wickes. When G. Schleicher died, his part of the estate went to Elizabeth Schleicher. She sold Lot 3, Block 44, in the original town of Menardville to Gus Wilson on April 6, 1899, for the amount of $40 cash, plus two notes, one for $45 and one for $40.

Gus Wilson and wife, Josephine, sold the lot to Dr. J.B. McKnight for $110 on August 15, 1899. J.B. McKnight and wife, Mable McKnight, sold this to A.L. Stroud for $250 on June 10, 1904.

The author found this information very interesting. She also found the ballroom on the second floor caused a local preacher to give a sermon about sin. He stated that some of the most prominent families in Menard had a dance hall in their own homes.

This big ballroom was used as a place to hold funerals when there was no funeral home. Ranchers had a place to stay when one of their kin died. Someone would sit up all night with the body the night before the funeral. One of these people who was taken there at his death was Bob Spiller.

Nancy Wilkinson, Ed L. Mears Jr.'s grandmother, died in the home. No further information was given on the subject of it being used for those in death, but she did find things about its use in life.

The ballroom seemed to be a very busy place, between dances and dead people. At this point, the author found someone was born there. Three upstairs apartments were created after Mr. Mears died. A wall was placed in the old ballroom to make another room. Jacques Noguess was born in this room. The author continued to discover this house and its property has quite a history.

The small house behind it was built in 1916, the same time the large one was constructed. It was used as the servants' quarters. Ed L. Jr.'s dad used to play poker in this small house with some friends. With a friendly smile on his face and a bright twinkle in his eye, Ed. L. Jr. told the author a story about how he could pick up a few extra dollars during this time:

"I remember when I was a little boy, my father would go play poker in the servant quarters with some friends of his. My mother would help me make a bunch of ham sandwiches. I'd take them over to the house and sell them. Sometimes I'd get a dollar a piece for them from some of those men."

Kate Mears, Ed L. Jr.'s wife, rented an apartment in this home. She intended to stay for one month, but she met Ed L. Jr. and stayed there. Many people in Menard either lived in this house at one time or know someone who lived there. To have gone through this many people, the house hasn't changed very much.

The large room downstairs has a beautiful hardwood floor. The wood is laid in the shape of a diamond. One can tell by looking at it that many hours were put in just to lay this one floor.

There is a small safe in the wall in the northeast room downstairs. Mr. Mears kept abstracts, deeds, and some gold coins in the safe. At the time the Mears decided to sell the house to Tom Nasworthy, Ed L. Jr. couldn't remember the combination to the safe where the deed was kept. Ed L. Jr.'s mother, Emma, was in the nursing home at this time. She was then ninety-three years old. He asked Emma if she remembered the combination and, at ninety-three, she did. The author found this very interesting because, at age sixteen, she found it quite hard to remember the combination herself.

Two beautiful chandeliers hang in the large downstairs room. They were installed when the house was built. Their cost now probably is at least $1,000 each. There are other valuable, timeless things about the house.

There are two footprints placed in the driveway. One is a small print, while the other is larger. The smaller one was placed there by Ed L. Jr. When the author moved into the house, her foot would perfectly fit the smaller one. Ten years later, when she moved out of the house, her foot was nearly the size of the larger one. Even though she never actually put her own footprint in the concrete, she had a feeling her footprints would always remain there.

This research supports the thesis that this house has been the home of many people, and probably will be the home of more people in the future.

The author found a lot of very interesting facts about the house in which she once lived. The following are the feelings she felt when she had to face leaving a place that she finally had accepted as her home:

The author walked out, onto the balcony for the last time and suddenly felt very lonely. She had become a part of this huge house, and she knew that it would be very hard to leave. It had a pleasant odor about it that she had smelled for ten years.

She saw the big trees and remembered when she used to climb them as a child. She turned and began her slow descent of the stairs. This house was totally empty now but seemed almost as if it were alive. The familiar creak of the stairs had a different meaning to her now. There seemed to be arms holding her back, not letting her go out the door.

She managed to make it out into the front yard and turned around for one last look. The windows seemed like eyes looking down at her, sad and gray. She swallowed hard to get the big lump out of her throat. When she turned and walked away, she knew that there would always be a part of her that would never leave this house.

Menard Theatre

By Chris Thornton

THE LAST SCENE
The stage is empty,
and the house is bare,
there's an extra program,
in the aisle lying there,
a Kleenex with make-up,
a coat hanger too,
I touch the front curtain
for a moment or two.
It stands there in wrinkles,
the way that I feel,
tired but happy,
with some blistered heels.
I cut out the lights
to turn to go home,
thinking how sad
that the year has gone.
When ghosts in the darkness
begin the applause
and the drapes come down
in a slow, steady crawl.
A record is playing a suicide song.
The emcee steps forward
to speak to the throng,
when suddenly two boys,
no longer afraid,
perform on the ledge
a comedy tirade.
A very odd couple
rock away the years,
and I stood frozen
amid the cheers.
Two witches are screaming,

"I want to live!"
And for one's convictions,
these were my students,
suspended in time,
for the old stage was lonely,
not wanting to die.
The music changed
to a frenzied blues song,
and I watched in the darkness,
while a doctor came on.
He also screamed,
to sooth his nerves,
and baffled his patient,
whose problems remained hers.
The music crescendoed
to a disco rock jive,
and the curtains opened
to a black ghetto dive,
where a hustler
mourned her son's early death,
he accused her of murder
in his spirit-world breath.
The laughs we all shared,
the practices, preps;
but the stage was then bared,
when on scraped a bed
with an irate old man
who harassed his nurse
with all she'd withstand.
I silently sat with the ghosts that night,
and laughed with as he dreamed he died,
while his sweet wife cried.
The windbag nagged,
the courier grinned,
and the angel died.
The doctor kept talking,

with poor choice of words,
and the nurses were thinking,
the patient was a nerd.
The interns were checking a fake bed chart.
Stage technicians were doing their parts.
Finally the thunder,
and sadly awake,
I, too, had been dreaming
while closing the drapes.
The seats were all empty
as I turned out the lights,
and fondly bid memories
a loving goodnight.
I held the fresh daisies
so close to my heart,
and blessed all of you
for your lives and your parts,
and whispered the words
to the stage so bare,
"You waz a heck of a good cast
I sweah!" —Patty Miller

The old Menard Theatre is part of every citizen in Menard, their own little Broadway. The purpose of this paper is to tell everyone of the greatest little theatre house in Texas. The author first researched the theatre through the eyes of Chet Hally. This is the transcript of that interview:

How long have you been associated with the old Menard Theatre?

"Since it started."

How long has that been?

"I've been with it, oh, about ten years. Since around seventy or seventy-one."

I thought it had been in operation longer than that.

"It started to become active, play-wise you know, when I became associated with it. Before that it hadn't been used very much."

How many plays have you been associated with?

"Oh, I really don't think I could tell you exactly, but probably around fifteen to twenty-five or thirty."

How many plays did you all have every year?

"We usually would have about four plays every year. Sometimes, though, we'd have 'em on special occasions, like the day of the big parade held every year around the middle of November. We would always have a pretty good size crowd then. That was always my favorite time of the year to stage a play."

Which was your favorite play?

"Oh, back in, uh, seventy-six, we had a play going on, and we had the best crowd we ever had. Everyone was enjoying themselves, laughing and all that. I don't think I enjoyed acting before a crowd as much as I did that night. It was a lot of fun."

Would you say that was the biggest crowd you acted for?

"Yeah, that was the biggest we had."

Did anything weird ever happen while you were acting?

"Yeah, I'll never forget this one night we were staging a play, don't remember which one or what it was off-hand, but while we were acting, I glance out to the audience during one of the actor's lines and saw this man, I'm not gonna mention his name, getting right into this play like you wouldn't believe. He was sitting there in his seat, clutching the arms, and cussin' like a wild man. Some people around him were getting mad. I could tell because they were giving him dagger looks."

What do you think led to the closing of the theatre?

"Well, what it all boils down to, I guess, is people just weren't interested in coming to see a play anymore. They would rather sit home and watch some television or listen to records. They just stopped coming."

So that was it?

"Well, that and that flood we had a few years ago. That messed the place up pretty bad. A lot of water got in there and messed the seats up pretty bad. Plus, we didn't have that much free time. Some of the husbands wanted their wives, who were the cast, to stay home more often, and vice versa."

How did you feel when it was decided to close the theatre?

"Oh, I was really disappointed. I knew it would happen sooner or later, but I really wished it had lasted a bit longer than it did. I'm a ham. I love getting in front of people and making a fool of myself more than anything else."

If you could, would you like to stage another play?

"Oh, yes."

The author goes back a few years to a play being performed at the Mission Theatre. His mother is in the cast, and her character is a dance hall girl. The play is entitled *Deadwood Dick*. The setting is in the eighteen hundreds, and the audience is fascinated by the stage props. At this time, few towns are so fortunate to have such cultural exposure. At this point, the author ponders the construction and activities surrounding that grand old stage.

The Mission Theatre stage resembles the design known as "full realistic setting" according to William E. Buys, PhD, in his book *Production in High School*.

The author visualizes all the tons of makeup applied to the actors who have acted on the Mission Theatre stage.

Makeup has been applied to the Menard actors to the same extent as is applied in one of the author's speech books. Rouge is applied to make actors look fat; dark lines makeup is applied to make actors look old. Dimple Noguess is one person who can boast as a makeup artist, as well as a successful farmer and one-act play director at Menard High School.

Dimple Noguess is known as a one-act play director for Menard High School in U.I.L. competition, and her students remember practicing on the Mission Theatre stage daily. She modestly smiles at having taken the one-act play to state five times and bringing back trophies five times.

The author learned the play *Blithe Spirit*, written by Noël Coward, is the play Dimple Noguess staged at a one-act play contest; the farce had seven characters.

Just as all winning seasons come to a close, however, so the curtain closes on the Mission Theatre. The author realized the paper's purpose has indeed been fulfilled. The research certainly proves that, at its peak, the Menard Theatre can be called the "Best Little Theatre House in Texas—Menard's Own Little Broadway." In retrospect, the author has his own personal reactions, which follow.

During the period of the author's research, he finds things he never thought imaginable. He finds out about the time and expenses, not to mention the dedication, put into each play ever put on at the theatre. He also grasps how important this theatre is to their lives. From now on, the writer thinks not of the theatre as just an old building, but as a monument in disguise. In closing, he leaves having these thoughts one day in English class:

As the author opens the doors to the old theatre, memories and a stale odor are there to greet him. Being taken by the hand, the researcher begins a journey back to when plays are being performed. He sees many faces that are familiar to him as the play opens, especially his mother and elementary school gym teachers. Turning slowly, he begins his walk back to the present.

Menard Public Library

By Dianna Lovelace

Experience is the child of Thought, and Thought is the child of Action. We can not learn men from books. —Benjamin Disraeli (sentence from his book *Vivian Grey*, Book V, Chapter 1)

As the author steps into the front room of the library, the musty odor of old books fills her nostrils. She looks around the dimly lit room and notices a bit of dust on the books. The boards creak and groan under the weight of the writer as she walks into another room. She can almost hear the books telling her of each of the adventures and stories they contain.

Picking a book from the shelves, she is aware that the pages are dog-eared and worn, the sign of a well-read book, the author thinks and moves on. As she stands in the center of the room, a warm, glowing sensation enters her, like a small fire just starting to burn. She realizes that a library is not just a place to get books, but a place to learn and read about new things as well as old. The purpose of this paper is to inform readers about the library, and to answer any questions they might have.

The Menard Public Library got its start in the arms of the women who sold books to start a library. According to Gertrude Westbrook:

"The women went house to house and solicited books to start a library. They had about 386 books and a little money. It wasn't a very big operation."

When enough money was raised to get a building, the library had its first home. It was opened February 1, 1934, in the south front room of the Mission Theatre. The library then grew until another building had to be found. This time it was moved to one of the buildings on Bevans Street.

When the library re-opened for the second time, people donated more books. Even though citizens were donating books and the women were working hard, there just wasn't enough money, so many fund-raising projects were started. According to a story in the *Menard News and Messenger Centennial Edition* published November 11, 1971:

"The main thing they did to make money was sponsor dances at Wilensky Hall on Saturday nights. I used to come over from Eden to dance. I can still remember Mrs. Jenny sitting up there taking tickets and keeping order."

The project was a big success, but again the library had to be moved because of overcrowding of books, thus the old American Legion Hall meeting room served as the library's next home. By this time, enough women were interested in the library and a club was formed. According to a story in the *Menard News and Messenger Centennial Edition*:

"Originally there was not a paid librarian. Of course, you can imagine what a mess it was. We now have a board of directors."

Charter members of the library club included: Mrs. R.H. Kidd, president; Mrs. J.R. Lovelace, first librarian; Mrs. James Bradford, Mrs. George Brown, Mrs. Fannie Ellis, Mrs. Henry Findley, Mrs. M.L. Mullins, Mrs. E.H. McTaggart, Mrs. N.H. Pierce, Mrs. Author Rodgers, Mrs. Nancy Wilson, and Mrs. Arch Wilkinson. Mrs. Lovelace served as the librarian for six months before Mrs. Findley was elected to the office.

Among the things a librarian needed to know were the parts of a book. The title page, copyright page, preface, table of contents, table of illustrations, body, appendix, glossary, bibliography, and index.

Mrs. McSherry served as librarian until September 1937, when Mrs. Frank Corder was elected. She worked as librarian until her death. After her death, Mrs. W.G. Westbrook was hired; she is now in her twentieth year as librarian.

Even though the women had helped the library tremendously, still more money was needed.

The Library Club met to decide on another fund-raising project. This time the project turned out to be the largest success of all. According to Gerturde Westbrook:

"After a few years, we fed the Rotarians for years and years. That is how we bought our property. When your momma was little, she used to hang to my skirt tails. I worked like a slave just like everybody else did to make money for the library."

The property that was bought endured and is the present location of library [1982]. At the time of research the Menard Public Library also boasted of more than 11,000 books and was still continuing to grow. [The current library opened in 2006 across the street from the library described in 1982; the old building was torn down and now is a public garden where Menard citizens have small plots for a nominal fee.]

The library came a long way from the arms of the women who walked door-to-door for books, to the house of the present-day library. Success did not spoil, it only made it better.

In conclusion, the Menard Public Library has remained basically the same. Throughout the years and many different locations, it carried on the tradition of helping to serve the public in the best way possible. This paper was written about the different events that happened to the library in hopes that it would be enjoyed by book readers in the future.

As the author sits alone in the front room of the library, she thinks about how she feels about the paper she wrote. She is glad that she got a chance to learn about the women who worked so hard to make the library a success. At the same time, she is also saddened that the spirit that the women had so long ago seems to have vanished today. The writer learned a lot about the library that she did not know, and she thought the effort was worth the while.

The writer picks up the shabby old book and begins to read. As she reads, the characters seem to jump off the pages, and the author feels herself being drawn into the story. She can smell the whiskey on the breath of the drunken man. The girl shudders as she sees the look of lust in the glazed eyes when he grabs for a painted doxy sitting at a table. The stench of the hussy's cheap perfume fills the reader's head, and she begins to feel slightly nauseous. The loudness of the intoxicated man and the hussy fills the author's ears as she watches them stumble up the stairs. The thought of what may go on when the couple finds a room disgusts the writer as she begins to look for the exit from this horrid place in which she has found herself.

Suddenly, everything is a blur, and the writer finds herself reading a book about Western bars and saloons. She shakes her head to clear the cobwebs from her mind. How could she have become so involved in a book? Replacing the book to its resting place, she once again notices the dog-eared pages. A slight smile comes to the girl's lips. She now realizes what a fact-filled place of adventure is packed into the Menard Public Library.

Menard Nursing Home
By Deborah Petty

IDEALS—GRANDPARENTS
Like the soft, steady glow of the sunlight,
May your lives continue to shine.
May the years toward tomorrow be richer
As your interests, devotion, entwine.

May you, too, shed your light along the pathway,
Guiding others to walk hand in hand.
May the light of the Father so bless you,
That your joys will be numbered as sand.

May today be a highlight forever—
Adding warmth you may constantly share.
Blessed with loved ones and friends all around you,
And the knowledge God's presence is there.
    —Thelma Anna Martin

The history of the nursing home in Menard is very long. The author intends to reveal some of its history, which spans more than a century.

The following is an interview with Dr. Herbert Westphal concerning the nursing home:

"There are forty patients in the nursing home. They have more people helping in medical care than anything else. They take special care of the patients who stay at the nursing home. If there are less than forty people in the nursing home, then the home loses money. They especially lose money when they only have twenty-five to thirty people."

Dr. Westphal came to Menard in 1958. The nursing home [also known as Menard Retirement Home] was located on the second floor of the Bevans Hotel at that date. Dr. Westphal continues:

"I worked at the nursing home from the time I came to Menard until the time that I retired in 1974."

At one time, the hospital was the Bevans Hotel. When it was

converted, the first floor was the kitchen and dining area. The second floor was the place for the old folks, and the fourth floor was the hospital, used when people needed a doctor's care. Dr. Westphal was one of those doctors. Dr. Westphal started practicing medicine in 1933. He practiced in West Texas for twenty-five years before coming to Menard.

Dr. Westphal and his wife went to Africa for a year after he retired. He helped the people there and helped with the work at the Central Nursing Home. The people there slept on the ground, and the hospital was the only place that had beds. Dr. Westphal continues:

"I think that Africa will gradually develop a system which will take care of the elderly, but right now most of these countries are only six to twelve years in existence as independent countries.

"The thing that Africa is working on mainly is on the education for the young. They try to get their kids to go to school so that they can elevate the standard of living."

The author asked Dr. Westphal about the morale of people in the nursing home. He responded that it depends on the individual. There are those who have many objections to a nursing home. Some people do anything to stay out of the nursing home.

If Dr. Westphal had to be put into the Menard Nursing Home, however, he says he would go without any objection. He has very strong feelings toward the nursing home and the people who work there. The only thing is that if he had a choice in putting his parents into a nursing home, he would not do it because he felt obligated, and his brothers felt obligated, to take care of them. He related that he enjoyed circumstances that would allow him to care for his parents.

"A nursing home is the very best place for elderly people who don't have anyone to look after them," Dr. Westphal explained.

This research reveals the reason the nursing home is needed.

The feelings the author has about this researcher's endeavor is that the nursing home is a place for people who can't take care of themselves, and for people who don't have anyone to take care of them. The helpers of the nursing home should support every-body who lives there. Everyone is important.

The senses paragraph sums up the author's thoughts prior to writing this paper:

Walking into the nursing home made the author see things she had never seen before. Smelling the odor of the freshly mopped floors gave her a funny feeling, like being in a hospital. It was like someone guarding something that can't be free. Later, when touching the walls, it seemed like being in a tub full of ice cubes. Her mouth had the bitterest taste it had ever had, just from thinking that some of the old folks couldn't do anything and didn't even have anybody around to visit them. In a way, she felt sad when hearing the old ones talk to themselves and mum-ble. She felt that old people were super, and, even though they are old, they have a lot of character.

The thoughts above are the feelings the author had before entering any nursing home and before doing this paper. It is a joy to find out that it is not true at the nursing home in Menard.

The Menard Country Club

By Cone McCain

THE GOLF LINKS

The golf links lie so near the mill
That almost every day
The laboring children can look out
And see the men at play. —Sarah Norcliffe Cleghorn

The Menard Country Club has served as a resort for members and is situated adjacent to the golf course. The purpose of this paper is to give a general knowledge of the country club.

In an interview with the author, Jacqúe Speck reported the country club was formed as a recreational facility for all accepted members. A limit of 150 members was set, with 138 members belonging to the club at the time this paper was written. Members conform to rules set forth by the board of directors.

The board of directors is comprised of Lila Gainer, president; Wayne Porter, vice-president; Richard Cordes, Bob Wilkinson, Louise Jennings, Lucille Tedrow, Ramona Goehman, Janet Rabun, Jacqúe Speck, Walter McGregory, Owen Wamuck, and Bill Austin, board members.

Each officer serves a two-year term and at the end of a term, the officers advance a position. The board meets on the second Monday of each month.

At each meeting, members vote on upcoming events. A dinner is usually held on Sunday nights twice a month. Each member attending brings a dish.

Being a member of the country club is not to be taken lightly, because expulsion from the club is a possibility.

A member who breaks the rules of the club more than once must have their case brought before the board of directors. A vote is taken for the member's expulsion or for the member to remain in the club. The same procedure is held for entrance.

To enter the country club, one has to have three letters of recommendation. The recommendations are submitted to the directors. If two or more "no" votes are recorded, the person has to wait at least a year before re-submitting his or her request for entrance. Two denials ends the chance for entrance as a member and use of the facilities.

The swimming pool can be used by all members and other residents of Menard County. The golf course, although located beside the club house, is not part of the country club's facilities. All the facilities are attended to by Johnny Gonzales.

Johnny Gonzales has been taking care of the club for the past twenty-one years. He opens the bar at 4:00 p.m. and closes at 1:00 a.m. He manages the grounds and the swimming area, as well as bartending.

Johnny Gonzales has seen everything that has changed in the past twenty-one years. He has been there when membership was low and when the buildings were much smaller.

During the past summer, $70,000 was spent remodeling the country club. The bar was transformed from a half-horseshoe to a full horseshoe design; $9,000 was spent on furniture and furnishings for the expanded facilities. The restrooms, game room, and lounge also were remodeled. Burk's re-did the restrooms, and Ray Rabun won the bid on the major renovations. The new facilities carried the Menard Country Club to standards above those of other towns.

Club members from other towns can use facilities at the Menard club, and any member in good standing can use facilities at other towns.

The club building is located only a short distance from the San Saba River. During the flood on 1980, the waters reached the building only slightly in the main room, however no damage was done.

There is room to accommodate the 150-member limit the directors have set. The hall can be rented for private use for $75. The club usually sponsors a few dances a year in this hall.

The country club was formed thirty years ago on land donated by Joe Aycock. There are 138 members governed by an eleven member board of directors. It is managed by Johnny Gonzales. The country club provides a pool, bar, game room, kitchen, and meeting hall.

As the author dives into the clear, blue water of the country club swimming pool, his breath is stolen by the icy water. Children can be heard laughing and playing in and around the pool. After swimming, a tantalizing aroma hints of the delicious meal to come.

MENARD
STORIES

Branding in Menard
By Alvin Kothmann

> *As the sun peeks through the darkness of the early morning, the author steps into the saddle, and he rides into the sunrise. He can see the herd grazing on the next hillside as the cool morning wind whips down his collar.*
>
> *In an hour the herd is gathered together in the corral, where preparations have been made for the branding of the cattle. The author can already smell the hot irons pressed against the flesh of a young heifer. At the same time, he can also hear the bawling of the heifer as pain from the red-hot iron agonizes her. The author can feel the money being rolled in his hand as she is let out the chute and another is brought in. He can taste the steaks that these heifers' feeder calves make. The result is a sneak preview of both steaks and future money doing what it does best from sun-up to sun-down.*
> *—Alvin Kothmann*

Branding cattle was an early means of reducing the chance of cattle being stolen or lost. A brand is simply a scar designed by a hot iron that is placed on the animal's hide. The brands are registered with county or state authorities. The purpose of this paper is to discuss one such event in Menard County.

Branding played an important role in the early days, and the brands were respected throughout the West. One example of the importance of branding is that a calf would wander off a range in the southern part of Texas and might end up in the northern part of the state. When this happened, whoever found the calf would try to make arrangements for sending it back. A dishonest person, however, caught trying to make the brand look like his usually was met with some heavy duty justice.

According to Raymond Kothmann: "A method often used by these dishonest people was altering brands by blotting. The brand burner used the original brand as the basic design and developed from that a design that was totally different and hard to recognize as being the old one.

"One who reads a brand does it as follows: from top to bottom, from outside to inside, and from left to right. The ability to read these symbols was referred to as callin' the brands."

Today's ranchers brand, for the most part, by using a chute. The animal is run into a narrow chute, a bar is placed in front of the animal and a second dropped behind him so he cannot move. He is the branded through the side railing.

According to Raymond Kothmann: "A stamp brand of the type in use today is made with a set branding iron which burns the complete brand with one impression. A newer piece of equipment, called the 'squeeze chute' has made the branding process, as well as other jobs, much easier than before."

This chute is placed directly in front of the cow chute, which is already in place. The squeeze chute is anchored with chains. This chute has wheels that make it easy to transport from one place to another.

"When a cow is run in the chute," according to Raymond Kothmann, "it can be squeezed tightly so it cannot move. A part of the side of the chute is then removed, giving more space for the branding iron to be placed on the cow."

Before ranches were set up with modern equipment such as the chute mentioned above, branding and most anything done in the pre-modern days was a completely different ball game.

"Branding the livestock required lots of help with plenty of muscle used for throwing the calf and holding it down while it was branded," according to Raymond Kothmann.

"Generally, there were two 'ketch' [catch] hands, two flankers, and a branding crew who worked to brand a calf. One would rope a young calf to be branded and drag the calf out of the herd for the ketch hands to get ahold. The calf is then stretched out and held down by the flanker men while it waits to be branded. Often, the hand on horseback would have fun with the hands on the ground by making it difficult for them to catch the four-legged critter. The side to which the calf is thrown depends upon the side to be branded. Flanking calves is no vacation.

"The calf is thrown by placing one hand in its flank and the other on the foreleg across the body. All in one motion the calf is thrown to the ground."

Once the calf is on the ground, the flanker holds the foreleg, pulling it back and placing a knee in its flank. A second man pulls the upper back leg back with his upper body strength.

"He pushes the calf's lower leg forward by placing his foot on the leg and pushing it forward," according to Raymond Kothmann.

The branding crew consists of the brander, who is the main man, and the iron tender. The brander's main duty was to place the brand on the calf. As soon as the calf was stretched out, the brander called for an iron with the name of the brand wanted. The iron tender then trotted over to the brander with the cherry-red iron, calling out: "hot iron" so the men would know that the iron was on its way.

The brander, upon receiving the iron, shook the coals off the brand and placed it on the calf's hide. According to Raymond Kothmann, "this was called slappin' or running a brand on."

The success of the brands depend upon the brander's skill in his business. He had to have expert knowledge in order to apply a branding iron properly.

According to Raymond Kothmann: "If the brand is not burned deep enough, it wants to peel, and if the iron is too hot it will burn too deep."

If the flank is burned too deep, it would cook the flank, blot the brand, and have a wound that would become infected. If too cold, it would leave no brand, only a sore. Yet it has to be hot enough to burn the hair and quickly sear the surface of the hide deep enough to place a scar which peels off in time but allows no hair to grow over it. The iron has to be free from scale and rust in order to make a sharp brand. Very little pressure is necessary to put on a good brand if the iron is at the right heat.

Different cattle react differently when approached with an iron. Thinking of all this, the author injects a few "don'ts" he learned as the son of a rancher:
· Don't let the brand get too hot; that starts a hair fire and results in a poor brand.

- Don't use a thin, used up brand; hair will grow over the brand.
- Don't try to brand a wet or even damp animal.
- Most important of all, don't get in a hurry because the cow has to wear the brand the rest of its life.

From the author's point of view, there were bright spots for both the old and new days of branding. During the old days, there was always work for everyone who wanted to work on a ranch. Because of the new methods, work is more likely to be more scarce than before.

The author's reactions about branding was that with such a process, there was a type of insurance for the owner's stock. In the old days, branding seemed to play an even more important role because of there not being as good fences as there are at the present time. Branding, thus, gave evidence as to whom the cattle belonged.

This paper hopefully helps any reader to learn more about branding in Menard County as it was at the time of this research, and as it was back in the old days.

A Tribute to Ranching

By Rona Bankhead

THE RANCHER

Hard old gray eyes, no pity in him
after years branding cattle—
a cruel man with cows & men.

he drove both hard & once when
he was 70 tried to kill
a young puncher for smiling at his

old wife, sat down & cried in fury
because his grown sons took his
ivory handled .45 away, held

his head in his arms & didn't
ever come back to the dance.
After a while his wife went slowly

out into the clear night
saying how late it is getting
now isn't it? without

pity for his eyes, him showing
nothing the next morning
barking at the hands to get

popping, the sun already up,
coffee on the fire & him
stiff legged, hard pot hanging

over the saddle horn, he led
fall's last drive
across the hazy range. —Keith Wilson

Ranching is a big part of the Texas economy. This paper will describe the ranching procedures of the Old West to the 1900s style.

A man who brought his family to ranch on the Western Plains usually had more ambition than he did money. The promise of unlimited open rangeland made it easy for a rancher to overlook the hardships he would face in a land where water was scarce and lumber for building more scarce.

A new rancher often spent his first year or two in a lean-to or a dugout on a hillside near a creek. If he was fortunate enough not to have to have his dugout swept away by spring floods, there was always a chance he would wake up to see the legs of one of his wayward cows sticking through the roof.

As a rancher began seeing his first profits, he built a ranch house and corrals. Even then, the housing was not much; the deeper into the prairies he went, the harder it was to find straight trees to use for logs. The only available alternative was the sod house, or "soddy".

Most houses had a sod roof. The gaps were filled with clay or cow manure. If it rained enough, the roof could turn into a garden. An Eastern bride traveling with her husband to their Montana ranch in the early 1880s recalled that they "kept passing low, cheerless looking log shacks, mud-dabbed, with weeds sticking up out of dirt roofs."

Finally she asked: "Is ours as bad as that?"

"Worse," her husband replied.

Along with the garden roofs came bedbugs and fleas. They were the constant companions of every ranch family, and mice were everywhere—unless bull snakes ate them. Some ranchers persevered, but others gave up, confirming the warning of Elinor Steward, a woman rancher in Wyoming that "persons afraid of coyotes and work and loneliness had better leave ranching alone. They were men who lived in the open, who tended their herds on horseback, who go armed and ready to guard their lives by their own prowess and who called no man master."

Teddy Roosevelt described the ranchers as a resolute breed who carved a great industry out of the western wilderness.

The ranchers—women as well as men—found a land that brought out the most in them. They made the most of the land, but not until they learned to cope with solitude and failure, back-breaking labor, and the hazards of fighting with nature and each other.

Many ranchers were lone enterprisers; other represented eastern or European investors. Together, they shared an independence that only open spaces can bring and a determination to build something lasting. Building something lasting meant working hands for both men and women.

The West was built by hands, from trail-blazing trappers and traders, to prospectors who panned for overnight fortunes, to enterprisers who transported people and goods across rivers and rough terrain. But the real foundations of the West were laid by men and women who became the first settlers throughout most of the wilderness, who stuck it out and made the land produce new wealth every year, long after the gold and fur-bearing animals were gone. They were the ranchers, a new breed of businessmen on horseback.

Besides the expected ration of courage and determination, the rancher needed a trader's acumen, a speculator's eye for opportunity, and a general's talent for action under fire. Some built up private baronies of land and livestock that gave them feudal powers at home and influence far beyond the borders of their domains. Large and small, barons and bitter-enders, a generation of ranchers engraved their indelible brand on western America. More than anyone else, they set its distinctive outlook, its dress, its vocabulary, its traditions, and its style of living. The pioneer ranchers branded the West.

In the heyday of western ranching from 1866 to 1886, ranchers shipped to markets in the east. They created jobs for some 40,000 cowboys and herders, founded communities inhabited by half a million people, and kept another million in the East and Midwest busy processing and transporting meat products.

In the early days, land was cheap or free for the taking and a lot of cattlemen put together great ranches that covered several hundreds of acres or more. In many places, ranches were on their own for years, even decades before they could count on effective protection from soldiers, lawmen, and the courts.

During that period, they had to defend themselves against not only Indians, but they also had to cope with natural disasters beyond their control. There were winters of killing cold, summers of wasting drought, market prices that fluctuated, and panics in the East that undid years of toil in the West.

Many of the ranchers shrewdly earned profits from cattle, then acquired newspapers, banks, hotels, stores, and political power. Many ranchers also made large amounts of money through investments in the enterprises of others.

In the 1870s, the fantastic success of the cattle kings caught the eyes of eastern financiers. They saw in the booming, cash-hungry West an opportunity to increase their capital faster than they could in their heavily industrialized home states. They knew Americans had taken a liking for beef, and they decided cattle prices, like the cow in the nursery rhyme, would surely jump over the moon. In anticipating the future for Western ranching, they hastened its arrival.

As individuals and corporations, Eastern investors grabbed up land, formed even greater ranches stocked with even larger herds, and trusted their business to skilled Western managers like R.G. Head, who in the 1880s, was paid $2,000 a month for running the far-flung operations of the Prairie Cattle Company. Western stock, however, was changing quickly even as it mushroomed. Change was in store from Eastern investors to barbed-wire fencing.

When barbed-wire fencing was introduced in the 1870s, it began cutting up the open range.

The cattlemen proved to be their own worst enemies. Aided by their enthusiastic Eastern backers, they had built up a business with an excess of optimism. Ranches became over-extended, over-stocked, and mortgaged to a point far beyond their cash value. The whole industry was badly shaken by cold weather, the prices were extremely high as the ranchers were ruined by the winter frosts and rushed to sell out. Stunned by widespread bankruptcies, ranchers finally moved to put their business on a stable footing.

Then even the farmers proved useful buyers for surplus ranch land. The ranchers concentrated on improving breeding and feeding techniques, producing more and better livestock on less and less acreage.

Much to the sorrow of old veterans, the excitement of that gaudy, slapdash, violent time now lived mainly in the imaginations of dude ranch visitors and readers of romantic Western novels.

The facts in this paper support the original thesis that the procedures of the Old West to the 1900s have changed and will continue to change.

The author closes with this senses paragraph:

As the author walks onto the field blooming with daisies, she see a mare nursing her colt, and can already smell the leather on the saddles as they rest in the barn, waiting to be ridden. The taste of wild bluebonnets lingers in the sunlit air. As she touches the fence posts, she hears the sound of horse hooves stomping the barnyard dust. The silence is everlasting in her mind.

Eastern Star

By Annetta Stephens

JUST FOR TODAY
My Father this I ask of Thee
Knowing that thou will Grant the Plea
For this and only this I Pray
Strength for today, just for today.

Strength for each Trial and each Task
What more, my Father Should I ask
Just as I need it, Day by Day,
Strength for my weakness, this I Pray.

I do not ask a Lifted Load
Nor for a Smooth and Thornless Road.
Simply for Strength to Bear
Life's Daily Burden anywhere.
    —Fort McKavett Eastern Star Chapter Golden Anniversary

Standing there in her lovely gown, the Worthy Matron made herself apparent to all who watched. Eastern Star became a part of life to many women in Menard and Fort McKavett between the years of 1925 and 1975. The purpose of this paper is to explain the organization first with a discussion about how Eastern Star began.

Eastern Star was founded by Dr. Rob Morris. He was born August 31, 1818. He served many years as an instructor in Masonry. He and his wife worked on the idea that females should have an organization as do the males. For years it was discussed, then, in Michigan in 1867, the first Grand Chapter of the Order of the Eastern Star was organized. Once organized, a traditional Eastern Star symbol was created for a pin. The pin is passed down through each Eastern Star generation, just as the purpose of the organization is passed down through each generation.

Eastern Star is an appendant organization of the Masons. It exists for the purpose of giving practical effect to one of the beneficent purposes of Freemasonry, which is to provide for the welfare of the wives, daughters, mothers, and sisters of Master Masons. It aids, comforts, and protects one's mother through life. Also, it was formed to hold the secrets of the organization; for instance, the title. Eastern Star was founded on a Bible verse, but it remained a secret about the true meaning of the name. Many of the secrets are still traditionally kept with some of Fort McKavett's first Eastern Stars.

Lillie Lehne was the first Worthy Matron of the Fort McKavett Lodge, and Henry Murr was the first Worthy Patron. One of the first members of that chapter was Teresa Tomlinson, who was the only charter member still living at the time of this paper; she is living in Houston, Texas. Some older members that were with the Lodge include Nugget Whitworth and Loraine Flutsch.

To become a member of Eastern Star, one could be a wife, daughter, legally adopted daughter, mother, widow, sister, half-sister, granddaughter, step-sister, or step-mother of an affiliated Mason in good standing. One had to be eighteen years old to be eligible to become a member. Once of age, she had to first show an interest in becoming a member, then be asked by a member, and then voted into the organization. Each member did what was asked of her, and was willing to help with community projects.

When asked what Eastern Star did for the community, Lillie's answer was, "they are all benevolent and charitable purposes." Eastern Star women served for the good of the community. They visited people who were ill, and prepared the meals for the funerals at Fort McKavett. Eastern Star also supported the home in Arlington that took care of some of the older members.

This paper indeed showed that Eastern Star was a fraternal organization founded by Dr. Rob Morris. It was full of many secret and meaningful purposes. The organization lived and served its community while also helping one another. It was a very close organization, full of people willing to commit themselves for the purpose of Eastern Star. It aided, comforted, and protected the members through life. Being a member of Eastern Star brought satisfying rewards.

As this author finished reader her paper, she felt a sense of accomplishment. She understood the true meaning of Eastern Star. The writer realized that there was still more information and secrets to be uncovered, but she also knew she must settle for what had been given to her. Through her research about Eastern Star, the author saw the importance of this organization. It especially helped her to understand the friendliness of some of the members.

The author was extremely grateful to have the chance to do her paper about Eastern Star. She ends with a paragraph written in class one day.

As the author stands at the entrance to the Fort McKavett Lodge, she can almost hear an Eastern Star meeting in progress. She is extremely grateful for having the chance to taste a little of Eastern Star. When the author enters the building, a familiar smell of friendliness envelopes her, and the writer suddenly is touched by an important love within the air. Because of her research, the writer sees the important of this organization, and wishes she, too, could be a member.

Home Remedies

By Frank Perez

> *Simple kitchen products such as sage, merit greater use as home*
> *medicine than some easy-to-take potent drugs that are being so*
> *freely dispensed with prescription in almost any type of store.*
> —*Clarence Meyer,* American Folk Medicine (1973 edition)

Home remedies were the only source of medicine the people of Menardville once had. This paper will describe the type of home remedies which people of Menardville used.

One of the many remedies for colds was to cut a lemon like one would to make lemonade, put it in a glass of cold water, and drink unsweetened. Put more water over it and drink as long as the lemon has strength in it , and then cut up another one and keep using it as long as needed. It is a sure cure.

Some of the other many ingredients used for getting rid of colds were ginger, sugar, Chinese black tea, honey, brandy, warm milk, salt, onions, and dried elder flowers.

Cold symptoms weren't exclusively caused by colds. Because there were no paved roads in Menardville, the dust blew into everybody's eyes. This brings up a new remedy for sore, inflamed, or irritated eyes.

Take two teaspoons of green elder and the bark of the roots of sumac, equal parts; one handful of double rose petals and live-forever, equal parts, pound them fine, put them into two quarts of water and boil for twenty minutes; strain off and boil down to one-half pint. Then add one pint of sweet cream and four ounces of clear rosin; set it on the coals and stir it until it melts down to an oil; strain it again. Then you put this ointment on your eye.

Some of the other ingredients for sore eyes are slippery elm powder, cheese plant leaves, sassafras, blue violets, roots of sumac, and tea.

The author found remedies for other ailments, too. One way to lower temperature is to slice a potato into several slices, take a slice and put pin holes in it, lay the slice on the forehead to draw out the fever. A second method is to place vine leaves on the head of the fevered person to draw out temperature.

The author's father recalled remedies for stomach aches such as using castor leaves placed in warm olive oil and placed on the stomach. This could be tied in place to hold the leaves on the stomach.

The author's father had another remedy. To rid the body of "mal de ojo" (evil eye), a member of the family would take a raw egg and rub it over the joints of a person's body while prayers were said. Before starting the procedure, the person would say "En nombre de Dios" (In the name of God).

Sore throats were taken care of by rubbing the chest with mustard oil and putting hot towels on top of that.

There were funny remedies, too. The author found many of the home remedies really funny and amusing. For instance, the remedy for being struck by lightning was to shower with cold water for two hours; if the patient does not respond, put salt in the water and continue to shower for one hour longer.

Of course, being hit by lightning would cause one's nerves to be a bit shaky, so the remedy for nervousness or nerves is a diet of celery, onions, and the next best, parsley. Vinegar removes the odor of the onions. To promote urine, sit over yard water or drink a concoction of turnips sweetened with clarified honey.

For intoxication, drink a glass of olive oil. It prevents the hurtful fumes from rising. For toothache, chew toothache tree bark or apply mashed bark around the aching tooth ["toothache tree" is the southern prickly ash and also is known as "tingle tongue"]. There were other dental remedies. The dentists of Menardville were few, and the ones who did practice were not really trained at college. Most trips to the dentist were very painful affairs. The people used home remedies for minor toothaches.

In the author's interview with Mrs. Rosa Turner of Melvin, Texas, he found out about toothaches and many other home remedies. She said to stop a toothache, she would mix salt with baking powder and a little water, place on the gum by the tooth and that this usually did the job.

When asked the remedy for insect stings and bites, Mrs. Turner said she would mix salt with tobacco and water and place on the sting or bite.

Organic cures went with the aesthetic cures also, and Mrs. Turner told the author that with different ingredients they used, they would also say certain prayers to get rid of an illness or disease.

She said that sore muscles were one thing she had to deal with almost every day. The remedy for sore muscles was to pour whiskey over the muscle and massage it deep into the muscle.

Sore muscles were mild compared to childbirth. Mrs. Turner told the author she knew a few things about delivering babies. She said that drinking raspberry juice helped ease the pain.

Mothers would often need laxatives, too. For a laxative, use the fruit of the cactus or algerita [agarita] berry. To be sure to have this on hand, they would can this when in season.

The author discovered a book of the Old West. The book, *Doctors of the Old West*, suggested that oil or grease from wolves, bears, or polecats be used for rheumatism. A poultice of slippery elm and Indian meal be used for burns. An ointment of crushed sheep sorrel leaves and gunpowder for skin cancer. Mashed cabbage for an ulcer or cancer of the breast. Mashed snails and earthworms in water for diarrhea.

There were many other home remedies in the book. A salve of lard and brimstone for itch. Common table salt with scrapings from pewter spoons for worms. Boiled pumpkin seed tea for stomach worms. Scorpion oil as a diuretic for venereal disease. Wood ashes or cobwebs to stop bleeding. Brandy and red pepper for cholera. Mashed potato poultice to drive out the core of a boil. A bag of asafetida worn around the neck to cure a cold. To remove warts, rub them with green walnuts, bacon rind, or chicken feet. Carry an onion in one's pocket to prevent smallpox. Use a poultice of flaxseed for pneumonia. Carry a horse chestnut to ward off rheumatism. Treat heart disease and dropsy with boiled oats. Treat goiter with burnt sponge. Use a soup and sugar poultice for boils. Use gold filings to restore energy. Watermelon seed boiled in water is used to treat kidney trouble. Sassafras tea thickens the blood. Use the juice of a green walnut for laxative and use the hot blood of a chicken to cure shingles.

There were remedies for very serious ailments as well. For snake bites he suggested you bite a mesquite tree and keep biting it for a day—or bite the snake itself! Wear a buckeye to keep away all diseases. For crazy people, tie them to a tree and feed them garlic. For boils, take the sap of an oak, boil it, and then apply to the boil. To get rid of lice, boil zinc with water and mix it. Burn zinc to rid your house of germs. For stomach ache, take garlic or put a lighted candle on the stomach and put a glass jar over that and it will suck out the ache. Treat shock with plenty of sugar. Arteriosclerosis was taken care of by sucking an acorn for a long time.

A gunshot wound was even more serious. When a person was shot or suffered a cut and either one got infected, the person was bled. This means the person was cut and their blood drained. This was supposed to rid the body of disease. When an arm or leg was severely injured, the limb was removed. This was done with only whiskey as the anesthetic.

The author has found that many of the home remedies are still in use today with a small name change, like castor oil. Times have changed, and the author reflects on this in closing.

As the author thinks of all the modern medicines which readers have today, he wonders how the people of Menardville ever survived. Looking back to the old days, he sees Grandmother picking the herbs and plants from her medicine garden. He thinks of what it must have felt like to have a slice of potato put on one's head to get rid of a headache or fever. He can smell the burning leaves and herbs, while hearing the agonies of the patient taking the medicine. He can almost taste the bitterness in his own mouth, and thinks how good it tastes only to look down and find he is eating a cough drop which is automatically helping with his cold.

MENARD PEOPLE

Pioneer Reflections—Edith Black Winslow
By Valeri Ledbetter

> NINE REQUISITES FOR A CONTENTED LIFE
> *Health enough to make work a pleasure.*
> *Wealth enough to support your needs.*
> *Strength to battle with difficulties and overcome them.*
> *Grace enough to confess your sins and forsake them.*
> *Patience enough to fail until something good is accomplished.*
> *Charity enough to see some good in your neighbor.*
> *Love enough to move you to be useful and helpful to others.*
> *Faith enough to make real the things of God.*
> *Hope enough to remove all anxious fears concerning the future.*
>   *—Johann Wolfgang von Goethe (disputed attribution; possibly*
>   *written by Rev. William D. Smith)*

In Those Days is a book written by Edith Black Winslow. It is her vivid story of the time she lived in Menard County. The author writes of her fearless, persistent, and continuous work with her father, Col. William Leslie Black, and with her husband and their family.

Col. William L. Black of Fort McKavett was born in New Orleans in 1843. At the age of nineteen Black joined the Confederate Army and served during the remainder of the Civil War. After the war, Black went to New York to become associated with the New York Cotton Exchange, of which he became a charter member.

In 1869, William Black married Comilla Bogert of New Orleans. The Blacks were very wealthy and happy with their home life and business. William Black sold his membership in the cotton exchange in 1873, then moved to St. Louis, where he was successful in buying cotton for American and European markets. Three years later, William Black came to Texas and bought a 30,000-acre ranch for ten cents an acre. The ranch headquarters was located at the headwater spring of the San Saba River, about a half mile from Fort McKavett.

Col. Black stocked the ranch with 700 head of native long-horn cattle, 1,000 head of native sheep, and imported a train car loaded with purebred Merino rams. Col. Black decided to devote the rest of his life to growing wool in Texas.

Col. Black first employed an Englishman to serve as on-site manager of the ranch, then in 1876 decided to move to Texas to take over operation of the ranch. Col. Black, his wife, and seven children [some sources say ten] traveled to Texas with all their household goods. They traveled by train to Abilene, Texas, and traveled by what was called an ambulance—a horse-drawn passenger vehicle with two seats and canvas curtain. Their beautiful furniture, carpets, and oil paintings followed in covered wagons.

After reaching Fort McKavett, they lived in the fort hospital until their ranch home was finished. The home was built in the shape of a cross. Col. Black also continued to acquire land, eventually more than 80,000 acres. He also had additional things on his mind.

Educational opportunities were limited for the Black children. The children had a governess and did not attend public school (there was none). The family had servants and cooks until some harder times came, and the girls had to learn how to keep house. At this time, it seemed Col. Black's career had turned into a comedy of failures, except for an experiment with Angora goats. The goats thrived and multiplied. Unfortunately, the goat herd expanded so quickly—to more than 8,000 animals—it threatened the health of his ranch. In response, Col. Black slaughtered and canned 3,000 goats in 1893 and 4,000 in 1894 and established the Range Canning Company, one of the first meat-packing operations, rendering plants, and tanneries of goat hides in West Texas. Sadly, he found the market was soft for his canned goat meat and the operation did not produce a profit.

Things got worse from that time forward, and money was not available for a governess, so there was no education for Edith after the age of sixteen. Instead, she had to help with the education of the younger children. Before Edith's brother, William Leslie Black Jr., was to enter college he was killed by a horse. The Black family did what was necessary to educate themselves and take care of what had to be done to operate the ranch.

According to Edith's book, their pleasures consisted of visiting neighbors, horseback riding, picnics, and playing tennis on their own tennis courts. The hard luck and setbacks would have made many people bitter, but Col. Black had a wonderful disposition and was liked by all.

Edith recalled privileges she enjoyed. As she grew up, she was allowed to go to San Angelo for pleasure. During the fair, trips were made over roads that almost were impassable. There were numberless gates to open and treacherous river crossings. She wondered if it was really worth the trouble, but she enjoyed herself when she got there.

Edith met the man she was to marry near the Black ranch. In 1883, R.S. Winslow wanted to see Texas and investigate the sheep business. He found the sheep business attractive, profitable, and the people friendly. Winslow began herding sheep, and within a few months he bought 500 ewes and leased 1,600 acres. He bought his first two sections of land in 1889, and pitched his tent at Dry Creek. Winslow had no well and had to haul water in barrels from Clear Creek ten miles away. Winslow wrote his parents in Philadelphia and told them of the deer, turkey, duck, and quail in abundance, also of the immense catfish in the rivers. The following spring, Winslow's parents came to live with him.

The Winslows soon built a four-room home, much like the style of those in Philadelphia. They also were able to drill a water well. They fought the lack of water, coyotes, and other worries without giving up. In his diary, Winslow would tell of lambs being born in a hard freeze and dying as soon as they were dropped. In the morning, he would haul and burn hundreds of these lambs. The Winslows almost gave up, but stuck with it until things were more ideal, such as a revolution in the water problem with the arrival of windmills. By the time R.S. Winslow met Edith Black, things were getting better on the ranch.

On June 9, 1896, Edith became interested in R.S. Winslow. He was fifteen years older than she was, but on October 14, 1896, at her home in Live Oak Park, they were married. Edith never was lonely—she loved the ranch and loved ranch life. Social gatherings were few and far between, but they went to a party now and then. The trip usually took longer than the party lasted. Soon the Winslow family increased.

When their first baby was due, rather than go to Menard, twenty miles away, Edith went to San Angelo by buggy sixty miles away a month before the baby came. She stayed with a nurse there. Elizabeth was their first child; shortly after that they had a boy named Robert. When Robert was six months old, he contracted whooping cough. The Winslows took Robert to the hospital in Menard, but could not enter the city because of the 1899 flood. Robert soon died. A friend made a casket lined with satin, and Robert was buried on the Black family ranch. Samuel Wallick, a friend, performed the burial service.

Each time a baby was to be born Edith went to San Angelo a month before her due date. Eventually eight children were born to the couple.

Tragedy struck again when Edith's mother, Comilla, suffered a stroke. The Black home was broken up after the stroke. Because of paralysis, her mother had to be moved to Brownwood. Col. Black continued to operate the ranch. Comilla designated each piece of furniture and silver she wished to leave for each child.

Soon after the Blacks moved to Brownwood, Edith and the children moved there, too, so Elizabeth could attend college there. Edith also wanted to help in Comilla's care. Brownwood was 130 miles from the ranch, so going back and forth was not unbearable. While living in Brownwood, the Winslows had another son, Samuel Bogert Winslow. Edith's mother lived to see her new grandson.

Comilla Black died two and a half years after she and the children moved to Brownwood. Col. Black already had given up the ranch to help his wife, but Comilla was taken back to the family cemetery on the ranch to be buried. After that, there was no reason to stay in Brownwood, so in order for the children to have the advantages of an education, the Winslows moved to Austin.

They bought a big, two-story home. They hated being away from the ranch, so at every opportunity they went home. Those trips were never forgotten.

To make the long trips, the Winslows bought a seven-passenger Cadillac in 1911 even though the roads were not truly ready for cars. The Winslows continued going back and forth for the next 15 years. This life was not what the Winslows wished, but the education of their children was of utmost importance.

As they traveled, sometimes the car would break down and they would have to sleep on the ground. There were many experiences during those trips, and World War I was on its way.

The war came, then the flu epidemic, and their youngest, Sambo died. Sambo was buried in a new cemetery in Austin. Edith returned to the ranch to help her husband in their time of sorrow, but as the flu was raging she went back to Austin to be with the other children and help them in their sorrow.

One by one the children graduated and married. After John left for Texas A&M, Edith returned to their real home—the ranch. They both had sacrificed very much for their children. They both were thankful they were able to maintain a home in Austin for the family and keep the ranch. The Winslows enjoyed those years being together and the children coming home with their children. Mr. Winslow lived to see all his children married. John married Mamie Wellington Mears, daughter of two of their old friends in Menard. Mr. Winslow lived less than a year after John was married, and John was left to manage the ranch.

Edith was left to begin life alone. She decided to stay at the ranch. John was nearby, and she had a good Mexican man to help her. Ezequiel helped her for seven years, and then he left. John went off to the Second World War, so Edith was lonely. Ezequiel had been the most reliable. Edith hired another ranch hand and continued to operate the ranch. Edith had no regrets and thanked God for William Black's goodness for more than fifty years of a busy life on the ranch before she died.

Edith Winslow died suddenly at the age of seventy while endeavoring to light a fire. Her book, *In Those Days*, was in the hands of publishers when she lit her last fire. Her daughter, Etta, then took over the ranch home.

On October 25, 1980, this author had the opportunity to talk to Etta Harrison about the life of her pioneer mother, Edith Black Winslow. Part of the interview was about Mrs. Winslow's father, Col. William Black, who brought his family to Texas in 1892. According to Mrs. Harrison:

"He bought the land at first as security for his wife. He was content in Texas; if not, he never let it be known. Grandfather never regretted moving to Texas, for he really loved the land and, after a few years, he really couldn't afford to leave."

Col. Black is buried in the family cemetery located near the highway on the old Black Ranch.

The Winslow family was separated when Edith Winslow moved to Austin and R.S. stayed at the ranch. Etta spoke of the time of separation:

"It was just something we accepted and thought nothing of it. We always looked forward to coming back to the ranch in the summer."

Mrs. Harrison remembered the old Cadillac her family used to travel back and forth to the ranch. She said eventually "it was sold for scrap iron." She also said she wished they had kept the car.

Mrs. Harrison dreamed of coming back to the ranch. She lived in Austin 30 years. She moved to the ranch in 1967, so she has been there for 13 years. Her husband died in 1979. She now lives on the ranch with her granddaughter from Austin. Her grandfather was a big part of Menard in the early days.

Col. Black played a large role in Menard's history even though he was not a native-born Texan. His family also was important to Menard. Edith Black Winslow's book certainly told of their saga in Menard and is a very good example of the times in Menard County "in those days."

The author of this paper felt it was very interesting to do research on such an important person, and the author learned a great deal about Menard doing the work. Someday people will

look back at the past and know a little more about their ancestors.

The author closes with a paragraph inspired by her research:

The author began to read the book *In Those Days*. She lingered on the high points of the early families of Menard and was
touched. One family, the William Black family, came from St.
Louis when William heard of land in Texas being sold for ten
cents an acre. His family later realized their dream near Fort
McKavett. To get there, they traveled by convoy from Abilene
to the Hill Country. They smelled the wildflowers along the way,
and when they finally reached Fort McKavett, the taste of the
spring water inspired them to want to build the most beautiful
ranch in Texas. In this paper, the author relived William Black's
dream.

The Lehne Legend

By Charla Kothmann

As the author listens to her grandmother talk about the Lehne family, she was not very interested. However, when her grandmother told her about the first Lehne voyage, the author felt a spark of interest. She could see two young brothers boarding a boat heading to a strange place. It touched her heart to think that if they had not been so brave, she would not be here today to enjoy this wonderful life, or write this paper to remind another generation.
—Charla Kothmann

The Lehnes are an important part of the author's life, and the purpose of this paper is to give you information on the Lehne Legend.

About 1852 in Brunswick (Branschweig), Germany, William Lehne, a boy—not quite seventeen years old—was deep in thought. He had to make a decision that affected not only his life then, but also the lives of his unborn children and all who would descend from them. There were many problems that influenced his decision, such as the Industrial Revolution.

The Industrial Revolution had come to Germany. Machines were taking the places of craftsmen. Thousands of men with inventive minds and agile fingers were no longer needed. The land was pressed to provide food for this over-populated area. Living conditions grew more intolerable each day. Fortunately, there were some people to help with the living conditions.

A few years earlier, a band of twenty noblemen formed a group to help improve people's living conditions. They called themselves the Adelsverein. Contracts were made between the Adelsverein and Germans who wanted new opportunities. Immigrants went to Texas by the thousands. Many came by ships.

Between October 1845 and April 1846, thirty-six ships took 5,257 countrymen to Texas. Things, however, were not as well in the new country as they thought they would be. There were a lot of opportunities, but also a lot of perils.

The Adelsverein promised three hundred twenty acres of free land to each family, and 160 acres to each male over seventeen years of age—half the land obtained from the Republic of Texas. The new settlers were also to be provided all materials for agriculture and livelihood at lowest prices from the storehouse of the Verein. They had plans to build many different types of buildings.

There was to be an establishment of churches, schools, hospitals, a means of communication, and the opening of rivers to navigation. There was also to be an overall provision for the welfare of the immigrants who had placed their trust in the Verein. This is what convinced William Lehne to go to the new land.

William had heard reports from his countrymen who had left their homeland for the new land. Letters from friends had come telling how thousands had been stranded at Carlshafen [later named Indianola] when Mexico declared war on Texas. Texas declared all wagons, oxen, horses, and supplies were to be used to transport immigrants inland. Dysentery, typhoid fever and malaria killed more than a thousand of these people before they could complete the walk of more than 150 miles to New Braunfels. Some managed to get as far as Fredericksburg, which had been established May 8, 1846. In Fredericksburg as well as New Braunfels, the people's inadequate diets caused them to sicken and die. William knew of all these bad happenings, but his will to go remained.

William was torn between the desire to stay with his parents where the pattern of life was known and the pull of the strange, unknown land. His older brother, Christian, and his new bride, Sophie, had arranged passage to the new land and the promises it held. William Lehne wanted to go, but he was not yet old enough to qualify for the free land. Then one day, even as he debated his situation, he shot a deer at the request of an elderly relation. The browsing deer was eating the old lady's hard-earned food supply she had grown in her tiny garden. The government authorities immediately exacted a heavy fine. This settled William's mind. He hurriedly packed his belongings, bid his parents goodbye, and departed with Christian and Sophie for a new life in a new land.

The ocean voyage in ships at that time took some two or three months, and it is quite likely that Christian, Sophie, and William disembarked at New Orleans. They were not listed on the ship records of those landed at Carlshafen, and there were no complete records of those coming by New Orleans. Even though there were no records of where they got off, later records show them to have been in Fredericksburg.

The young Lehne brothers made their way to Fredericksburg, named for Prince Frederick of Prussia. A bustling settlement of wide streets—to accommodate a U-turn by oxen teams and wagons—and stone buildings greeted their eyes.

It was not long before Christian and William had built a home for themselves and Sophie. William was too young to receive land and soon became a teamster, plying his wagon back and forth between Fredericksburg and Carlshafen, where all the supplies for the colonies were landed.

It was in Fredericksburg that William Lehne met and married Miss Theresa Jung. Many of the present-day Jungs trace their ancestry back to Switzerland via Germany. Theresa was born in Nassau, Germany.

Theresa and William became the parents of seven children: Mitzi, William, Louie, Lena, Ed, Mary, and George. In 1868, they moved from Fredericksburg to Fort McKavett, where they established a general store.

On April 5, 1877, William Lehne returned from a buying trip for his store. Along the way home he stopped to eat a sack lunch and have a drink with a friend. He suddenly became ill and died. He was buried on the banks of the San Saba River.

William's death at age forty-one left his wife and seven children in a bad financial situation. The boys had to take the responsibilities of men long before they should have. Lonely cow camps and trailing longhorns became their life. Nowhere on earth was true manhood put to a more severe test than on the frontier, and this is the way Willie, Louie, Ed, and George became a legend. Here are some of the stories they told their grand-children, nieces, and nephews.

According to Nella Mae Lehne: "Willie, Louie, and Ed were still boys and decided to go fishing. They hitched the mules to the wagon and drove to the river. Willie removed the harness from the mules and left them to graze. The fishing wasn't very good, so they decided to go for a swim. The brothers removed their clothes.

"They had a great time playing in the water, and it wasn't long before they began to get hungry. Willie, Louie, and Ed were shocked speechless when they discovered a herd of grazing long-horns had consumed their clothes. Then they discovered a far worse catastrophe. The cattle, to satisfy their hunger for salt, had chewed the mules' harness until there were only strings left. By using the bits and pieces remaining and a lacing of vines, the managed to attach the mules to the wagon. Then Willie, Louie, and Ed waited for the cover of darkness before they crept home."

That is only one of many stories told by Nella Mae Lehne; here is another:

"When Ed was a young man, he kept a group of steers in Oklahoma. He was out of grub one day, so he shot a wild hog and, laying his six-gun on a rock, he proceeded to butcher the animal.

"During this he looked up and there were three Indians standing beside his gun. Ed calmly finished his work while they watched. Ed then cut the hog in half and offered it to the Indi-ans. They took the pig and departed without uttering a word."

The boys had many stories to tell as they grew up, but William grew restless as he got older. In 1893, William and his wife, Clara, and their small baby moved to Sandstone Creek, now known as Roger Mills County, Oklahoma. On this ranch, Charles Lehne, Dema Clara Lehne, and Varian Lehne were born.

William and Clara lived a good life. They spent their old age with Dema, their oldest daughter, in Portland, Oregon. Clara died on March 30, 1964. William died on April 8, 1964, at the age of ninety-nine years and five months.

Charles William Lehne, only son of William and Clara, was

born on April 4, 1894, at Sandstone Creek. He married Addie Lusby on December 26, 1918. Their first child, Nella Mae, who is quoted above, was born October 27, 1923. Three years later, they bought and moved to a farm near Foss, Oklahoma. Their second child, Clayton William Lehne, was born on March 22, 1931.

Charles William Lehne died suddenly from appendicitis at the age of thirty-nine on September 21, 1933. His widow, Addie, continued to operate the farm, paid off all the debts in a short time, and lived through the "Dirty Thirties." Her daughter, Nella Mae, also helped Addie through this time.

Nella Mae grew up sharing the burden of the farm work. She married Russell Johnson on June 18, 1944. Their children are Charles Preston Johnson, born December 1, 1946, and Allen Ray Johnson, born January 13, 1950. Charles Preston married Marilyn Adcock, and they are the parents of Jennifer Lehne Johnson, born November 7, 1975. Allen Ray married Chana Maupin; Allen Ray in particular inherited the distinctive, humped-up Lehne nose.

Clayton William Lehne does not have the distinctive nose, but he does tend to toe-in when he walks, another Lehne trait. He married LaRue Ainsworth, who gave birth to Chris William on March 30, 1960, and Karen LaNell on August 21, 1962.

Chris William does have the Lehne nose, and when asked about it he said not having run into anything, he wondered why it humped up.

Dema Clara Lehne, the third child of William and Clara, was born October 16, 1895. She married Charles Clayton and the couple moved to Portland, Oregon. They did not have children, but in their later years they adopted John and Emily who still live in the Portland area.

Dema was a diabetic and died suddenly of insulin shock. Charles Clayton died a year later. They are buried near Alfalfa, Oklahoma.

Varian Lehne, the third daughter of William and Clara, was born on March 3, 1903, when Clara was thirty-three years old. Varian married, but the couple had no children.

Louis Henry Lehne, the second son of William and Theresa Lehne, was born June 11, 1867. He never married and lived with his mother and sister, Mary, who was a deaf mute. Louis died February 16, 1961, fourth months shy of his ninety-fourth birthday.

Lena Lehne was born to William and Theresa Lehne about the time they moved from Fredericksburg to Fort McKavett. Lena married a Bridges, who died at an young age. Their children included Henry, Joe, George, Evie, Theresa, and Ruby. All members of this family died at young ages.

Mitzi Lehne, the fourth child of William and Theresa, was born about 1870. She married Robert Holbert. Their children include a daughter, Selena Byrd, and a son, Robert. The Byrds had a son, Robert Byrd. Robert Holbert had two daughters: Allie, who married Vestal Askew, and Bobbie, who married a Fawcett.

Mary Lehne was born a normal child on October 25, 1872, but a severe childhood disease destroyed her hearing. She attended the School for the Deaf in Austin and learned to read and write. Mary lost her eyesight completely about 1940 and died on May 9, 1950, at age seventy-eight.

George Lehne Sr. was born June 5, 1877, one month after his father died. George married Maggie Burlson. George was a Menard county commissioner for more than sixteen years. George Sr. suffered from poor circulation in his later years and died October 5, 1966. Maggie died January 23, 1967.

George Sr. and Maggie had five children: Annie Inez, who died of a childhood disease at age seven on July 15, 1915. James Dennis was born December 12, 1909; James married Ruth Helen Talbot and they had two sons—James Dennis Lehne Jr. and Edwin Ruthben Lehne. Lillie Margaret Lehne married Fred Ellis Jr.; they had one child, Fred Ellis III, who married and has three children—Gaye Lynn, Wade Kevin, and Holly Elizabeth.

Louis Leslie Lehne finished his education at Shriner Institute in Kerrville. He served in the Army Air Corps during World War II and never married.

George Lehne Jr. married Mary McGuffin; their children include Mitzi, Candace, and William Louis. Mitzi married Kent Rabon; their children include Brandi, Kendal, and Kenneth Zackery. Candace and her husband have two children, George Travis and Lexy. William Louis married Ann; they live in Dallas and both are pharmacists.

Edwin Ruthben Lehne, better known to the author as Papa Lehne, was born November 5, 1874. He grew up loving and caring for horses and was considered an excellent horse trainer, a hard worker, and a good manager. He married Lillie Arnold; their children include Theresa (Aunt Theresa) and Mae (Mother Mae).

Ed (Edwin) and Lillie soon owned a small ranch near Fort McKavett where Lillie loved to entertain and Ed pampered his livestock. Ed was considered more congenial than the other Lehne men and had a lot of friends. He had the classic Lehne marks—light blue eyes, a little humped nose, and small feet. He died August 21, 1959, after a long illness following a stroke.

Aunt Theresa is married to Wade Tomlinson, and they recently celebrated their fiftieth wedding anniversary. Their children include Lou Ellen and Ed Lehne Tomlinson.

Mae Lehne (Mother Mae) married Merlin Rogers (Daddy Merlin). They had one child: Lillyth Ed Rogers. They lived in Fort McKavett for five years. In 1943, they moved to Menard when Lill started school. Lill married Charles Kothmann on December 27, 1958. Lill always named her dolls Merlina Ann and her first child was named that, too. Charla Elehne, this paper's author, was born August 2, 1963, and named after her father, Charles. Mae Katherine was the last daughter, and she was named after both her grandmothers.

This paper goes far back in time in great detail. It tells the facts as the Lehnes lived from one generation to the next. Generations are born, they live their lives, and they pass on.

This author really enjoyed writing about the generations of families in the Lehne Legend. She learned a tremendous amount about her family. It is information that always will be helpful to her. She closes with an Old Testament quote reflecting the mood in which she researched the pieces of the Lenhe Legend:

The sun also ariseth,

And the sun goeth down and hasteth to his place where he rose.

All the rivers run into the sea;

Yet the sea is not full: unto the place from whence the rivers come, thither they return again.

One generation passeth away.

And another generation cometh: but the earth abideth forever.

    —Ecclesiastes 1

Grandma Sides

By Carla Sides

ALL PATHS LEAD TO YOU

All paths lead to you
Where e'er I stray,
you are the evening star
At the end of the day.
All paths lead to you
Hill-top or low,
you are the white birch
In the sun's glow.
All paths lead to you
Where e'er I stray,
you are the evening star
At the end of the day.
All paths lead to you
Where e'er I roam
You are the lark song
Calling me home! —Blanche Shoemaker Wagstaff

This paper is a tribute to a very lovely grandmother, Velma Sides. The author would like everyone to know of the wonderful and exciting life she enjoys. Her outlook on life is unique and could be a pattern for others to follow.

She tells her story: "I was born in Voca, Texas, in 1898. I lived there 'til I was six years old, when we moved to Lohn, where I was later able to attend school.

"I didn't start school 'til I was nine years old because we lived so far out, and I had no way to get there. At age nine, I attended school in the Lohn school building. It was a big, one-room building with about seventy children attending. I wore gingham dresses every day. The part of the day that wasn't taken up with school was taken up with chores.

"Being's my mother died when I was thirteen years old, I had to do many chores. I washed clothes on a washboard, cooked the meals on an ole' wooden cook stove, I kept the house, and I worked out in the fields."

The responsibility of all that was something the author can really relate to because her life has led a similar pattern. The author asked if her grandmother graduated from high school.

"No, I 'quituated' in the ninth grade," Velma said. "I was sixteen years old. I quit school and married. I married L.W. Sides Sr. on October 4, 1914.

"Your grandad and I lived in Kimble County for seven years. We then moved to Menard County and made our home. While living in Menard, we lived in four different houses, two of them very near the San Saba River. We were happily married and had four sons.

"David Sides, the oldest, was born on August 7, 1915. L.W. Sides Jr. was born April 8, 1923. Next in line is your [the author's] father, Joe Dan Sides, born August 16, 1928. Mack Levi Sides, the baby of the family, was born on September 16, 1931. My sons and I have had good and bad times. One of the bad, I guess, was when I had to watch them go off to war.

"My sons and I have had many experiences with wars. My only brother fought in World War I. He survived it and came home. My oldest son was working in an airplane factory at Grand Prairie, so he didn't have to go fight.

"Junior [L.W. Sides Jr.] fought in World War II and was overseas three and one-half years before he returned home.

"Joe Dan fought in the Korean War for two years, then returned home. The Korean War ended with my youngest son, Mack. He fought in that war for two years, and when it was over he returned home.

"Mack had been home for two years when an accident happened—he was killed in a car wreck on July 22, 1956. This was a hard time for the entire family."

The author's grandmother raised her sons to be very fine men. Her grandmother had a very happy life despite the hardships, as Velma asserts:

"Your grandfather and I had a happy life together. I can remember back yonder in 1925 when we bought our first car. It was a Model T Ford. You had to crank on it to get it to go. Well, we lived out on Bear Creek during this time, and I would have to drive that ole' car all the way to town jus' to buy a few groceries. Pa never did like to come in with me, and David was barely walking. I would load him up in that car, then I'd crank and crank on that ole' car 'till I rubbed many a blister on my hands. I used to say 'If I ever get a son old enough, I will never crank another one of these here ole' cars again.'

"That was one of our hardships, but really it was a blessing compared to the horse and buggy I had been used to. Of course, there were a lot of people less fortunate than me back then.

"A hard time for many people was back in 1938 when we had that terrible flood! We were living up on the side of a hill. We had just moved out of a house that was right on the bank of the river. That little ole' house we had been in got washed plumb off its foundation. That flood was really large!

"It was so large, young 'un, that your daddy himself rode in a motorboat down the main street by the post office. No sirree. People couldn't get home. I tell you, I wore out daggome every mattress I had by throwing 'em out on the floor for people to sleep on when they couldn't get home or their homes had been washed right out from under them. Let me tell you, it was a pitiful sight to see.

"I didn't get to see a lot of the water itself because at this time we were taking care of Louie's father. He was an eighty-six-year-old man and blind. This took up a lot of our time and truly was a hardship.

"Other than that, we didn't have too many more hardships. I broke my ankle when I was about sixty, but I got over that, and I'd say I haven't been in the hospital but just maybe a couple of times since then. I've only had one other really major hardship, and that was when we lost Pa.

"We had just celebrated our sixtieth wedding anniversary—one month and twelve days before he passed away. He died on November 12, 1974."

One might think after all this the author's grandma deserves to just sit back in her rocking chair and take life easy. Well, that's not the way she feels about, and it is not the way it is.

"After grandpa died, I knew I had to get interested in something to keep busy. A friend of mine told me about the Country Store, and it wasn't long after that I became a member. I work one day a month there. I usually cook anywhere from eight to ten loaves of bread, two German chocolate cakes, and one or two other kinds of cakes a day.

"Some other things I do are crochet, watch television, fish, and go visiting. I always have plenty of people to visit. I have seven grandchildren and eight great-grandchildren. Once a year I try to visit with each of the kinfolks that live out of town. I have a grandson and families in Rankin, a nephew in Midland, and a cousin in Odessa. Sometimes I take a bus to their homes, sometimes they come and get me, or I'll catch someone else going that way. I even flew on a jet down to the valley last summer!

"One of the latest trips I have been on was one up to New Mexico. A friend of mine and I drove up there and stayed in a little cabin of hers. We drove around a lot just looking. It surely was cold up there. It took us a day to come and a day to go. We spent two nights there. I really enjoyed it, and I'm enjoying my life today just as it is."

This is certainly true for Grandmother Velma whether she is on a fancy jet or in a simple kitchen.

The author's grandmother is a very good cook. She cooks a large Christmas dinner and supper each year at her house. All of the family eat and then we open presents. It's a very special thing to the author. The author would like to pattern her life after her grandmother's life.

"My life is very filled up," Velma says. "I never regretted a minute of my marriage despite our hardships. Today, I enjoy being able to drive my own little car and go and do as I please."

The facts in this paper support the original thesis that the author's grandmother's life is a pattern for anyone to follow. Despite all of her hardships, she is still carrying on a very happy life and loving it.

In conclusion, the author realizes that this paper is truly a tribute to the author's grandmother. It will be something she can read and remember her grandmother's wonderful life. This is the type of thing a person may pass down from generation to generation.

The author wants to leave a few feelings about the subject in general:

Stepping into grandmother's house, one feels as if she's just walked into a bakery. She can smell the aroma of German chocolate cake baking in the oven and can almost taste the homemade bread that she is so carefully applying butter on top.

She sits and listens carefully as grandmother tells of her life from her childhood to her trip just yesterday, delivering three cakes and six loaves of bread to the Country Store.

The author can feel the mist in the air from the steam of her iron, which she just finished using to press smooth a basket full of shirts for her many customers.

As the writer leaves her house, she knows that each day she will watch her grandmother with great astonishment, wishing she will be just like her.

Life of a Jockey—The Merlin Lemons Story
By Vanessa Welch

FIRST

SPIRIT...
   DRIVE...
      PRANCING BEAUTY...
Muscles flexing...
   A fire burning hot within
Which escapes from the eyes.
   TO RUN...
      TO WIN...
To be GREATEST...
   STRONGEST...
      FASTEST...
Possessed by the will to win.
The world stops.
   No green pastures.
No colts beckoning to play.
Just the will to run and reach
   The finish line
   FIRST —Vanessa Welch (original poem)

Merlin Lemons grew up on a ranch at Voca, Texas, where he started his career as a jockey. His grandfather, Johnny Lane, was a jockey and started teaching Merlin the track at a very early age.

"From the time I knew what it was all about, I knew that is what I wanted to do," Merlin said.

Merlin started by cleaning stalls and walking the horses. After galloping or exercising a horse on the track, it must be walked or led around the track for twenty-five to thirty minutes to get it cooled off. After a race, the horse must be walked an hour to an hour-and-a-half. At thirteen years of age, Merlin started galloping, or exercising, horses on the track.

"Boys get five dollars for galloping a horse today," Merlin said. "I used to get twenty-five cents."

In 1938, at age sixteen, Merlin rode in his first race at Brady in a three-quarter mile race. He said he must have gotten too excited, because he dropped his stick and had nothing to swat the horse with. It slowed him up, but he came in third anyway.

Merlin's second race was a half-mile and seventy yards. He came in second in that race.

His third race was the charm: he came in first on a two-year-old that had never won a race. Those three races were considered a very good start for a new kid on the track. Merlin went on to continue to prove his ability.

Merlin married Guelda (Doodie) Lee Horton in 1940. They had two boys, Harold Dean Lemons and Gerald Lemons. During his jockey career, Merlin rode in eighteen different states and also Mexico City. While Merlin was racing, Doodie and the children traveled with him.

Merlin told of his many different experiences while traveling to the various races. They would go from race to race in New England from spring until the snow fell. They went from Rhode Island, to Boston (Suffolk Downs), to Salem, New Hampshire, then back to Rhode Island. These races were about seventy-five miles apart and this route lasted for thirty to forty-five days.

Merlin explained that jockeys must maintain a certain weight. The weight consists of the man plus the saddle. In 1940, he weighed 103 pounds with his saddle. He explained he would gallop horses every afternoon, drink some liquids, eat supper (which often was his only meal), and then go to the YMCA and take a sweat bath every night. Afterwards, he could not have any liquids or he would gain weight. He recalled one night he came from the YMCA and felt he had to have a glass of water. Doodie asked him if he needed some, why didn't he just have a glass of water? In order to show her what a difference one glass of water made, he weighed, walked to the restaurant next door, and drank a glass of water. He then went back home and weighed again. He had gained a pound, which could make a lot of difference for a jockey.

A jockey must maintain not only his own physical condition,

but that of his equipment. Jockeys must furnish all of their own equipment, including saddle and everything else except the "colors", which consist of the blouse and cap.

Merlin talked about many of his experiences on the track. He had two horses fall dead under him. The first one was in Nebraska in a five-eighths mile race. He was head-to-head with the leader when Merlin felt it.

"His head just got heavier and heavier, so I knew something was wrong," Merlin remembered. "I first thought he had a broke leg."

At the head of the stretch, Merlin "pulled him out" in the middle of the racetrack. Just as he got to the finish line, the horse fell across the line dead. They gave him third place in the race. They later discovered the horse had bled internally because he was a "bleeder." When the horse went down, Merlin was thrown against a post, which knocked him unconscious. He recalled that he could hear talking, but could not answer. After Merlin regained consciousness, he found he was not seriously injured, but he could not ride his other six races that day. He rested a week and then was able to ride again. Merlin came out of this accident with only minor injuries, not knowing he would experience a similar incident in years to come.

The second race in which a horse died under Merlin on the track was in Fredericksburg. The horse's name was Relic. It was a five-eighths mile race and, as before, the horse's head got heavier and heavier. Merlin started feeling this near the quarter-mile post. He rode him on past the finish line. When he pulled him up and turned his head loose, the horse fell dead. The horse had suffered a heart attack and his heart had burst, but he had won first place in the race.

Merlin had nine falls in races and seven falls while exercising a horse during this career. He once received a fractured jawbone that laid him up from July to September. This was one of the worst injuries he would have while racing.

Merlin told of one race which he and his family traveled to in Mexico City. He was riding Reynolds Brothers' horses, and Clyde

Loftier was the trainer. They took the horses to Laredo in a van, crossed the border, and unloaded the horses in some stock pens. They then had to wait to have some stalls specially built in box cars so the horses could be shipped on a train. A few men rode along with the horses to take care of them. Merlin and family spent the night in Monterrey. Gerald Dean, Marlin's oldest son, celebrated his first birthday there. The baby became dehydrated, and they almost lost him. After he recovered some, the doctor suggested taking him indoors and just letting him play. They had all gone down to the stables and let Gerald down to go play. After a few minutes, they missed him, so Merlin went to look for him. There was a mean stud in a stall there.

"I guarantee he'd take an arm off ya," Merlin said.

When Merlin found Gerald, he was in the stall with that stud, standing, hanging onto its front leg. Merlin eased in and got him. The stud never moved a muscle. Merlin said no one to this day knows why that stud didn't hurt the baby.

Merlin and Doodie also remember a time in 1941 when they were at a race in Omaha, Nebraska, before the children were born. It had been raining for days and Merlin had not been winning many races. The two of them decided they wanted to come home. They left Omaha with a tank of gas and ten dollars in Merlin's pocket. They ate crackers and cheese all the way home and had five flats on their 1939 Chevy. They finally made it to Goldthwaite, Texas, with the tank sitting on empty and two cents left in Merlin's pocket. They said back then they just didn't worry about "what if something happened?"

Merlin returned home to Texas, in 1959, after twenty-one years as a jockey.

"I lived out of a suitcase for too many years," Doodie said.

The lifestyle was very hard to live with children, so they returned to Texas, where they settled.

Merlin's grandfather, Johnny Lane, taught Merlin everything he knew. They often rode match races against each other. The pride and rivalry between them caused highly competitive races.

"Ah, but me and my Grampa, we used to have at it," Merlin remembered.

At one time, three generations rode in the same race—Merlin, his grandfather, and an uncle. Merlin also had cousins who were jockeys. Merlin, therefore, was born into a long line of jockeys in his family.

Merlin rode horses that set track records and still holds them. He rode a horse named Hodey in Del Rio in a two hundred fifty yard race, and the record still stands. He also rode a horse named Black Walnut in a five-eighths race in Albuquerque, New Mexico, and set a track record, then lowered the record each time he ran there thereafter. Later, Black Walnut was taken to California, where he set yet another track record. He was then sold and shipped to Chicago, where he got shipping fever and died.

The biggest race of Merlin's career probably was in Mexico City where Blue Stripe won the seven-eighths mile, $100,000 race. The best two-year-old was Yava-Pie; at Narragansett, he set a track record and was nominated for the Kentucky Derby, but broke down before he was entered in the race. With Blondie and Miss Panama, Merlin had a world record in the three hundred yard race with eleven wins and one loss. These days were a big part of Doodie and Merlin's life and now are fond memories for the couple.

Merlin and Doodie now own the Handy Liquor store between Menard and Eden. They had two boys and now have five grandchildren—two girls and three boys—and they are happy to show you the pictures. They have many happy memories of their exciting lives and many travels.

Merlin told the author that once in Lincoln, Nebraska, he was riding in a race. The track was very muddy, and when he was going into a curve, the horse in front of him fell. This could have been a very serious accident, but—instead—a really freaky thing happened. Merlin's horse stepped on the fallen horse's tail and cut off the hair part cleanly. Then he jumped the horse, jockey and all, without hitting them. Merlin continued galloping his horse around the track with the other horse's tail looking as though, "someone had cut it off with a pocket knife," according to Merlin.

The author concludes with these thoughts: The author was very fascinated with this subject and the interview. It is amazing that such an interesting person could live in our midst, yet only be vaguely recognized for his accomplishments.

The author would like to thank Merlin and Doodie Lemons for all their cooperation and for sharing the exciting moments in their lives.

The author closes with this senses paragraph:

As the writer looked at the bred perfection of a species standing before her, she was in awe. These were fantastic creatures of speed and beauty, whose famous sires were yesterday's great winners. The reason for their existence was for that one moment when they could taste the excitement, thick in the air, hear the exuberant cheers of the crowd, see the blue of the finish line ahead, and feel their entire bodies being pushed to their ultimate ability, later to smell the sweet fragrance of victory as they flew past statuesque others. At last, to feel that one treasured pat from the human hand of the trainer... standing, as is the writer, in awe.

A.H. Murchison

By Susie Kothmann

The cattle drives, a common occurrence in the county until the early 1890s, deposited many settlers in Menard, as they liked the country so well that they made it their home. Among the better known of these was Andy H. Murchison, Menard County rancher and businessman. —Menard News and Messenger

As the author stared at the old crumpled picture of Andes Henry Murchison, she saw him playing a large part in Menard's history. This writer creates this tribute to A.H. Murchison in hopes of preserving his memory for future generations. First, she walked back in time.

A.H. Murchison was born of German and Scottish ancestry on March 9, 1855, in New Braunfels, Texas. His father, Dan Murchison, was a captain in Sam Houston's army. The following was an article in the *Austin Intelligencer* in 1867 announcing Dan Murchison's death:

"We are in receipt of a telegram from New Braunfels, Comal County, announcing the demise of Captain Dan Murchison, at that place, at 10 o'clock a.m., of the 22nd instant. Mr. Murchison was an old soldier of the Republic, and served his country in the brilliant campaign of 1836, terminating in the achievement of its independence. He was ever the faithful friend of his country, and the fearless, outspoken advocate of whatever tended to her honor and advancement of her national interests. He has served the State of Texas in many responsible civil positions, with honor to himself and advancement to his immediate constituents. He was a member of the last Texas Convention for revision of the State Constitution, and also a member of the House in the last Legislature. When the 14th Article, proposed as an amendment to the Constitution of the United States, was voted upon in the House, his name was recorded as one of the fearless, sagacious and patriotic five who favored its adoption. Crowned with many honors, fairly won and modestly worn, he has been called to lasting repose. His memory will be cherished by his numerous friends, and his name will be coupled with terms of praise, when hereafter spoken of by his countrymen, who now mourn his death as an individual bereavement and a great loss to the State, whose honor and interests were ever safe in his keeping."

A.H. Murchison, Dan's son, was born March 9, 1855, and began his married life in 1889 with his first betrothed, Jacqueline Dupree. They were married in Burnet County. Jacqueline Murchison died in 1930. Mr. Murchison then married Mrs. Jim Lee, the former Clara Elizabeth Barton, in 1935. Mr. Murchison passed away November 5, 1952, in his home in Menard at age ninety-seven.

Memories of him and his life came from an interview with Jo Anne Potts, Mr. Murchison's step-granddaughter:

"From 1886 to 1889, Papa was a trail boss. He made as many as twelve trips up the trail, driving herds of cattle to Abilene and Dodge City, Kansas, where the trail met the railroad. In 1887, Papa drove one of his largest herds, 2,500 head to Clayton, New Mexico, for Felix Mann."

Continuing up that ladder of success, from 1886 to 1889 Mr. Murchison was a brand inspector for the Panhandle Cattleman's Association at the Chicago Stock Yards. He was still a very young man. In 1889, Mr. Murchison returned to Texas, where he settled in Menard. Jo Anne Potts continues:

"Papa first stopped in Menardville in 1885 and liked it so much he stayed all winter visiting his only sister, Flora, and her husband, Dr. E.G. Dora. He—Papa—always thought Menard County had some of the best cattle country he had ever seen and he liked the people he had met there, so when he decided to settle down, he chose Menardville to be his home."

N.H. Pierce in his book *The Free State of Menard* told of Mr. Murchison's settling in Menard, in part using Murchison's own words:

"'The first time I stopped in Menardville was the fall of 1885, and I liked it so much that I stayed here all winter, then came back here to make a permanent home when I quit the trail,' says

Andy H. Murchison, 87-year-old businessman of Menard. Mr. Murchison made at least twelve trips up the old trail from Texas to Kansas with great herds of cattle before he 'retired,' only to open up a business here that he operated more than 50 years, having observed the 50th anniversary in 1939."

The home Mr. Murchison built when he settled in Menard still stood at the time this paper was written [1982]. Mr. Murchison built his home in 1889. The home was included in the tour of homes during the Menard Centennial Celebration. The home was still inhabited at the time of this paper. Also at this time, Mr. Murchison and his brother, Ed, built Murchison and Bro. Dry Goods and Groceries. According to the *San Antonio Express* in 1915:

"In 1890, in company with his brother, Ed Murchison, he (A.H.) embarked in the mercantile business. In 1901 the brother died, since which time A.H. Murchison has conducted the business alone. His store is one of the largest and most complete in the county."

In the early years, Mr. Murchison, with other local merchants, stored valuables for local people in his safe. The store received damage from a fire, but the contents of the safe were unscathed. In some cases, as this one, fire was a hazard, but, as the interviewer learned, first, used in the way it was for A.H. Murchison and the train, began more wheels turning for the new little town.

The author learned that until 1910 the nearest railroad to Menard was Brady. Cattle had to be driven to Brady for shipping to market and supplies had to be hauled by wagon to Menard. Menard, thus, needed a railroad.

The scene was the same in the movie *Red River*, depicting the driving of herds of cattle to railheads. Ms. Potts made the comment that, in her opinion, this movie was closely tied with the stories Mr. Murchison told.

The idea for a railroad began in 1910 when the president of the Frisco Railroad, Mr. A.J. Davidson, came into Menard unannounced and quietly contacted Mr. William Bevans, a local banker, and A.H. Murchison. Mr. Davidson told the two men that Menard could have a railroad, but they had to decide before the end of the day and sign the contract he had placed before them. The three men conferred at length and before the day was gone the president of the Frisco Line had the signed contract in his pocket.

Mr. Murchison and Mr. Bevans, however, were required to keep the deal a secret for one month, and they were obligated not to buy land in the vicinity of the proposed depot. In the signed contract, they agreed to provide a right-of-way from Brady to Menard, to furnish land for the depot and stock pens, and to furnish funds for the building of the depot. Each of those men invested a large sum of money in this project.

After the building of the depot, a big celebration was held. Ms. Potts recalled the story of that celebration's events:

"The people of Menard, along with Papa and Mr. Bevans, fulfilled that contract, and on February 10, 1911, the first train steamed into town. The whole county turned out for the celebration. There were welcoming ceremonies at the depot and then a huge barbeque on the San Saba River. Papa remembered it as a great day with visitors and local people getting into the spirit of the celebration early in the day. Some folks never did find the barbeque."

Maybe Mr. Murchison was one of the people who did find the barbeque, but if he didn't he made up for it when he found the land, which he started acquiring in the early 1900s. According to Ms. Potts:

"He—Papa—started with a few hundred acres of land and a few head of cattle. In a few years, he owned several thousand acres and hundreds of purebred Hereford cattle, branded with the Forked Lightning brand. Papa's idea for the Forked Lightning brand grew out of many nights on the trail when the sky lit up with lightning. It was beautiful at times, and it was awesome. It could remind a man of a power greater than his own, and once you saw it, you never quite forgot it."

Mr. Murchison carefully chose that name for his ranch,

therefore he was particular about what livestock he ran on his land. Ms. Potts explained:

"It was in the late 1930s when Papa first allowed sheep on his ranch. Someone paid a bill they owed him at the mercantile with livestock instead of cash. Cash was hard to come by in those times. Papa accepted the sheep as payment, but never did like them. He would often ask his ranch hands if they had found any dead sheep that day. If they said 'no', Papa would say, 'Well you haven't been out in the pastures.'"

In later years, Mr. Murchison admitted that sheep made money for him. Nonetheless, he still did not like them. Even at the time of this paper, no sheep roamed on the Forked Lightning Ranch. Ms. Potts also noted Mr. Murchison's distaste for mares:

"It was 1949 before Papa allowed a mare on his ranch. He thought mixing mares and horses caused trouble more often than not. I was living in San Angelo, and I found this mare at a riding stable and fell in love with her. I asked Papa if I could buy her and bring her home to the ranch. He said 'Yes' without a moment's hesitation. I don't know why he let me buy that mare. Maybe it was because he knew how much I loved horses, and if I found one I loved more than all the rest, then I should have her. Maybe he just wanted to make me happy. I only wish Papa could have lived to see how much pleasure that mare brought me for more than twenty years."

Much the same pleasure was experienced by Mr. Murchison himself with his continued involvement with his mercantile. A.H. never really retired from the store business, even after he turned over the management to his nephew, Ike Murchison. He continued to go to the store until the last couple of years of his life. He also continued operating his ranch until the last months of his life, as remembered by Ms. Potts:

"A man like Papa never retired. A man like Papa could only be separated from the things he loved by death."

The interview with Ms. Potts then turned back to the days of Mr. Murchison's trail driving:

"Occasionally, after a trail drive had begun, a cowboy would ride into camp asking to sign on. Papa hired one such man who, unfortunately, was killed before the drive was over. Right away, Papa could see this man was not an experienced cowboy, but he worked hard and did his job. He didn't talk much, and when in camp, he would stay off to himself. One night, a bad thunderstorm came up, with wind and hail, and the rain coming down in sheets. Streaks of lightning flashed everywhere. Every hand was out riding around the restless herd, hoping and praying they wouldn't stampede. Well, they didn't this time, but when the storm passed and the cowboys returned to camp, they were one man short. The quiet man had not returned to camp with the other men. Papa sent the men back to look for him. Near dawn, he was found in a draw beside his horse, both dead, killed by lightning. He was buried on the trail where he died. Nobody knew where the boy came from or who to tell of his death.

"More than a year later, Papa was contacted by the young man's father, a wealthy businessman from New York. The man had not heard from his son in years, but somehow had heard the boy might have worked for Papa at one time. Papa had to tell him that his son was dead, killed in a cattle drive. The man had his son's remains brought home and buried in his family plot."

Each new trail drive brought new faces to the scene, but there were regulars who made trail driving their lives. One such regular was the character of Ms. Potts's next story:

"One man who had been the cook on several of Papa's cattle drives got into trouble on his last drive with Papa. The drive was done, the cattle were delivered, and most of the cowboys were in a bar, celebrating the successful ending to another long cattle drive. They had their pay in their pockets and a lot of them seemed to feel the need to empty their pockets as soon as possible. After weeks and months on the trail, men had to blow steam. Well, something happened between the cook and a local man. Words were exchanged, and then so were bullets. The cook killed the man. The cook and the cowboys that were with him figured he had to get out of town, even though it had been a fair fight, the way they saw it, because the law in a cattle town did not look kindly on rambunctious cowboys disturbing the peace. The cook's friends got together and gave him part of their pay, and he rode out of town before the law came calling. As it turned out, the law decided that the cook acted in self defense."

Self defense was an important word in those days, especially when the word "self" included an entire crew of cowboys. Ms. Potts's next story showed Mr. Murchison's defense against Indians:

"More than once, Papa and his cowboys ran into Indians on the trail. On one drive, a band of six or eight Indians rode into camp and demanded that Papa give them several head of cattle from his herd. Papa said no, but he would give them some flour and beans. The cattle were not his to give away. The Indians rode off, only to return a couple of hours later with thirty or more braves, armed to the teeth. Again they demanded cattle, and flour, beans, and tobacco if Papa wanted his herd and men to go on. It was then that Papa decided discretion was the better part of valor and said, 'Let's talk'."

Mr. Murchison gave the Indians ten head of cattle, twenty-five pounds of flour, a few pounds of beans, and a little tobacco. The Indians rode off satisfied, and the cattle drive proceeded without incident.

"Papa never had trouble with that tribe of Indians again," Ms. Potts noted.

Thus ends my story of Andes Henry Murchison. The reader could see he was a true pioneer of Menard. After retiring from trail driving, an occupation he loved, he settled in Menard. Andy Murchison, as he was known to close friends, fell in love with the country in Menard County. He started a general store, which helped supply people settling in Menard.

Mr. Murchison started the Forked Lightning Ranch, which at the time of this paper was still owned and operated by family members. The home he built for his first wife, Jacqueline, was one of the first homes built in Menard. In Mr. Murchison's memory, his family donated the funds and land for the A.H. Murchison Memorial Barn for the FFA and 4-H club. Mr. Murchison played an important part in the growing of this town. His memory became indelible on the past, present, and future of Menard.

As the author neared the final pages of her paper, many thoughts of relief and satisfaction filled her body. She sat down in her chair and sighed. Finally, after many weeks of deliberation, her term paper was completed. Even though there were many frustrations and trying moments, she was grateful for the opportunity to learn of Menard's heritage. The writer enjoyed the moments when she read through old data and learned of many happenings. Never could she forget what she learned. A thank you went out to Ms. Potts for her cooperation in the project. Also, a thank you went to A.H. Murchison for his involvement in the development of the writer's home: Menard.

To find the proper closing for her paper, the writer visited the Pioneer Rest Cemetery in Menard, where Mr. Murchison now rests. As she gazed at the final resting place of Andes Henry Murchison, she smelled the curl of smoke from the campfire. Listen! Was that the lowing of the cattle? She could taste the last bitter dregs of the coffee. The author rode out to join the trail drive of days gone by. The rich heritage left by this man enveloped her. She reached out and touched the cold, hard surface of the monument and was abruptly returned to reality. She knew, however, that she was richer by far for having the opportunity to share a part of the history of this man, Andes Henry Murchison.

Sol Mayer

By Stefan McCoy

> *A bad boy can spoil a dozen. A good boy can save as many.*
> —Sol Mayer

In 1880, an eleven-year-old boy of emigrant parentage roamed the hills around Fort McKavett swapping yarns and horses with the soldiers on duty there at the time. Sol Mayer also was a respected businessman later in his life. He was well known for his honesty, courage, and loyalty. The purpose of this paper is for the readers to become better acquainted with a great man of Menard's and Texas's history.

Soloman "Sol" Mayer was born in San Antonio, Texas, January 18, 1869, the son of Ferdinand and Jette "Yette" (Steiner) Mayer. A native of Germany, Ferdinand came to the United States in 1852 when he was twenty years old. He resided in Hondo County, Texas, in 1860 [likely Medina County; Hondo is the county seat], engaging in the mercantile business there for a number of years and also running cattle. He later went to San Antonio and was postmaster and clerk in a store north of San Antonio for several years. Ferdinand lived in San Antonio for half a century. He later moved to Fort McKavett in Menard County and had the largest mercantile store there for many years. He had a large trade among ranchers and others coming into this section. The trade building still stands. Ferdinand died on April 11, 1913, in San Antonio, where he was buried. Sol Mayer followed in his father's footsteps.

According to *The Free State of Menard* by N.H. Pierce, it was said that Sol Mayer, like his father, once took a horse, a bridle, and a cash capital of eighty cents, left home, and was gone for about thirty days. When he showed up at the end of the month, he was riding one horse, leading five others, and carrying $1.50 in his pocket.

This knack of shrewd trading stayed with Sol Mayer all down the years until, at the age of seventy-one, he was reputed to be one of the wealthiest men in Texas, his fortune being counted in the millions. Sol Mayer, however, started out just like any other cowboy.

At the age of fifteen Solomon, or Sol as he was familiarly called, started out in life as a cowboy at a wage of thirty dollars per month. As his years advanced, his salary was raised accordingly. Young Mayer worked here and there, sometimes for his father, then for outside parties and wherever he could secure the best salary. He was not permitted to devote the time and attention to books and studies that he deserved, however, because of his eyes having been affected by an explosion of powder when he was young. In an interview with this writer, Robert Flutch said:

"Yep, I remember when ol' Sol nearly got his head blown off. Sol Mayer was playing around with some powder, and it went off, Sol burned his hair a might, and when he had to get it cut, he wasn't pleased."

Sol Mayer, nevertheless undaunted, had ranches all over the place by the time he was thirty, one of which he later donated to the Boy Scouts of America. The ranch was known as the Opp Ranch or Brown Ranch. According to a story in the *San Angelo Standard-Times* in 1945:

Sol Mayer said to his wife, Ernestine, that the ranch would make an ideal site for the Boy Scouts as the couple stood on the banks of the San Saba River on their Menard County ranch. The donation of a three-hundred acre campsite to the Concho Valley Boy Scout Council by Sol Mayer was a continuing reminder of the good that the material resources collected by Mr. Mayer and his wife did.

Mr. Mayer had no schooling; however, from his contact with people, young Mayer seemed to have absorbed an education superior to anything he could have obtained from the ordinary common schools. He was a good conversationalist, and his manner was as affable and pleasing as could be desired. To become acquainted with Sol Mayer was to like him, and one could readily see that his rapid success was entirely attributable to his force of character and indomitable energy.

Perhaps beginning life when the average boy was still confined to the nursery, he had by tenacity and honesty of purpose gradually advanced. At the age of thirty-six, for example, he found himself general manager of, and chief factor in, a livestock concern which, in 1893, handled $120,000 worth of cattle and 9,000 sheep. To give an idea of the competence of the young general manager, the author noted: years ago Mr. Mayer leased for his firm a pasture containing about 52,000 acres, located in Sutton and Schleicher counties. In the leasing of this pasture, he spent $20,000 in improvements. He had two other pastures besides the one mentioned containing 20,000 and 13,000 acres. He generally kept from 8,000 to 10,000 head of cattle on the pastures and an equal number of sheep. During the month of April, 1894, he sold $43,000 worth of cattle, besides shipping 2,000 head to the Indian Nation and 500 additional head to the market in July and August.

There was one thing of which young Sol Mayer was very naturally proud, which was the amount of confidence his business associates had in him. He had not, in all of his numerous deals, had a single purchaser inspect a herd of cattle and demand the price be changed. This fact alone spoke volumes for young Mayer, as it was well known there was more caution and hesitation exercised in the buying and selling of livestock than any other commodity.

Sol Mayer was indeed a respected businessman of Fort McKavett and Menard County, as the author learned from this research. Especially notable was his rise from being the son of emigrants to a prominent businessman in the cattle industry.

In writing this paper, the author increased his knowledge about some of the old timers who lived to see Fort McKavett being built. The old timers to whom the author talked filled him with awe him as they told how the country used to be. Some of the old-time ways seemed far better than those used now. Robert Flutch said it best: "I wish the country was still the way it was, full of Indians and wildlife such as wolves and bears."

This paper, in total, was a tremendous experience for the author, and he hopes the readers will enjoy the uncovered history of Sol Mayer. Pondering Sol Mayer's life, the author imagines what he might have felt being in one of his cattle drives. In closing, the author wrote a senses paragraph in English class to leave with the hearts of the readers:

As the author drives a herd of cows to the train station, he can feel the dust in his eyes and taste the dirt in his mouth. The writer looks at the cows and sees a pile of money. Once the cattle are at the station and the money is in his wallet, the author searches his mind to find out what he will invest his money in. A nice, cool drink of beer sounds good to the author.

The Man of Clear Creek—Jack Wilkinson

By Joe McKinney

TWENTY YEARS AGO
The spring that bubbled 'neath the hill, close by the spreading beech,
Is very low—'twas once so high that we could almost reach;
And kneeling down to get a drink, dear Tom, I even started so!
To how much that I am changed since twenty years ago.
—excerpt from poem/song attributed to several authors

As the author looks over the creek and the old homestead, he is reminded of a time some years ago, a time when men were men and women stayed home. Also, he thinks of the freedom of all to live where they please. One can feel the vibes of the old creek and the people who lived there—Clear Creek and Jack Wilkinson, two important characters of Menard. The purpose of this paper is to describe Jack Wilkinson's life in the Clear Creek area.

To tell about Clear Creek, one must start with W.J. "Jack" Wilkinson. Mr. Wilkinson was born in November 29, 1833, to Daniel Wilkinson and Elizabeth Osborn Wilkinson. His childhood days were spent in Tennessee on the family's farm.

Though raised on a farm, W.J. Wilkinson found he did not like agriculture and began seeking a more desirable and profitable calling. According to the book *Cattle Industry of Texas*:

"He had been accustomed to work from his boyhood for when he was not in school there was always employment awaiting him in his father's crops. He had been given a common school education, and upon starting out for himself faced the world with the assurance that his mental and muscular abilities would prove sufficient to conquer all difficulties encountered and eventually land him near the high-tide mark of prosperity."

He first found employment in the forests of Louisiana, working in the timber and rafting business for five years. He returned to Mississippi when his health failed. He stayed there for two years. He then went westward, eventually settling in Coleman County, Texas. There, he turned to cattle raising. Money saved from his former business helped him start in good shape.

Mr. Wilkinson bought a herd of cattle in Parker County and drove them through to Coleman, locating them on the range in Parker County. He continued to hold them there during the years of the Civil War and was very successful. His losses, however, were very heavy from Indian depredations, and he sold many hundreds of cattle to the Confederate army and was paid in money which was worthless after the war. In spite of the losses, he gained in wealth rapidly and became generally known as one of the leading stockmen in his section.

W.J. Wilkinson also saw a great deal of active service on the frontier during the war. He had enlisted in a regiment which was retained on the border as protection against Indian raids. Fights and skirmishes were frequent occurrences, and Mr. Wilkinson was in many of them, the most important, perhaps, being the famous Dove Creek fight with the Kickapoo in 1865.

In 1870, Mr. Wilkinson moved to Menard County and bought a ranch. He also continued his business in Coleman. After two years, he made his first trip over the trail to Fort Sumner, New Mexico, with 3,000 head of cattle, all of which were his own. He sold the cattle at Fort Sumner for a good price, but, as generally mentioned earlier, he never received hard currency. He consented to accept notes which later proved worthless. The following years, however, he drove two herds to Louisiana, both of which were disposed of to his advantage.

Jack was first married to Miss Martha Spiller in Coleman in 1869. There were two children born of this union, Neil and Carrie, who both lived in Menard County.

After the death of Martha, Mr. Wilkinson married Miss Nannie Myres in 1875; they had nine children: Emma, Alice, Willie, Lamar, Frank, Arch, Charley, Earnest, and Edgar. Shortly after his second marriage, he invested his surplus money—$25,000— in land in Menard County. It comprised about 20,000 acres and was well-stocked with cattle and horses.

Mr. Wilkinson was largely interested in sheep until 1892, at which time he disposed of his entire flock, and decided to focus on cattle.

His next residence was near a large spring, one of the most picturesque in the state, forming the headwaters of Clear Creek. With the construction of a large dam, he succeeded in bringing fifty acres of fine land under irrigation.

Mr. Wilkinson served twenty-one years as a Menard County commissioner. He represented Precinct Four from 1876 to 1879. After a thirteen-year absence, W.J. served from 1892 until 1910 serving Precinct Two. After 1910, he became a full-time rancher. He was regarded as one of the richest and most respected businessmen in the area. He died May 15, 1919.

Because Jack Wilkinson moved to Menard in 1870, not many people remembered anything about him. This author, however, found Vera Wagoner, J.W.'s granddaughter, who did remember some things about him and Clear Creek.

Mrs. Wagoner descends from the first marriage of W.J. to Martha Spiller. Mrs. Wagoner told this author of some times at Clear Creek. She told him of the time that she and her cousins would scrape cream off the milk in the spring house. Their grandmother thought the loss of cream meant the cows were going bad. Another tidbit she told about the family was that Mrs. Wagoner's grandmother was also her aunt by her grandfather's first marriage.

In summary, W.J. Wilkinson was a man who one can be proud to say that he is kin. Jack's accomplishments will never be forgotten by this writer, nor by the people of Menard.

This author was pleased to say that, after this research, he knew more about his family tree. He learned about the time that his family came to Menard. The author also hopes that other people will read this and drink a cup of the past.

This author stands on the dam. He can see the clear water of Clear Creek. He can also hear the water coming up from the spring underground. When he walks into the spring house, he can smell the coldness of the water and, thinking back, can almost taste the cold milk. When the writer walks on the old floor of the spring house he can feel the worn wood give way to his weight. The author now knows the past of the old ranch, and that it will not be forgotten.

The Midwife—Nicolosa Rodriguez
By Vicki Mays

Therefore God dealt well with the midwives: and the people multi-plied, and waxed very mighty. —Exodus 1:20 (KJV)

Many people in the country still have their children at home. In this paper, the author tells the midwife's and mother's view of having a baby at home.

Being from Fort Worth, the author did not know people still use midwives. She found out that many people in the country use them. Nicolosa Rodriguez is the local midwife. She was born December 6, 1906, in Brady, Texas. She has delivered 286 babies in her fifty-four years of being a midwife. Nicolosa told the author how she became a midwife:

"My sister lived in Brady, and she was going to have a baby. My brother-in-law called a doctor. And, well, I hadn't married then, and he called me over there and said, 'I want you to learn how to bring babies.' I said, 'Well, I'm not married.' And the doctor made me bring that baby. He told me how, you know. Just one time. That's the way I learned."

One and a half months before her first child, Nicolosa had a wreck and her stomach "came loose." She told the author that when she moved, her stomach moved in the opposite direction. Her husband made her go to the doctor to have the baby. She delivered the other nine of her children herself, however. She told the author what she did when she had the children:

"I fix my bed, have the baby, and get up and fix my bed again. Go to bed and get up the next day and start cooking again."

Nicolosa claims she can tell if the baby is going to be a boy or a girl before it is born by putting something the mother cherishes in front of her.

"Sometimes I lose... When it turns, that's the way you can't tell... When it comes face down, it's a boy. When you can see the face, it's a little girl."

Nicolosa told the author that a small baby often will be larger when it grows up than a large baby will when it is grown. One of her sons weighed one-and-a-half pounds at birth.

"He was little, tiny. I never seen one as tiny as that. My sister said, 'Well, take him to the doctor and put in the incubator.' I say, 'I'm the incubator. If he is going to live, he is going to live. If God gonna take him, he's gonna take him. And I'm not gonna take him nowhere.'

"I put diapers on him, double, twice at three weeks. When he was four months and eight days, he weighed twenty pounds. And he was the biggest little devil. And now he is the biggest boy I have. He weighs 210 pounds."

Nicolosa has delivered most of her family.

"I brought my sister's daughters. One weighed eleven pounds and the other weighed thirteen pounds at birth. She said, 'I'm gonna die!' I say, 'No you won't. Got in, have to come out.'"

Nicolosa started working for the McTaggarts when she was sixteen and stayed with them for the next fifty-five years. She cleaned the house, took care of the baby, washed and ironed.

"He (Mr. McTaggart) moved over here (to the McTaggart Hotel) when the boy (Col. McTaggart) was about seven or eight, something like that. And I help her in the hotel. Oh, I work like I don't know what. And then we didn't have washing machines. We had to wash on the board and stick them in a pot of hot water. Her husband helped me. He was a good man."

The author then interviewed two mothers who had some of their children at home. She obtained two totally different views of delivering one's child at home. Barbara Estrada said:

"I love Westerns, and all those old-timey women just had a lot of courage. I thought, 'If they could do it, I could do it.' I was just really testing myself more than anything, because I didn't have to have her at home. It was just an experience I wanted to try, just something I wanted to see if I could do it. And, besides, my husband told me he would pay the hospital bill, and since he was going to pay it, I could have the money. And that was really why I had her at home."

Barbara Estrada had complications with the second child she

had at home. She said: "So, if I had another one, I wouldn't have it at home. I do know that."

Ellen Rodriguez's mother-in-law, Nicolosa, asked Ellen if she could deliver the baby. Ellen agreed because at that time Nicolosa charged only $100. She now charges $150. Ellen told the author why she prefers having her children at home:

"It's so much easier at home. I guess it's okay to have your children at the hospital if you don't mind the shots. I have had seven children and never did I go to the doctor until my first labor pains."

When the author asked Barbara Estrada if she would advise having one's children at home, she said:

"I couldn't say if I would advise it or not, but usually it is all right. It is just one out of a very few that are not."

The author asked Ellen Rodriguez what the town will do without a midwife when Nicolosa retires. Ellen said Nicolosa's daughter, Betty, who helps her mother, will probably take over.

Barbara Estrada told the author some things she doesn't like about having her children at home:

"She (Nicolosa) doesn't tell you what you are supposed to do. As soon as you have that baby and she fixes the navel cord [umbilical cord], well, she goes home and you're there by yourself... They just leave you there by yourself with these little babies, and you don't know what to do... she doesn't tell you a thing. She didn't bathe them or clean them up or anything when they were born, you know. Just get a little olive oil she rubs around on them, you know. But she didn't bathe them and get that ol' afterbirth and stuff off. It'll be all over them. She don't clean you up. That's left for your husband to do or whoever else is there. If there's nobody there, well, that's your problem, you know."

Ellen Rodriguez told the author a couple of tales. When she started her pains, her husband called his mother. Because it was the first child she had at home, she was afraid. The fright made her pains stop. She took Nicolosa's advice and walked until she couldn't take another step, then went to bed. The next pain she had woke her up. She had her baby with the next pain.

Ellen Rodriguez also told the author of a tea that Nicolosa gave her. If it is time for one to have the baby, the Ruda tea will cause one to have more pains. It will stop one's pains completely if it is not time. Nicolosa boils the leaf and gives one cup of tea. Ellen couldn't keep but one swallow of the tea down, but within three hours she had the baby.

The author also found some home remedies in books. When labor is prolonged in childbirth, blow snuff held on a goose feather, up the mother's nose. This will induce a sneezing fit, resulting in delivery.

Here is another remedy: Golden seal, an herb tea, cures morning sickness. Vitamin E prevents stretch marks (take the capsule orally). Coffee decreases absorption of Vitamin C. A pregnant or nursing woman needs twice as much Vitamin C as other people. By drinking alfalfa-mint tea instead of coffee, you can get calcium and many vitamins.

The author found another remedy. If, after the birth, the mother is constipated, prunes or dried figs will help remedy this. A cup of sarsaparilla tea will quiet the muscles after the birth because it contains the hormone progesterone. Navajo women were given watercress as a tonic after a birth. Red raspberry leaf tea has been used in Europe for centuries for the same purpose—it relaxes the vaginal muscles and is good for menstrual cramps. And, if she can, the mother should eat some of the placenta.

Here is another remedy: When the baby is born, he or she will be blue until they take their first breath. If he or she has trouble doing so, hold the baby upside down, clear the baby's mouth, and tap the baby's back. Put the baby to the breast soon after birth and/or massage the breasts to stimulate contractions which expel the placenta. Don't wash the baby; leave on the coating. Apply castor oil to breasts to increase flow of milk if necessary.

There are more precautions and advice which the author discovered. Do not cut the cord until it is white and all pulsation ceases. That way, all its blood will have flowed into the baby. It is not necessary to cut it; left alone, the cord eventually will shrivel up and detach itself from the baby.

The facts in this paper support the original thesis that many people still have their children at home and use midwives. Unlike what many people think, midwives are not a thing of the past. Many small communities still have midwives.

The author enjoyed doing this paper. She met many people and learned many things about Menard and its people. She leaves the reader with the following feelings and two appropriate quotes from the interview:

When the author walked into the room, she envisioned the midwife standing over the bed, working by candle light. She heard the baby cry as the experienced hands gave it a swat on its seat to help it start breathing. The sight of blood made her sick, but the smell of Ruda tea helped smooth her queasiness.

"Raising children is the hard part. Having them is the easy part."—Barbara Estrada

"After you have one at home, you'll never want another one at the hospital."—Ellen Rodriguez

Adolph Beyer, Blacksmith

By Don Menzies

THE VILLAGE BLACKSMITH
Under a spreading chestnut-tree
The village smithy stands;
The smith, a mighty man is he,
With large and sinewy hands;
And the muscles of his brawny arms
Are strong as iron bands.

His hair is crisp, and black, and long,
His face is like the tan;
His brow is wet with honest sweat,
He earns whate'er he can,
And looks the whole world in the face,
For he owes not any man.

Week in, week out, from morn till night,
You can hear his bellows blow;
You can hear him swing his heavy sledge,
With measured beat and slow,
Like a sexton ringing the village bell,
When the evening sun is low.
—Henry Wadsworth Longfellow (excerpt)

The blacksmith played an important role in the early days of Menardville, keeping the wagons rolling and the jail doors swinging. In this paper, the author intends to describe in detail one of the largest blacksmith shops in early Menard, the Wheelright.

Although there were numerous blacksmith shops located in the small town of Menard, the author has chosen to tell of the Wheelright. The owner of this fine establishment was a man named Adolph Beyer.

Adolph Beyer originally was from Eufort, a small town located somewhere in the central portion of Germany. Adolph was born on November 17, 1874, to his mother, Emma Schultz Beyer, and his father, Gus [Gustav] Beyer.

When Adolph was a very small boy, his father decided to sell everything they owned and sail for North America, the land of opportunity.

Adolph Beyer and his family arrived in Menard in 1879. In 1898, Adolph married a girl named Ellen Wyatt. They had four sons, one dying at birth. The first son was Edward B. Beyer, born June 8, 1902. The second son died without explanation after being born in 1905. Joseph A. Beyer, was born in 1907. The fourth son was Wyatt Beyer. At the same time, Adolph took over the job of the town blacksmith.

The blacksmith, a man of sweat and brute strength, holds a place in the history of small towns. Without the blacksmith's trade, wagons and buggies would not have rolled through the early history of the West. The trade of blacksmith kept Adolph very busy because people depended upon him every day for one thing or another.

The blacksmith had a wide range of tools, but not very many when compared to the many jobs he performed with them. The shop contained a large anvil for hammering out steel. It also contained a large furnace which was formed by placing a steel pit with coals in it over an air blower. The shop contained everything from hinges to wagon rims. In the middle of the shop stood a large whiskey barrel which had been cut in half to hold water for cooling the hot metal.

The cooling pot was used by the blacksmith in a process called wheel rimming. In this process, the blacksmith took the metal wagon rim and heated it so it would expand. After the rim was heated throughout, it was placed around the wooden wagon wheel. When the metal cooled, it contracted around the wheel, making a tight fit for a longer lasting wheel. If the rim was still a little bit loose, it would be placed in water to swell the wood.

Many of the other jobs of the blacksmith were just simple repair jobs, such as windmill repair, gun repair, wagon repair, and plow sharpening. Adolph Beyer also was a manufacturer.

He made branding irons, de-horners, knives, bolts, and even hinges. According to Alex Menzies:

"Old Adolph Beyer did some babbitting work, too. This is where you take a mixture of lead, tin, antimony, and you melt it. Then you pour it into the place where the axle fits onto the hub of the wheel. This gives the wheel greater flexibility."

Adolph Beyer and the author's great-grandfather [Alex Menzies] were very good friends. Sometimes during the deer season they would pack up to leave on a hunting trip. Great Grandad Menzies would furnish the wagon and team. Adolph would fill up the chuck box, and then they would head for Saline Creek. They would hunt for two or three days. One day, when asked about their hunting trip, Adolph said, "Mr. Menzies shot the biggest buck that roamed the woods."

Joe Decker ran a nearby wagon yard for supply carriers to stop and sleep for the night. Feed was sold for "two bits" [twenty-five cents] a gallon. Hay was sold for fifty cents a bale.

Adolph Beyer died May 3, 1964, at the ripe old age of eighty-nine. He is buried in Menard next to his wife, Ellen, who died December 2, 1934.

This paper supports the thesis that the blacksmith did, indeed, play an important role in early Menardville. In gathering research for this paper, the author was left with these thoughts:

The blacksmith, a man of sweat and brute strength, the tamer of the unforced steel, was the picturesque vision the author pulled out of the magical hat of time. Suddenly, he could feel the heat from the red-hot steel horseshoes being bent into shape.

The amazed researcher could see the steam rise from the cooking pit as the smith cooled the glowing metal which would soon thunder under the hooves of a fine quarter horse. As the blacksmith placed more burning rocks into the melting pot, the author could smell the charcoal smoke as it billowed up into the air. The researcher could detect the sound of metal being driven into shape by a hammer backed by the blacksmith's powerful arm.

Whiskey was the sudden, staggering taste in the author's mouth as the tamer put away the once wild metal and lay his whip aside with the other hammers, then headed for the local pub.

Personalities of Menard
By Kenny Parker

With any elder whom one may presently chat, some knowledge of Menard's past will be gained. They'll tell of times during the Depression, and the people who soothed the disabled. One will learn of the boarding house, as a main point of interest, and the manager that flattered people with complements. Knowledge of the saloons and the gangsters it enhanced, and of the wise-guy who would exit if lucky, will be shared. How would these elders detail their discussion without the personalities who gave culture to their youth? These paint images that your minds can perceive.
—N.H. Pierce, The Free State of Menard

When one thinks of leaders with an influence on society, William Bevans was Menard's Louis & Clark. The purpose of this paper will be to pay tribute to William Bevans and other citizens experiencing the pain and glory of Menard.

William Bevans was a pioneer stockman. He also was a West Texas banker and financier with a huge influence on Menard County. William was the president of the Bevans State Bank of Menard, and his influence is easily envisioned. William is remembered as being a versatile person, involved in many activities, particularly stock raising both directly and indirectly in Menard.

Bevans was self-educated and began ranching at age fifteen using meager funds his father left him after he was killed by a Comanche. With a limited amount of money, Bevans bought some cattle and sheep and began ranching the free range. He would slowly increase his herds and eventually graze them in Oklahoma and Texas. Bevans bought lands from many different regions of the United States and became involved in trading and ranching. Bevans led many of the ranchers to use different ideas and techniques for ranching, making him one of the top leaders of Menard's past.

In 1896, Bevans purchased the Col. Black ranch in Schleicher and Menard counties. The ranch contained 47,000 acres; Bevans and his partner R.R. Russell paid ninety cents an acre for the big ranch. This property now is owned by Harold Bevans, one of William's sons. Harold remembers his father as a true pioneer.

Bevans was one of those pioneers who helped to carve the destiny of the Southwest from a wilderness of Indians and wild beasts. He herded his stock on the high plateaus and in the river valleys at a time when a stockman on the open range was constantly beset by challenges. Having fared well in his operations as a stockman, Bevans continued his pioneering activities by establishing a private bank.

During the drought, when conditions were hectic, the Bevans Bank was a true lifeboat in the ensuing recession. Loans were given elsewhere to ranchers with no method to regain any of their capital loss. Unfortunately, William Bevans died soon after the drought ended.

The *San Angelo Standard-Times* noted Bevans was put to rest leaving an immense mark, well thought of in the minds of his many friends and the society to which he had given great value.

Another member of the society, Aunt Bet Pearl, was held in high regard at this time, too. Aunt Bet, a pioneer in Menard for eighty years, claimed to have seen the "white owl". She experienced sixty-four consecutive years of farm life on the same place in the Little Saline community.

On the Saline property, Aunt Bet experienced many hard times with Indian intrusions. There was one defenseless time when a tribe of marauding wild Indians seized Aunt Bet's house and captured her brother when he was just ten. He was kept prisoner for several days before he was rescued. He said the only food he was given was a piece of raw meat. He was hungry enough to eat the meat, he said, but he cooked it because he had the option of using a fire. Only a few months later, however, Aunt Bet's two brothers were captured again.

The brothers did not show up one morning, and Aunt Bet began to believe they were dead. The next day her little brother was rescued, but one of her friends had been killed.

This was one of many major losses Aunt Bet suffered. She was a most tolerant person with a clear knowledge of Menard's hard times during the country's past. She was one of many remarkable people in the Hill Country.

Adam Bradford is another disaster-experiencing citizen worthy of mention. Bradford was one of the first settlers in the new village on the San Saba River in 1863. Bradford experienced many Indian disasters; in one he was allied with his oldest surviving son, James Bradford [Adam had twelve sons]. Adam and James were in the midst of rebuilding a cedar break on the Las Moras Creek when they were attacked. They were with a group of men with guns containing only four cartridges. They fired the cartridges, terrorizing the Indians, repelling their plans for assaulting Adam and his crew, and causing the Indians to flee. The personalities of Menard's past were engaged in many disastrous eras such as wild Indian marauding.

Disasters also included drought, which was a time of terror and immense destruction for Menard's citizens. In normal times, this part of Texas was used to receiving about twenty to twenty-three inches of rain each year. During the drought of the 1950s, the rainfall drastically narrowed to five to eight inches a year. The ranchers were helpless as they were extremely dependent on the rain for their production. Surviving was a major ambition as finances were hard to acquire because of the closing of banks. Water had quickly evolved into a scarcity. It was fortunate the river had not been totally devoured. The businesses that profited from this disaster were feed companies, who were the last source of feed for ranchers who had any remainder of livestock and money.

Though the drought was a critical mark of destruction, Menard's citizens did not lose the desire for rebirth. When the drought ended, rebirth began with a society contributing their faith and desire. Throughout the town, integrity flourished and recuperating was the major event. It was revivers such as William Bevans and characters such as Aunt Bet Pearl who salvaged Menard's healthy, distinguished outlook.

This author was full of admiration as he glimpsed the past in contrast with the present. He was able then to clearly define a leader of yesterday as an independent prospect, a leader who gave the town a true sense of dignity. Society had learned to cope with the drawbacks of the past. Because of their will to continue, disasters of the past had no crippling effect on the future.

The author leaves the reader with a closing paragraph about the feelings he sensed during his research:

A town was struck with misfortune. The chances of recovery looked slim. A group of people led by a band of conquering prospects extinguished brutal misery and began a period of reconstruction. The feelings I possessed passed beyond definition. The love of a town was seen as a never surpassing song of belief.

The days slip by as my grip shows little resistance to the lingering past. A river of thoughts possess me. I envision those days in contrast with now, wondering how we differ in lifestyle. I taste the challenge of reliving those fabled days with a curious desire.

The trip of reliving the past has begun, and I hear the townspeople chattering. I next inhale the scent of the steam from the train that once was an integral reality here; now only a painted image. I end my trip with an engraved impression that will never depart from the present.

Grandpa Ruff's Days of Ranching

By Terri Ruff

I Would Go with You

Because you walk through ways of charm and beauty
I would go with you down the lanes of time; my glad heart leaps as
*   to call of duty.*
As poetry pens, it speaks the beat of rhyme.
Because you lead matched minds to epic meetings in gardens that
*   are given to fair thought, Bright joy, like rainbows, is mine for*
*   the keeping.*
Alive are dreams that my soul deeply sought.
Because you picture life as good and treasured,
Mankind, a valued occupant of earth, closer sees the merits time
*   has measured.*
Clearer are the images of worth.
Sweet inspiration thrives while beauty reigns;
I would go with you down ethereal lanes. —Maxine McCray Miller

Grandpa Carl Ruff was a rancher in Menard. The author is writing her paper about her Grandpa Ruff's years in ranching.

It is interesting to look back on this. Her grandfather is eighty-six years old. He was reared in Schleicher County, west of Fort McKavett, on a 320-acre ranch with a 100-acre farm on it. Grandpa tells a lot of stories of how they ranched and farmed. He picked a lot of cotton in his young years. There were twelve people in his family. He had a lot to do taking care of his little brother and sisters.

Grandpa went to school at Fort McKavett. In those days, they had a governess visit the farm and teach them. He quit school in the seventh grade. He worked until he went overseas to France when he was twenty-two years old. He was in the Army in World War I for about a year and a half, then he came home.

Grandpa began buying land when he returned home. In 1925, he bought two sections and moved on these. He then bought 874 acres of land in 1926. He lived by himself for a long while. He worked, saved his money, and bought two sections and 500 acres of land with his savings. Land was not expensive then. He loved the land and ranching.

Grandpa married Ora Leakey when he was thirty-six. There were married on October 31, 1930, on a Friday night at the Baptist preacher's home in Menard. Mr. and Mrs. Hugh Spinks, the preacher and his wife, were there.

Grandpa's car was a little two-door, one-seat Ford Roadster. He had it when he got married. Since then, they have always bought Ford cars.

The couple had a son on March 31, 1933. He was born in Brady. They named him Duwan L. Ruff; he is the author's father. Duwan was an only child.

The author's grandfather is half German—Grandpa's father came over from Germany when he was in his teens. Grandpa loved the ranch and ranching. He raised Hereford cattle, sheep, goats, and some chickens. He always kept about three horses on the ranch. It was expensive to feed them because there was no vegetation on the ground.

The author's father, Duwan, grew up on the ranch and attended school at the Palmer School house a couple of years. He went the rest of his school years in Menard and graduated from Menard High School in 1951.

Duwan's parents gave him two sections of land as a gift, and he and his wife, Alice Marie Wallace Ruff, my mother, moved a house onto his land and Duwan and Alice lived there and Duwan began his ranching business.

In 1951, the second drought set in. Father sold everything by 1953. He and mother moved to Amarillo, and dad went to work for the Livestock Sanitary Commission. He also worked for the state. Grandpa also sold all his cattle, except for one regular cow and two milk cows. Grandpa also kept his horses and chickens. Grandma said she milked the cows, made butter, and sold it and eggs to people during the seven-year drought.

The drought was almost over when the author's parents came back to the ranch. It was a hard time for people.

Then Grandpa and Father started the ranching business again—Hereford cattle, sheep, and goats. Father and Mother fixed everything up, and they had chickens and a milk cow. Everything was fine. They had rain that fall, and flowers, ragweed, and other vegetation started growing.

The author's grandparents loved the outdoors and ranching. They always butchered their own meat. Grandpa and a Mr. Pearl always shod the horses. Grandpa loved to ride and always raised about one hundred little chicks a year. He and Grandma also raised turkeys for a while. One other thing they enjoyed was a big garden they both worked. They did a lot of canning. Both of them always raised little doggie lambs, too. They raised twenty-five one year. Father got his start with goats from that group.

Grandpa enjoyed hunting and trapping when the season came. He also was a real "fixer". He was always building and fixing things. In 1968, he was up on a windmill working. He fell off, broke some ribs, and hurt his back really bad. He was fine in no time at all, and oh how times have changed.

In Grandpa's days of ranching, he used the old ways. They did not have all the modern technology they use today. He said that these were the steps to follow: roundup, marking, vaccinating, shearing, doctoring, and selling them. And then start all over again, year after year.

Today, there are a lot of new and modern things. All water at the ranch comes from wells. There are dirt tanks and cement tanks. Some windmills are still used. Electric pumps, however, are used the most.

The author's grandparents moved to town in Menard in November, 1978. It was hard for them at first—they had lived on the ranch for forty-eight years.

Grandpa and Grandma celebrated their fiftieth wedding anniversary on Friday, October 31, 1980, here in Menard. They go to the ranch often, but are adjusting to town now. They may live in town, but to me they will always be country people.

The facts learned in this paper made clearer to me that Carl Ruff was a rancher during tough droughts in Menard. I enjoyed going back in the past and getting this information. It is a nice memory of times past. Change comes and goes, I hope the reader enjoyed learning about them.

I close with these thoughts:

As this writer drove down the rigid, old, muddy dirt road feeling every bump, she tried to imagine what it was like to have no grass, just rocks. At the author's grandparents, it was not unusual to see musty things left from those days. In the barn, the earthy smell of cow cake, chicken feed, and the leather of the worn saddles fill one's lungs. It was easy to taste in one's mind the fresh, good buttermilk pies and rolls Grandma used to make. Upon leaving, the author had some funny feelings not believing that the old times, which are not really so old, are gone.

Fritz and Anna Luckenbach

By Roger Q (Jake) Landers Jr.

The note reads: "Miss Anna, As I have no good chance to meet you, will send you a little note by Albert. If you will stay until Sunday & if it is your desire to take a buggyride, we will do so, if so please let me know as soon as possible, so I can secure a team, & state at what time and where. Trully yours, Fritz."

It was a successful buggy ride, and they promised to exchange letters when she returned home. So the love story between Fritz Luckenbach and Anna Nauwald began, he a lonesome young blacksmith, far from the friends of home, and she the granddaughter of a prominent family in Fredericksburg out to see the frontier city of San Angelo. She, not yet eighteen, had ridden with a wagon load of goods with brother Albert Nauwald and bosom classmate Adele Brockmann to visit her Uncle Ernest who owned the Nimitz Hotel.

Anna, Adele, and brother Albert had probably begged their parents to allow them to go on such an adventure with two drivers and a wagon load of goods for the hotel. Chances are they did not know they would see one of their singing and dancing friends from home on the main street of San Angelo.

Fritz at twenty-three had been blacksmithing in San Angelo for several months working in his own stall across Rio Concho Avenue from the Nimitz Hotel. Often he would stand and stretch his back and look across the river where the soldiers at Fort Concho were drilling or take in anything interesting going on at the hotel. You might imagine that he dropped a hot horseshoe when he saw two pretty hometown girls unload.

Fritz's parents and Anna's grandparents had emigrated from Germany in the years following statehood and settled in the Fredericksburg community. His parents were farmers at Grape Creek in Gillespie County, and her grandfather, Charles Nimitz, owned the Nimitz Hotel in Fredericksburg.

Letters began flowing when Anna returned home. Soon she asked for his picture and he asked for hers, but their letter writ-

ing was interrupted by Anna's parents who said, "No more letters to Fritz". What does Anna do? Ingeniously, she gets Fritz to
send her letters to Adele, then when Adele moves away, to Mrs.
Weyrich, whose husband had helped Fritz learn blacksmithing.
More than sixty-one letters were exchanged from October 1886
to November 1888 which tell a story of tender love developing
despite her parents' interference.

A critical letter was written two years after the buggy ride. It
was Fritz's letter to Anna proposing marriage, and closely crafted
with her help to get the words just right for her parents. The next
letter from her begins: "The battle is over and the parents have
consented."

Once the marriage was settled, Charles Nimitz along with
his granddaughter and favorite daughter-in-law, Anna Henke
Nimitz, Chester's mother, traveled to Menardville to check it
out. Was it a decent place for a member of the family to settle
and raise a family? They approved, and the wedding was held in
Fredericksburg on November 27, 1888, and Fritz and Anna were
on their way.

Fifty years later Fritz told the story of his life at their Golden
Wedding Celebration giving some of the background that might
have been reason enough for Anna's parents to dismiss him as
a suitable son-in-law. He had a poor record in school, leaving
school and his large family at age thirteen to find work. Jobs included setting pins at a bowling alley, building fences, working
livestock, and finally learning the blacksmith skills.

Eventually he decided to seek his fortune in San Angelo, a
bustling city soon to get a railroad. He left Fredericksburg, de-
jected because his girlfriend Math had jilted him and told some
bad stories about him. In one of his first letters to Anna, he was
not as much interested in her as he is in finding out something
about what Math had been saying about him.

Anna was the first granddaughter of Charles Nimitz. Her parents, Bertha and Charles Nauwald, began living in San Antonio
where Anna was born and started school, but soon they moved
to live next door to the hotel in Fredericksburg. They dealt with

buying and selling produce from the store front in their home, and at least by age seventeen, Anna was out of school and caring for her young siblings, one brother and six sisters, and helping in the store.

In the second year of their letters, Fritz started blacksmithing again after his shop and tools were destroyed by fire in San Angelo, this time in Willow City, northeast of Fredericksburg, where he was raising horses with his father and brother. Felix Mann, passing through with some cattle, hired him to help drive them to Mason where he was hired on by A.H. Murchison to drive them to Menardville. There he was introduced to the opportunities for blacksmithing. Menardville, although tiny, was on the northern route from San Antonio to El Paso, and many horses passed through carrying the load before railroads were extended.

Soon Anna was cooking meals and running the City Hotel in their home, and Fritz, in addition to blacksmithing, began selling hardware, fencing materials and tools; autos and windmills came a little later. He bought the old county courthouse, and ten years later constructed the stone hardware building in 1900 that stands next to it today.

There was no bank in Menard, but Fritz had a safe in which he was willing to hold money for other people. He was loaning money from accounts in Brady and Ballinger before the Bevans Bank was built in 1903. He had sold his blacksmithing business earlier to Adolph Beyer and started expanding his hardware business selling Ford cars and windmills assembled on the second floor of the hardware building.

Tragedy struck the family in 1903 when Henry, their first-born, was hit in the head at the school playground with a baseball and died. The anguish of the family is expressed on his tomb stone: "How many hopes lie buried here". At age thirteen he was recognized as a budding young businessman developing the skills of business in which his father was so successful. Henry was followed by the birth of four daughters and another son.

Anna was active in starting the Presbyterian Church and

soon gave up the hotel business to live in the newly constructed family house in 1910 on the corner of Bevans and Houston Street. She remained active in cooking chicken soup for the ill and helping new mothers in childbirth.

The family grew up in the big house. Sophie, we called "Putty", married Weck Mears, who soon died of typhoid. Infant Mamie was fatherless until Putty married Henry Reeve, who fathered two daughters—Margaretta, "Betto", and Katherine, "Kappy". Bertha, "Badda", married Wilkes Kothmann, acquiring Norman, Charles, and Anna. Norma married Hugh Spiller and had Dorothy, Hazel, and Hugh Bob. Emmie married Roger Landers and had Susanna, "Zanna", Roger Jr., "Jakie", Fritz, and John Brooks. Fritzie married Frances Smith to whom Angela was born.

The fourteen cousins enjoyed many happy occasions, especially at Christmas in the big house, as did their parents growing up. Mamie, older than the rest, married John Winslow, and bore Johnny, Diane, and Robert Keith, who were close enough in age to be included as cousins with the other fourteen.

Fritz had been a generous supporter of the railroad coming to town in 1911 and many other civic projects. Shipments of autos, windmills, and other materials came into the community, and livestock, wool & mohair were shipped out. He established the Luckenbach Motor Company of which Emil Toepperwein, his brother-in-law, was dealer. Albert Nauwald, another brother-in-law also became a partner to expand the hardware business. Menardville was thriving and the name was changed to Menard.

Fritz and Anna celebrated their Golden Wedding Anniversary in the ballroom of the Bevans Hotel with as many guests as the structure was designed to bear. By then Fritz had acquired the Jackson Ranch near Five-Mile Crossing with land irrigated by the Ditch Company of which he was secretary for many years. Closer to town were his pecan orchards with several hundred trees of improved varieties planted in the 1920s with water supplied by The Ditch.

The Davis Ranch, 15 miles south of town, was managed by J.C. Appleman who had roomed with Fritzie at Texas A&M and became almost a member of the family. Halfway to Junction was the Baker Ranch in a joint venture with Ed Mears, but when he died suddenly in the 1930s, with no agreement on paper and Fritz heavily invested, the land was retained in the Mears Estate and his investment was returned.

In his earlier years he had made many small loans, mostly for purchases of tools and equipment, and some to young couples just starting out. In his later years he was often seen sitting in front of the hardware store making notes in his little black book as a payment was made. He had grown in wealth as he had helped to make the community successful.

Fritz had no will. Son Fritzie guided the division of his assets among the five children after many family meetings in which his main directive was "no squabbling". Fritz passed away on March 7, 1951, and Anna on March 21, 1956. Their love letters were discovered in a box in the big house in 1997, one hundred and ten years after they were written.

INDEX

This is an index of people's names, not a complete index of every event, place, and concept. With 53 authors, there is inconsistency in name styles. Some authors used initial letters for first names, others full names. In some cases, spelling of names differs between authors. The index uses the style and spelling of the author when there is doubt about the name, thus some names are indexed under more than one style and spelling. Not every name is indexed because some obscure people were not deemed relevant to the work. The index does not include names of authors who appear in bylines (those can be found in the table of contents) except when their names appear in the body of a story.

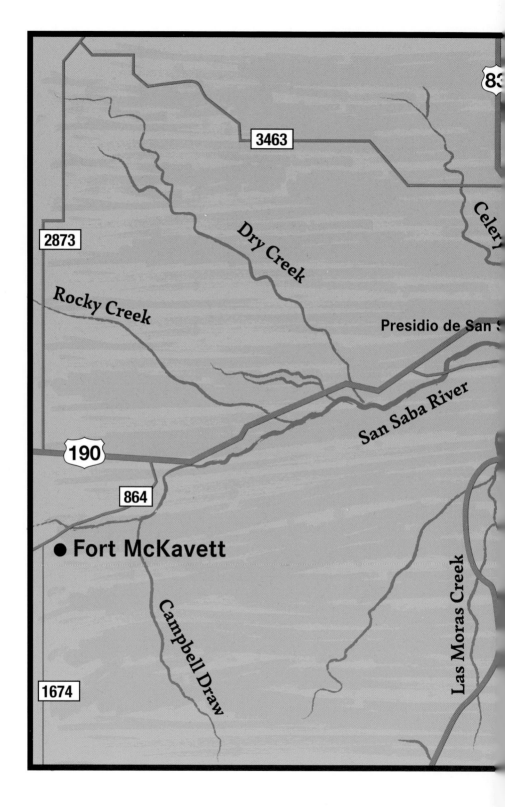